15.45
ท
7/02

D0300635

WITH

RURAL HOMELESSNESS

Issues, experiences and policy responses

Paul Cloke, Paul Milbourne and
Rebekah Widdowfield

WITHDRAWN

The POLICY
P P
PRESS

First published in Great Britain in March 2002 by

The Policy Press
34 Tyndall's Park Road
Bristol BS8 1PY
UK

Tel +44 (0)117 954 6800
Fax +44 (0)117 973 7308
e-mail tpp@bristol.ac.uk
www.policypress.org.uk

© The Policy Press 2002

COLEG RHYL COLLEGE
CANOLFAN ADNODDAU LLYFRGELL
LIBRARY RESOURCE CENTRE
CEFNDY ROAD, RHYL   LL18 2HG

| 067631 | 362·5 CLO |
| 7\|02 | RHYL |

British Library Cataloguing in Publication Data

A catalogue record for this book is available from the British Library

ISBN 1 86134 284 5 paperback

A hardcover version of this book is available

Paul Cloke is Professor of Geography in the School of Geographical Sciences, University of Bristol, **Paul Milbourne** is Senior Fellow and **Rebekah Widdowfield** is Research Fellow, both in the Department of City and Regional Planning, Cardiff University.

Cover design by Qube Design Associates, Bristol.

Front cover: photographs supplied by kind permission of Mark Simmons Photography and Jonathan Tooby.

The right of Paul Cloke, Paul Milbourne and Rebekah Widdowfield to be identified as authors of this work has been asserted by them in accordance with Sections 77 and 78 of the 1988 Copyright, Designs and Patents Act.

All rights reserved: no part of this publication may be reproduced, stored in a retrieval system, or transmitted in any form or by any means, electronic, mechanical, photocopying, recording, or otherwise without the prior permission of The Policy Press.

The statements and opinions contained within this publication are solely those of the authors and not of The University of Bristol or The Policy Press. The University of Bristol and The Policy Press disclaim responsibility for any injury to persons or property resulting from any material published in this publication.

The Policy Press works to counter discrimination on grounds of gender, race, disability, age and sexuality.

Printed and bound in Great Britain by Hobbs the Printers Ltd, Southampton.

Contents

Acknowledgements

We gratefully acknowledge the financial support of the Economic and Social Research Council for our research (award number R000236567). Local research in Gloucestershire and Somerset was undertaken by Jenny Cursons and Phil Cooke. Their contribution to this project has been invaluable, and we fully acknowledge their very significant support. Rebekah Widdowfield acknowledges financial support from the British Academy fellowship scheme. We also thank Anna, Polly and Theresa in the Bristol office for their help with the manuscript. Finally, we acknowledge the contribution made by those homeless people and representatives of rural and homelessness agencies who willingly gave up their time to talk to us about their experiences of homelessness in rural areas. Without their help we would not have been able to write this book.

We are grateful to the following for permission to reproduce extracts from papers we have published in their journals:

Taylor and Francis Ltd (http://www.tandf.co.uk/journals) for:

Cloke, P., Cooke, P., Cursons, J., Milbourne, P. and Widdowfield, R. (2000) 'Ethics, reflexivity and research: encounters with homeless people', *Ethics, Place and Environment*, vol 3, pp 133-54.

Cloke, P., Milbourne, P. and Widdowfield, R. (2000) 'Change but no change: dealing with homelessness under the 1996 Housing Act', *Housing Studies*, vol 15, pp 739-56.

Cloke, P., Milbourne, P. and Widdowfield, R. (2001) 'The geographies of homelessness in rural England', *Regional Studies*, vol 35, pp 23-37.

Pion Ltd, London, for:

Cloke, P., Milbourne, P. and Widdowfield, R. (2000) 'The hidden and emerging spaces of rural homelessness', *Environment and Planning A*, vol 32, pp 77-90.

Cloke, P., Milbourne, P. and Widdowfield, R. (2000) 'Homelessness and rurality: "out-of-place" in purified space?', *Environment and Planning D*, vol 18, pp 715-35.

Blackwell Publishers Journals, for:

Cloke, P., Milbourne, P. and Widdowfield, R. (2000) 'Partnership and policy networks in rural local governance: homeless in Taunton', *Public Administration*, vol 78, pp 111-34.

Cloke, P., Milbourne, P. and Widdowfield, R. (2001) 'Homelessness and rurality: exploring connections in local spaces of rural England', *Sociologia Ruralis*, vol 41, no 4, pp 438-53.

Elsevier Science, for:

Cloke, P., Milbourne, P. and Widdowfield, R. (2001) 'Interconnecting housing, homelessness and rurality', *Journal of Rural Studies*, vol 17, pp 99-111.

Cloke, P., Milbourne, P. and Widdowfield, R. (2001) 'The local spaces of welfare provision: responding to homelessness in rural England', *Political Geography*, vol 20, pp 493-512.

RHYL COLLEGE
CEFNDY ROAD
LL18 2HB

ONE

Rural homelessness: an introduction

Homelessness 'you don't see'?

> It has been documented that there are four times as many animal shelters
> in this country as there are shelters for battered women. While
> emergency shelters do very important work, there are not enough of
> them to provide shelter to everyone knocking on their doors. For
> every homeless person you see on a street corner, there are another
> nine homeless people you *don't see*. People using couches for makeshift
> beds in the homes of friends and relatives, two or three families sharing
> a mobile home meant for just one, people living in substandard housing,
> people living in their cars, people living outside in parks, campgrounds
> and primitive wooded areas. The list goes on and on. (Stoops, in
> Lewallen, 1998, p 9)

This book is about some of the 9 out of 10 homeless people you do not
see – those living in *rural* areas. In terms of numbers, the hidden rural
homeless cannot 'compete' with those in urban areas, and by adopting a
rural focus in this book we in no way seek to underestimate or undermine
the significance of issues faced by homeless people in various urban
situations. However, we do want to claim loudly and clearly that rural
homelessness exists as an important, but often invisible, social issue of our
time. If you read this claim as a statement of the obvious, then you are
probably one of a relatively small minority of people who recognise that
homelessness is not confined to the sites and sights of the city. *Not*
knowing about rural homelessness is entirely forgivable. Popular discourses
of homelessness repeatedly focus on images and ideas relating to on-
street homeless people – usually labelled as 'rough sleepers' or 'beggars' –
in major cities. Highly publicised policy responses to homelessness, such
as the Rough Sleepers Initiative in Britain, tend to reinforce the
interconnections between homelessness and the city.

Rural areas by contrast are associated with, and often defined by, very different discourses. Increasingly, many rural areas are constructed as 'ideal' places to live. If you want to be part of a close community; if you want to live close to nature; if you want to escape from the pollution and crime of the city; if you want a safe, happy, unspoilt environment in which to bring up your kids; then a house in the country is the commonly constructed answer. This 'idyllisation' of rural areas varies significantly in different international situations, but it has taken a firm hold on how rural areas are perceived in much of Britain. As a result, rural areas are often tagged as 'problem-free' in social terms, and come to represent places where supposedly 'urban' issues can be left behind. It is easy to see why discourses of poverty and homelessness do not find common purchase among idyllistic ideas of 'rural'. It is all too easy to subscribe to a simple view that anyone becoming homeless in a rural situation will be forced to move to an urban centre where they can better cope with their problem and their problem can better be coped with. As we suggest in Chapter 3, rurality and homelessness have become almost mutually exclusive in contemporary society. In this book, then, we join with other researchers and pressure group representatives in the task of understanding and publicising the plight of rural homeless people; of rendering visible the problems of hidden rural homelessness.

There are very few published accounts of 'encounters' with homeless people in rural areas. As we discuss in Chapter 7, being homeless in a rural area often involves the deployment of tactics of invisibility. One such encounter, though, is recorded by Jim Lewallen in his book *The Camp* (1998) (Figure 1.1):

> Each day after work I took my five dogs for a run on an undeveloped 80 acre tract of fields and woods near my home. Surrounded by subdivision and apartment complex walls, and rarely visited by anyone, it was the perfect place for them to exhaust themselves racing through the woods and fields. On this particular day we were on a narrow dirt trail in the wooded section, a heavily shadowed area beneath a canopy of ancient oaks. The dogs had ranged a good 100 yards ahead around a bend in the trail when they began barking loudly at something I couldn't yet see. I ran ahead, expecting to have to save a treed possum or cat, and instead found Will, surrounded by my undisciplined 'pack' and not really sure what to do next. When he asked simply 'Dogs bite?' I assured him that they didn't, apologised for the scare, and spent the next hour or so talking with him beneath the branches of the oaks. Will, I learned, was a homeless man who lived in a clearing further back in the woods with some other homeless friends. (p 13)

Figure 1.1: *The Camp* (1998) by Jim Lewallen

Lewallen goes on to recount a year of regular evening visits to 'the camp' resulting in involvement with, and insights into, the personal circumstances of these homeless men. The space concerned may well have been suburban rather than rural, and the sleeping out/living rough at the camp may represent only one form of hidden homelessness, but what is important about Lewallen's account is its value as an *encounter*. He is introduced to the day-to-day lives of homeless men, not as an abstract unemotional concept, but as a committed involvement with the (often tragic but also sometimes funny) experiences of hidden homeless people.

It is precisely this kind of encounter that is necessary to demystify rural homelessness. Although part of the research which underpins this book deals with issues relating to the enumeration of homeless people, and thereby signifies their problems as a statistical entity, our motivation for undertaking the research stems from a strong political sense of the injustice of homelessness and from a desire to provoke practical policy responses to the needs of homeless people hidden away in rural areas. Too often any glimpse of rural homelessness in public discourse is immediately romanticised. Consider the following story from the *News of the World*:

VILLAGERS BUY THEIR TRAMP HIS OWN WOOD

Supertramp Max Smith has been crowned king of the road by kind-hearted locals who chipped in £26,000 to buy him his own wood. They raised the cash so the happy hobo can live out the rest of his days under his favourite bush amid 90 acres of ancient forest.... Shopkeeper Graham Dando, 49, said 'Everybody knows Max and there's a small network of us who keep an eye out for him each day.... If we don't see him we go and make sure he's all right. That wouldn't happen in the city'. (Johnson, 1997, p 10)

This particular 'encounter' with a homeless man in a rural setting merely serves to reinforce the status quo of the idyllised rural. Instead of homeless people, rural areas entertain 'happy hobos'. Instead of being socially excluded, the happy hobo is cared for by a supportive community. Instead of being forced to move on, he has his wood bought for him by kind-hearted locals for whom a supertramp somehow fits their romanticised view of the idyllic life-styles of country living. Readers can sleep safe in their beds as their rural idyll is being enhanced by the mysterious romanticism of the somehow ageless tramp, rather than being transgressed by the harsh social reality of homelessness.

Part of our task in this book, then, is to unpack the cultural context of rural homelessness and to demonstrate its impact in terms of more specific discourses of it. Such demystification is an essential prerequisite for the encouragement of appropriate encounters with hidden homeless people in rural areas. In the remainder of this chapter we set the scene for the research we have undertaken. We review how ideas of home and homelessness have been defined. We then discuss the evidence for, and of, rural homelessness, focusing in particular on the US and the UK. Finally, we contrast what is clear numeric evidence of the significant existence of rural homelessness with the common perceptions of the nature of housing problems in rural areas, finding once again a discursive mismatch which lies at the heart of ineffective policy responses to homelessness in rural areas.

Encompassing homelessness

Homelessness

There is little agreement over what constitutes homelessness. A number of commentators (see for example, Watson, 1984; Blasi, 1990; Hutson and Liddiard, 1994) have conceived of homelessness as a continuum of housing situations ranging from life on the streets to people living in inadequate or insecure housing. However, while there is a general consensus that those without any form of shelter are homeless, as the definition is extended to encompass people with recognisable but less extreme housing problems – for example those living in insecure or overcrowded accommodation – it becomes increasingly difficult to draw a distinction between those with and without a home. This difficulty feeds into a broader debate on the distinction between a house as a shelter and as a home, which implies much more than a physical structure. As Hutson and Liddiard (1994, p 29) contend, "in its broadest sense, the term 'homeless' means not having a 'home' ... the problem, however, lies in defining what one means by the term 'home'. A 'home' ... clearly means more than a house". Indeed Watson (1984, p 70) argues, "in policy and research terms what is needed is a recognition that material conditions and standards, the need for space, privacy, control, safety, self-expression and physical and emotional well-being, are all important aspects of a dwelling and have to be taken into account".

The wider definitions of homelessness likely to develop from such considerations, "begin to embrace all the elements normally included in discussions of housing needs" (Johnson et al, 1991, p 8), a link which has been emphasised by a number of writers. Thorns (1989, p 254) for example claims "homelessness is but one, albeit extreme, situation along a continuum of housing needs", while Neale (1997, p 48) writes that "homelessness is a highly ambiguous and intangible phenomenon which lies at one end of a spectrum of housing need/experience" and regards homelessness as "inseparable from other aspects of housing need". The advantage of framing homelessness in terms of housing need is that it highlights the similarity between homeless households and other households experiencing housing difficulties. As Bramley (in Bramley et al, 1988, p 27) writes, "although the homeless may at times appear to be in competition with the waiting list for scarce resources, they are also people in housing need. They may indeed be on a waiting list or have the same problems as other people at the top of the list". In addition, grounding the concept of homelessness in more general terms of housing insecurity and inadequacy as embraced by the term housing need may provide a more adequate basis for understanding and preventing more extreme forms of homelessness (notably rooflessness) which, as Nord and Luloff (1995, p 475) have argued, generally occurs, "as a relatively short period of a much longer residential crisis episode characterised by residential insecurity, residential instability and residential inadequacy".

However, despite widespread acceptance of the notion of a continuum of housing need, there is still a tendency in much of the literature (especially in the US) to define homelessness simply in terms of rooflessness (see for example, Golden, 1992; Wolch and Dear, 1993; Jencks, 1994; Piliavin et al, 1996). Such a narrow definition is inadequate as "it ignores all those who may at present have some kind of roof but not a 'home' in any meaningful sense of the word. Further it ignores the great mental and physical stresses and pressure that having some kind of roof may ease but certainly not eliminate" (Wright and Everitt, 1995, p 8). In addition, as Johnson et al (1991, p 5) point out, simply equating homelessness with rooflessness fails to address the issues of access to housing, insecurity and the circumstances which affect the ability to attain or retain housing.

Broader definitions of homelessness talk of the lack of a home or inability to live in one's own home, "... not being in, nor having immediate or easy access to secure accommodation" (Liddiard and Hutson, 1990, p 165) and a commonly cited definition regards homeless people as those lacking "a right or access to their own secure and minimally adequate housing space" (Bramley et al, 1988, p 26). Yet these wider definitions have also been criticised as unduly restrictive. For example, Somerville (1992, p 530) criticises Bramley's definition for embracing only two aspects of homelessness (lack of control and privacy and poor material conditions) and neglecting the emotive aspects of homelessness (such as lack of 'hearth' and rootlessness). However, at a time of resource constraint and withdrawal of welfare provision, it is perhaps not surprising that the statutory definition of homelessness embraces only some of the aspects identified by Somerville (including lack of shelter, lack of hearth, heartlessness, lack of privacy, rootlessness and lack of abode) and focuses predominantly on the more material meanings of homelessness.

Statutory definitions in the UK

Under the 1996 Housing Act a person is homeless if they have no accommodation available in the UK or elsewhere. Accommodation is only available for a person's occupation if it is available for occupation by them, together with any other person(s) who normally live with them as a member of their family or can reasonably be expected to reside with them. In addition, the Act stipulates that a person shall not be treated as having accommodation unless it is accommodation which it would be reasonable for them to continue to occupy. However, being accepted as homeless under these terms does not automatically guarantee rehousing. In order for the local authority to have a statutory duty to rehouse a household a further set of criteria has to be met, namely that applicants are in priority need, have not become homeless intentionally and have a local connection with the area in which they are seeking to be rehoused. "What the Housing (Homeless Persons) Act does therefore, is define a concept of homelessness and then delimit it to exclude certain categories of the homeless" (Watson, 1984, p 66).

Determining whether or not an applicant is homeless, and the nature of the duty owed to them by the local authority as laid out in the legislation, is complicated by the use of terms that are themselves ambiguous and contestable. For example, the 'reasonableness' criterion can embrace factors relating to the condition of the property, conditions of occupancy and household circumstances. While Section 177 of the Act stipulates that in determining whether it would be (or would have been) reasonable for a person to continue to occupy accommodation, an authority *must* take into account whether the accommodation is affordable to them and whether it is not reasonable for them to continue to occupy accommodation if it is probable that this will lead to domestic violence against them. Beyond that, local authorities have substantial freedom to determine what is reasonable. A local authority *may* choose to consider the criteria posited in the Code of Guidance (DoE, 1996) – namely: physical conditions, overcrowding, type of accommodation, violence or threats of violence from persons not associated with the applicant, and security of tenure – but there is no compulsion upon it to do so.

Similar flexibility exists in defining vulnerability and intentionality. Although again the code offers some guidelines, local authorities have considerable discretion in determining which households to consider vulnerable and the circumstances that constitute intentional homelessness. Whether or not a household has a local connection is more clear-cut and is usually based on length of residence, residence of immediate family and employment, but it still rests with each individual authority to decide the time in an area deemed necessary to establish a local connection.

There are consequently a number of points in the homeless application process at which subjective judgements are made. Indeed statements in the Code of Guidance would seem to positively *encourage* subjectivity and discretion in the assessment of applications and warn against local authorities laying down too clearly defined strictures. The statutory definition of homelessness is thus

> a mixing of objective statements about current housing situation and judgements about why that situation has arisen, whether the household involved deserves to benefit from policy action and what priority they should have compared with other people. (Johnson et al, 1991, p 3)

Given such room for manoeuvre, it is perhaps not surprising that studies (for example, Evans and Duncan, 1988; Hoggart, 1995b) have found considerable differences between authorities with regard to the interpretation and implementation of the homelessness legislation, resulting in substantial disparity in the proportion of applicants accepted as homeless. The way in which terms are defined is thus not simply a debate about semantics but is critical to application outcomes. For example, the study of local authority policy and practice conducted by Evans and Duncan (1988) found that only half of all local councils accepted those in statutorily unfit accommodation as homeless. Furthermore, the variation between authorities with regard to who is and who is not considered homeless, "provides a simple indication of the contested nature of this concept" (Hoggart, 1995b, p 60) and suggests that failure to be defined as homeless in legislative terms does not necessarily mean that a household is not homeless. However, actual homelessness does not go away because it has not been recognised or alleviated but, as Webb (1994, p 25) contends, it may become concealed or hidden.

Hidden homelessness

The majority of studies and policies relating to homelessness have tended to focus on the more visible forms of the problem – those living in the streets, in hostels or emergency accommodation and those who are statutorily homeless. As a result, the size and scope of homelessness has been considerably underestimated with the definitions and foci adopted serving, albeit perhaps by default, to conceal some types of homelessness. For example, defining homelessness in terms of rooflessness excludes those in temporary or emergency accommodation, while extending the definition to include those in hostels still fails to consider those living in insecure and/or intolerable housing. Similarly, focusing on London and other major cities hides homelessness in non-metropolitan and rural areas, while a reliance on statutory definitions means that those not presenting as homeless or not accepted as being in priority need are in effect hidden (Webb, 1994, p 28).

This has particular ramifications for identifying the homelessness experienced by particular sections of the population who tend to experience it in a more hidden form. The relative invisibility of young women in single homelessness statistics, for example, reflects the fact that women in need tend to use hostels less than men and are less likely to sleep on the streets but tend instead to stay with friends and relatives. As a result, the housing needs and homelessness of many women is likely to go unrecorded, thus remaining hidden and, consequently, unaddressed.

Like the more general term homelessness, hidden homelessness is itself subject to debate, with the boundaries which delimit such a situation more or less tightly drawn. Acknowledging that 'hidden' homelessness is ill-defined, Bramley (in Bramley et al, 1988, p 40) offers a threefold definition comprising:

- people whose objective circumstances are indistinguishable from those officially accepted as homeless, but who do not register under the formal system, for whatever reason;
- people who are or are about to become homeless, but who are not in the Homeless Persons Act priority groups;
- people whose circumstances clearly put them 'at risk' of becoming homeless within a finite period.

Webb (1994) accepts these households as forming part of the hidden homeless population, but also broadens the definition to include, for example, those who sleep rough but not regularly or in known sites;

those who live in some form of institution primarily because there is nowhere else for them to live; those who want to live as a separate household but who have to share with another household, irrespective of whether or not they can technically stay there; and, perhaps most controversially, those who describe their own situation as constituting homelessness or who say their present housing is not their home.

Home

As Watson (1984, p 70) notes, "to a large extent the difficulties inherent [in defining homelessness] derive from the notion of a 'home' and what that means". Homelessness thus cannot be adequately defined without some consideration of the meaning of 'home'. Like the term homelessness, home is, "a multi-variate concept with meanings varying across individuals, culture and time" (Moore et al, 1995, p 10). As Neale (1995, pp 54-5) points out, meanings of home "change according to the households involved, according to the individuals within it, and according to the prevailing economic, social and political climate. No single definition of the home can be considered absolute, because meaning is relative and varies historically across different regions and/or societies". These variations highlight the importance of the *context* in which meanings are formed, yet this is something which is frequently overlooked in the literature. This omission is noted by Despres (1991) who criticises studies examining the meaning of home for what she refers to as their "interpretative bias", neglecting "the impact of societal forces and the material properties of the built environment on individuals' perceptions, judgements and behaviours, and experience of and about the home" and giving "little indication of the socio-political context of the settings under investigation" (p 98).

At its most basic level, home as 'abode' defines home as anywhere one happens to stay, while home as 'shelter' connotes the material form of home but still provides an essentially restricted definition, with home considered simply as a physical structure which affords protection against the elements. Less tangible are the notions of home as 'hearth' and 'heart'. Somerville associates these aspects of home with warmth and love respectively, both of which may be obtained through relations of mutual affection and support. A number of writers have stressed the role of family and social relations as marking the difference between house and home. Harrington (quoted in Giamo and Grunberg, 1992, p 20) for example contends that, "a 'home' is not simply a roof over one's head, it is the centre of a web of human relationships", while Dupuis and Thorns

(1996, p 496) refer to a house as being "transformed over time into a home by the presence and practices of the occupants, the family".

Social relations are also likely to contribute to home as 'roots', that is 'a familiar environment, a place that provides its occupants with a sense of belonging somewhere' (Despres, 1991, p 98). In this sense, home provides a sense of identity. Indeed Havel argues that our homes are "an inseparable element of our human identity. Deprived of all aspects of his home, man would be deprived of himself, of his humanity" (quoted in Daly, 1996, p 149). A person's home communicates information about their social position – their profession, personality, life-style and family status – and, as such, is significant in joining personal identity with identity with place and the social world (Dant and Deacon, 1989).

Home is also identified as 'privacy' – a certain territory from which the occupant(s) has the power to exclude others. Indeed Despres (1991, pp 99-102) regards the establishment of this inside/outside boundary as "fundamental to the experience of being-at-home". This ties in with the notion of home as a refuge from the outside world (although home as 'refuge' does not form a distinct aspect of home in Somerville's categorisation), "a place to get away from outside pressures, a place where one can control the level of social interaction and a place for privacy and independence" (Despres, 1991, pp 98-9).

As Table 1.1 shows, each of the various aspects of home identified by Somerville can be deemed to provide some form of security. Thus home as shelter and privacy are a source of physical and territorial security respectively, while home as hearth and heart afford less tangible, but equally if not more important, psychological and emotional security. Despres (1991, pp 98-9) refers to home as "providing an atmosphere of social understanding where one's actions, opinions and moods are accepted".

Table 1.1: The meaning of home

Key signifier	General connotation	Sense of security	In relation to self	Others
Shelter	Materiality	Physical	Protection	Roofing
Hearth	Warmth	Psychological	Relaxation	Homeliness
Heart	Love	Emotional	Happiness	Stability
Privacy	Control	Territorial	Possession	Exclusion
Roots	Source of identity	Ontological	Sense	Reference
Abode	Place	Spatial	Rest	Living/sleeping space
'Paradise'	Ideality	Spiritual	Bliss	Non-existence (?)

Source: Somerville (1992, p 533)

However, the extent to which home is a source of security is subject to tenurial and, in particular, gender differences, with a large number of studies questioning the extent to which women experience home as a place of security and refuge. For example, Kearns and Smith (1994, p 422) point out that "occupants may be 'at home' in that they are literally within their dwellings but they may be less than 'at home' in terms of feeling safe, secure, and at ease. Many women do not feel at home within their dwellings on account of domestic violence"; while Tuan's (1997) contention that home is a place which holds meaning and significance can be expanded to suggest that home "is not only a place we can escape *to*, but it also can be a place we want to escape *from*" (Tomas and Dittmar, 1995, p 496, emphasis added).

The implications for studying rural homelessness

As the above discussion demonstrates, homelessness is an ambiguous and contested concept and defining the term makes for a contentious debate. There are a large number of definitions which could be adopted, the scope of which reflects "arguments about human needs, political agendas and social priorities" (Chamberlain and Mackenzie, 1992, p 294). The importance of these definitions should not be underestimated. As Daly (1996, p 9) argues, "words, concepts, values and beliefs shape our behaviour and our views of others. By exercising our power to name, we construct a social phenomenon, homelessness, the criteria used to define it and a stereotype of the people to whom it refers". This in turn affects the way in which a problem is dealt with, with definitions being of fundamental importance in informing resource and policy decisions.

While in the academic and policy literature there is a general acceptance that homelessness encompasses a whole range of circumstances, the tendency for homelessness to be equated with rooflessness and other more visible forms of homelessness, such as households living in hostels and other forms of temporary or emergency accommodation, obscures the existence of homelessness in rural areas where the occurrence, or at least visibility, of rough sleeping is less obvious and where a lack of hostels reduces the number of sites at which homeless people might congregate. As a result, there is a substantial amount of 'hidden' homelessness. As Webb (1994) notes, anyone with no home of their own or who cannot reasonably be expected to continue living in their present accommodation – but who is not accepted for priority rehousing as homeless by their local authority, is not sleeping rough or using hostel accommodation – is likely to find that their homelessness remains hidden. Similarly, Fitchen

(1991, p 186) points out that "for people who move in and out of the homes of relatives and friends because they lack security of shelter, the period of being 'potentially homeless', 'sometimes homeless', or 'near homeless' may last for several months. Yet they are never classified or counted as homeless because they are not sleeping in the village park or in an agency shelter".

While such an approach is understandable given the difficulties involved in trying to identify and quantify problems of 'hidden' or potential homelessness, the failure to examine the nature and extent of such less visible forms hinders attempts to raise the profile of and subsequently to take steps to deal with the issue of rural homelessness. As Fitchen notes in relation to rural North America, "because homelessness ... is hard to define, to count and even to see, it goes unnoticed and unaddressed" (1992, p 191). Consequently, in order to gain a clear picture of homelessness in rural areas it would seem paramount to adopt a broad definition that embraces not just those who are roofless, but poor households within inadequate or insecure accommodation 'living on the edge of homelessness' (Fitchen, 1992).

The idea that someone can have accommodation but still be homeless highlights another key theme which emerged from the literature, namely that the concepts of home and homelessness are inextricably linked. Homelessness can only be defined in the context of home and it is not possible to fully understand the former without some conception of the latter. Once again this suggests the need for a broad definition of homelessness. If home is conceived as more than a dwelling, it is a logical step on from this to conclude that homelessness encompasses a range of situations other than simply lacking a roof (people in such a position perhaps more accurately defined as 'houseless' or even more simply as 'roofless'). As Chamberlain and Mackenzie (1992, p 280) contend, people "may have a 'home' when defined by certain physical structures, but in other senses they are 'homeless', because the dwelling to which they return is not 'home' in an emotional or affective sense". This is recognised by Kearns and Smith who employ the notion of metaphorical homelessness to describe a 'state of being' in which "someone ... might be adequately housed but spatially removed from their acutely felt sense of home (ie some other place of greater felt meaning or value)" (1994, p 420). Thus "even among the adequately housed there are groups or sub-groups within the population who do not feel 'at home' in the existential sense of 'home is where your heart is'" (1994, p 422). "Individuals can therefore be roofless and yet maintain that they are not homeless because their home is on the streets. Similarly people may have a good material standard of accommodation, but nevertheless consider themselves to be homeless" (Neale, 1997, p 55).

Such differences between people in their expectations and beliefs about what constitutes a home make it perhaps impossible to draw a dividing line between what is home and what is homelessness. Indeed Veness (1993, p 324) regards the distinction drawn between the two concepts as an artificial dichotomy, arguing that "the criteria traditionally used to establish what home and homeless mean, and thus the boundary between them, are a contested domain" and adopts the term 'un-home' in recognition that, "homeless is not a temporally and spatially circumscribed category that puts those people who fall into it in a time and space limbo until the boundary conditions of home have been met, rather the environments and experiences of home are negotiated".

Studies of rural homelessness

In rural America, homelessness is hard to find. Visible homelessness, in the sense of people sleeping in community shelters or out of doors, is quite rare in small towns and the open countryside. However, a growing number of rural low-income people have housing that is so inadequate in quality, so insecure in tenure, and so temporary in duration that keeping a roof over their heads is a preoccupying and precarious accomplishment. Many rural residents who are living below the poverty line are potentially homeless much of the time, and an unknown number of them actually do become homeless. Because they are few in number and dispersed in space, they are seldom seen; they do not sleep on sidewalks where the public side-steps them, so their plight is unknown. From media coverage to scholarly writings, the homeless of rural America are hardly mentioned. (Fitchen, 1992, p 173)

This account by the late and much lamented US anthropologist Janet Fitchen astutely summarises the dilemma of circular argument that pervades discussion of rural homelessness in the developed world. Because homelessness in rural areas is usually hidden rather than visible it tends to be neither recognised nor quantified, and as a consequence it hardly gets a mention in public discourses. This in turn renders the problem even more invisible, reinforcing the tactics deployed by rural homeless people to keep their situation hidden. As part of our research we have conducted widespread searches of bibliographic databases and found very little by way of significant research or academic publications on the subject of rural homelessness. A variety of reasons have been offered to us as explanations for this phenomenon. The most common is that in many rural areas housing is inexpensive compared to that in cities, and that as a consequence there are very few circumstances in which an individual or household cannot gain access to some kind of cheap housing. Therefore, homelessness does not exist as a problem per se. This conflation of discourses of housing and homelessness is a recurrent theme in this book. We argue that it is often more *comfortable* to address rural issues in terms of housing than to 'admit' that problems of homelessness exist. Yet as our review of homelessness definitions suggests, and as the above statement from Fitchen reinforces, inadequate and precarious housing must be recognised as an essential edge of homelessness alongside the more 'obvious' signs represented by rough sleeping. The claim that rural homelessness does not exist in rural areas may be erroneous. Rather, it can be argued that homelessness exists but lies hidden due to a matrix of discursive convention, cultural representation, political disinclination, and self-chosen invisibility on the part of homeless people themselves.

Homelessness in rural North America

Despite Fitchen's claim that rural homelessness receives scant mention in North American scholarly writings, the 1990s have witnessed (due in no small measure to Fitchen's own work) some considerable study of rural homelessness in the US, particularly by rural sociologists (see Patton, 1988; First et al, 1990; Fitchen, 1991, 1992; and also Lawrence, 1995). It is possible to highlight four key findings emerging from these studies. The first concerns the hiddenness of homelessness in rural areas. With rural spaces characterised by more disperse settlement structures and relatively few hostels and other public sites for homeless people, it is difficult to encounter 'literal homelessness' – those people living on streets or in shelters – in rural areas. This is not to suggest that literal homelessness is not present there, but that it tends to be positioned in more hidden spaces, such as woods, cars and farm buildings, than in large towns and cities. Consequently, it is argued that these different scales of visibility lead to literal homelessness being socio-spatialised out of rural areas and connections between homelessness and urban space being reinforced within the dominant social imagination.

A second feature of rural homelessness highlighted by researchers in the US is its statistical significance. Official counts of poverty, included as part of the decennial Census, point both to persistent levels of rural poverty (at around 16-17% over the 1980s and early 1990s) and to a higher rate of poverty in rural areas than in metropolitan counties – in 1990, the respective rates were 16% and 13%. The collection of information on homelessness levels by government, however, is less comprehensive. Unlike in Britain, where statistics are collected on all homeless households who approach local authorities for assistance, estimates of the scale of homelessness in the US are limited to street counts of homeless people in known sites of concentration on the night of the Census. Consequently, not only are these official statistics seen to underestimate the overall extent of homelessness in the US, they also can be viewed as spatially biased, in that the most visible sites of (literal) homelessness are located in towns and cities. It is hardly surprising, then, that the 1990 Census recorded a much lower level of homelessness in rural areas (at 1.2 per 10,000 residents) than in urban areas (17.5 per 10,000).

But studies conducted in rural parts of the US using different methods of counting homeless people have revealed much higher rates. Research by First et al (1990), for example, in a range of US states over a six-month period, has highlighted a level of rural homelessness for any one week of six per 10,000 residents, rising to 14 per 10,000 if counted over a six-month period. A second study in the state of Kentucky utilised information supplied by a range of agencies and reported a one-day level of homelessness in rural parts of the state of 13 per 10,000 residents compared with 22 per 10,000 in urban areas (see Aron and Fitchen, 1996).

Third, homelessness in rural North America is characterised by considerable spatial unevenness in terms of its scale, profile and causal factors. Highest rates of homelessness are found in those remote rural areas characterised by declining local economies based around farming, mining and forestry. It is these remote areas that also record high levels of poverty. Over recent years, though, rising levels of homelessness have been reported in a range of accessible rural areas with more vibrant local economies. In such areas, in-movements of jobseekers and rising levels of local taxes and property prices have pushed many lower-income households out of local housing markets and into new situations of homelessness (Aron and Fitchen, 1996).

A final feature of rural homelessness identified by US researchers relates to important connections between rural housing structures and homelessness. Work by Fitchen (1992) has shown how inequitable systems of rural housing not only result in situations of homelessness, but also create difficulties for people when they become homeless in rural spaces.

Homelessness in rural Britain

Rural studies in Britain have a rich heritage of research into the problems and policy issues relating to rural housing (see, for example, Rogers, 1976; MacGregor et al, 1987; Clark, 1990; Shucksmith, 1990; Williams et al, 1991). These studies have explored the broad issues of how to provide affordable homes for local people in contexts where the in-migration of adventitious middle-class newcomers often results in gentrified housing markets. More recently, specific issues of housing conflict (Milbourne, 1997), changing public housing stocks (Hoggart, 1995; Milbourne, 1998), home occupancy rates (Hoggart, 1997) and planning for rural housing (Cloke, 1996; Tewdwr-Jones, 1998), have provided a more critical edge to the broad awareness of rural housing problems. This long-term acknowledgement of housing issues in rural areas is reflected in the policy pronouncements of a range of agencies associated with the countryside. For example the new Countryside Agency (1999) suggests that:

> There is an increasing need to accommodate growing numbers of households in rural England. It is projected that a quarter more households will exist in rural England in 2011 than in 1991. A supply of affordable, accessible housing is needed to alleviate the rural problem of high house prices, low incomes and a lack of social rented housing. (p 23)

Over recent years we have also witnessed a growing engagement on the part of researchers with sets of rural social welfare issues. Studies conducted over the 1980s and 1990s have focused on issues of poverty and social exclusion in rural Britain (see McLaughlin, 1986; Scott et al, 1991; Cloke et al, 1994, 1997a; Shucksmith et al, 1996; Chapman et al, 1998). However, while we undoubtedly have a clearer understanding of the nature of housing problems and social welfare in rural areas, these studies have avoided rural homelessness as a research focus. Rural poverty research has concentrated on groups living within conventional properties, while studies of rural housing problems have not moved beyond groups located within different rural housing sectors.

We want to suggest that the ready emphasis on rural housing and welfare issues has been associated with a relative invisibility of rural *homelessness* issues within academic and policy discourse. It is certainly true that studies of rural homelessness in the UK have been far less numerous and detailed than those undertaken in the US. The following parliamentary exchange highlights that up until quite recently the UK government was unaware of the scale of homelessness in rural areas:

Mr Cunningham:"... to ask the Secretary of State for the Environment what has been the level of rural homelessness: (a) in total; and (b) as a percentage of total homeless households in each year since 1989."

Mr Clappison: "The information is not available centrally. The data collected on homeless households accepted for re-housing does not differentiate between households from rural and non-rural areas." (*Hansard*, 20 March 1996)

While this exchange relates to official statistics on homelessness, it is also the case that homelessness research in Britain has tended to be aspatial. The majority of studies have focused on the shifting policy contexts of homelessness (see Burrows et al, 1997; Hutson and Clapham, 1999; Kennett and Marsh, 1999), different homeless groups (for example, on young homeless persons – Hutson and Liddiard (1994), and the single homeless – Kemp, (1997)), and changing profiles of homelessness at the national spatial scale (Greve, 1991). Furthermore, the limited amount of research that has been undertaken at the local level, for reasons that we set out earlier in this chapter, has been conducted in the spaces of the city, and particularly in London.

This limited academic coverage of rural homelessness is compounded by policy considerations of homelessness in the UK, as a whole suite of recent central government initiatives aimed at tackling homelessness has been characterised by particular urban spatial foci. For example, the Rough Sleepers Initiative has tended to concentrate on the most visible manifestations of homelessness – rooflessness – in London and other large cities, while the initial programme of policies implemented by the Social Exclusion Unit has also contained implicit assumptions about the (urban) spatiality of social exclusion. In combination, then, this twin neglect of the rural components of homelessness within academic and central policy discourse has led to certain assumptions about the limited, or even non-existent nature of homelessness in rural areas.

There have been a small number of studies undertaken over recent years which have touched on the subject of rural homelessness. Perhaps the first was that by Newton (1991), who analysed government figures on homelessness for the period 1978-91 according to a three-fold spatial categorisation – London, metropolitan areas and non-metropolitan areas. In 1978, non-metropolitan homelessness stood at roughly 26,000

Table 1.2: Changing levels of homeless households in England, by area (1978-1990/91)

	1978	1982	1986	1990/91	Total change 1978-90/91	% change
London	14,400	21,750	28,700	36,800	22,370	155.3
Metropolitan	12,500	19,000	27,600	47,800	35,340	282.7
Non-metropolitan	26,200	34,050	47,300	63,200	36,980	141.1
England	53,100	74,800	103,600	147,800	94,690	178.3
Non-metropolitan homelessness as % of total homelessness	49.3	45.5	45.7	42.7		

Source: Newton (1991)

households which represented 49.3% of the total for England (Table 1.2). By 1990-91, this non-metropolitan total had increased by 141.1% to around 63,000 households, although in proportional terms it accounted for less of the national total – largely due to the dramatic rises in homelessness levels recorded by metropolitan areas over this period. However, Newton's analysis did indicate that levels of homelessness were increasing faster in non-metropolitan areas than in London between the mid-1980s and early 1990s.

The first, and until quite recently only, piece of research to focus specifically on rural homelessness was published by Lambert et al (1992). Commissioned by the then Rural Development Commission (RDC), the research consisted of an analysis of data on statutory homelessness relating to rural local authority areas[1] for the 1980s and early 1990s and brief case studies drawn from six local authorities. The study provided detailed information on the scale and changing scale of rural homelessness in relation to that in London and urban authority areas. It was calculated that in 1989-90 there were 14,590 households recorded as homeless and in priority need by local authorities in rural areas – 12,347 in mixed areas and 2,243 households in deep rural areas – representing 12% of the homeless total for England in this year. The research also highlighted that the level of homelessness in rural local authority areas had increased at a faster rate over the 1980s than that in urban areas.

Further statistical information on rural homelessness emerged in a published paper by Bramley (1992) – a co-author of the RDC rural homelessness research report – which examined variations in the incidence of statutory homelessness between local authority areas in England over the 1980s and early 1990s. Utilising homelessness returns for 1990 and key findings from an earlier study by Duncan and Evans (1988) of local authority homelessness policy and practice, Bramley was able to provide a number of comparable indicators of the profile of, and local policy responses to, homelessness in rural areas. The paper highlighted a dominance of families among the statutorily accepted homeless in both rural and urban area types, accounting for over 80% of households in mixed rural, deep rural and urban authority areas. In terms of the factors contributing to homelessness, Bramley's analysis again revealed strong similarities between rural and urban authority areas, with four factors – parents or relatives unwilling to accommodate the household; relationship breakdowns; mortgage arrears; and loss of rented housing – accounting for slightly more than 8 out of 10 accepted cases in each of the three area types.

Notwithstanding these broad similarities concerning household types and contributory factors, Bramley identified three distinctive features of homelessness in rural areas. First, a higher proportion of rural homelessness cases (than among London and urban authority areas) were resulting from a loss of private rented and tied housing, which Bramley argued was linked to declining private rental opportunities in rural areas and losses of tied agricultural accommodation. Second, a distinctive feature of rural homelessness was a lower level of rural households being made homeless by parents or relatives being unwilling to accommodate them, which Bramley suggested could be linked to more pronounced incidences of 'social stress' in urban areas and/or different interpretations of homelessness legislation by local authorities. Third, a lower proportion of rural homelessness acceptances were found to fall within an official category of homelessness labelled 'other' (which includes households previously sleeping rough or living in hostel accommodation), confirming "the casual impression that such types of homelessness do cluster in urban centres" (Bramley, 1992, p 142).

In addition to these academic studies of rural homelessness, over recent years a growing number of homeless agencies have developed an interest in homelessness occurring beyond the limits of the city. In 1995 the British homeless charity, Shelter, organised a national conference on rural homelessness which brought together a range of national and local homeless organisations to discuss the nature of homelessness in rural areas and a range of practical and policy responses to it. More recently, two other national homeless organisations, Crisis and Centrepoint, have begun to turn to rural homelessness issues, with each funding research projects focused specifically on rural areas (Evans, 1999; Gunner, 1999).

Perceptions and causes

The studies of rural homelessness surveyed in the previous section suggest that rural areas are by no means immune from the problems of homelessness. Indeed, there is considerable evidence to suggest that significant numbers of people experience homelessness in rural areas, and that these numbers are not disappearing either by simple transfer to urban areas or by dint of national-level policies which are claimed to be dealing effectively with homelessness nationwide. In fact, taking account of how such statistical evidence almost certainly underestimates the problems of homelessness, particularly in rural areas, it seems entirely legitimate to argue that rural homelessness is underrepresented in academic, political and policy discourses. Yet it remains the case that popular perceptions of rural space, and rural life, continue to deny the existence and importance of rural homelessness as an issue and the rural homeless as people experiencing serious social problems.

Some insights into this political invisibility of rural homelessness can be gained by brief reference to a survey we have undertaken of the local authority officers with specific responsibility for dealing with homelessness (see Chapter Two for details of the survey). Sixty per cent of officers responding to our survey regarded rural homelessness as a significant issue. Given the broad invisibility of homelessness in rural areas, this figure perhaps represents a significant affirmation from practitioners, although the fact that the remaining 40% did not attribute significance to rural homelessness confirms an underlying reluctance to connect homelessness and rurality in policy discourses. Indeed, only 12% of authorities surveyed use the term 'rural homelessness' in their official documentation – again indicating that it is housing rather than homelessness which represents an acceptable discursive tag for the problems involved.

Given that many officers regarded rural homelessness to be a significant issue, there was an interesting range of responses to questions about the exact nature of *rural* homelessness:

> "We do not have obvious homelessness – people living on the streets. Due to close-knit communities, everyone seems to know each other; people tend to assist by being a good friend/neighbour." (Monmouthshire)

> "Homelessness applies to anyone in that position irrespective of whether they live in a city or a small country village. The words 'rural homelessness'

is a phrase used to separate between urban and rural areas, and really is quite pointless." (Shropshire)

"If someone comes to us as homeless, we look into it. I cannot really see the difference in being homeless in a rural or an urban situation, except the general public do not perceive there is a problem with homelessness in rural areas." (Somerset)

"I feel our district is what rural homelessness is about – widely spread-out villages, no provision of hostels or emergency accommodation (apart from bed and breakfast in local public houses). A huge public transport problem." (Essex)

"Rural homelessness is where those inhabitants who have a local connection with either a small village or an outlying area are unable to secure long-term affordable accommodation. This may lead to two categories: homeless, living in non-secure accommodation, ie family/friends; or roofless, having no access to accommodation whatsoever." (Lincolnshire)

The different ways in which rural homelessness is rendered invisible echoes clearly through these responses. The first separates out on-street rooflessness as the leading indicator, suggesting the absence of this visible form of homelessness in the rural context. Other related problems are conceived as being dealt with by the positive self-supporting nature of rural communities, where the close knit idyll of everybody knowing each other sponsors the necessary assistance. Both material and socio-cultural strands of invisibility are in evidence here. The second response seems to deny any spatiality of homelessness, and clearly rejects the need to raise the profile of rural homelessness in order to counteract any assumed urban spatiality. A similar even-handedness in the response from Somerset is tempered by the recognition of a common discursive perception that homelessness is not a problem in rural areas. Here, then, the spatiality of homelessness issues is problematic at least in terms of a blindness in public perceptions to the plight of homeless people in rural areas. Some of the more material and morphological influences of rurality are indicated in the response from Essex, whereas the final respondent confirms the presence of a range of homeless people (including those experiencing rooflessness) in rural areas.

Further insight is given by homelessness officers on the issue of why rural homelessness is a hidden problem. Some of the officers indicate once again that the lack of street homelessness in rural areas contributes strongly to the lack of visibility. More generally:

"The scale [of homelessness] is different in terms of absolute numbers and concentration of problems. Street homelessness is very visible and mainly an urban issue. Voluntary sector activity is greater and better organised in urban areas." (Kent)

The visibility of urban homelessness and its related agencies, then, casts a shadow over homelessness in rural space, which itself has to compete with other, more visible, indicators of affluence and idyll:

"... villages have been seen as mutually supporting networks (a romantic myth still promulgated, and which serves to mask, rather than highlight, the problem)." (Derbyshire)

These relative spaces of visibility and invisibility are further stylised by news media coverage:

"Concentration and media impact make metropolitan areas newsworthy. Much better to see 12 homeless people on one street in London than one person sleeping in a car in a town." (Northamptonshire)

"The media focus is on rough sleeping." (Bedfordshire)

Significantly, although many of the authorities surveyed had carried out localised housing needs surveys in rural areas, only three reported having undertaken studies of local rural homelessness per se. One respondent commented on why such a study had not been done:

"... it would [take] far too long. What will it achieve? Evidence is already there and known." (Devon)

While accepting that many authorities lack the resources to undertake the detailed ethnographic work needed to uncover hidden homelessness in rural areas, it is much less certain that evidence of rural homelessness is already widely available and acted on. Indeed, the only evidence that is 'already there' concerns numbers of households statutorily accepted as priority homeless, a measure which clearly underestimates the scale and scope of hidden homelessness in rural areas. It seems to us much more likely that the stance adopted by many rural local authorities is underpinned by the different strands of discursive non-coupling of rurality and homelessness. In this way, 'housing needs' concerns elide with concerns for homelessness, with the latter rendered invisible with the continued insistence that a focus on homelessness necessitates emphasis on rooflessness in cities. Far from evidence of rural homelessness already being 'there and known' it would seem that homelessness officers in rural authorities generally struggle to present informed discourses of the scale and scope of the problem, let alone generate innovative policy responses.

This, then, is the context in which rural homelessness needs to be understood. In one sense, homeless people in rural areas are merely those unfortunate enough to be experiencing a 'housing problem', and although housing problems are often acknowledged to be serious, they lack the edge of emergency or crisis which homelessness can convey. In another way, the idea of rural homelessness can be seen to be statistically valid, but such validity suffers from a lack of reinforcement in terms of visible reminders of the issue. Rural areas offer few sites/sights of homelessness, and so numeric indicators to the contrary are easily deprioritised.

Our concern is to convey the homeless as people. The most likely causes of homelessness in Britain relate to a series of key processes and circumstances:

- *loss* of a job, and of income, leading to rent or mortgage arrears;
- *crisis*, involving relationship breakdown, domestic violence, family dispute, disagreements with landlords and so on;
- *release* from care, from the armed forces, from institutions;
- *benefit traps*, especially involving teenagers and asylum seekers;
- *shortage* of affordable, secure, rented housing.

Many of these processes and circumstances are aspatial, meaning that the risk of, and occurrence of, homelessness is not diminished in a rural location. There may even be 'special' rural factors that add to such risk, especially in high-value and prestigious rural housing markets where the shortage of affordable housing is exacerbated. Unless we really believe that all people experiencing problems of homelessness immediately vacate rural space and somehow by magic migrate to urban centres, it seems safe to assume that people in rural areas will be experiencing different forms of homelessness.

The structure of the book

The research discussed in this book seeks to unpack the cultural and political contexts of rural homelessness. It surveys the legislative framework for dealing with the problems experienced by homeless people, and charts the significant localised variations in how agencies respond to homeless people within their jurisdiction. Above all it emphasises the experiences of homeless people and the spaces which they inhabit, arguing that it is only these kinds of real encounters – as described in Lewallen's *The Camp*, discussed at the beginning of the chapter – that will break down the discursive reluctance to acknowledge rural homelessness and to instigate targeted and effective policy responses to the needs of homeless people.

The remaining parts of the book have been brought together under seven main chapters, which reflect the key themes discussed in this introduction. The first of these, Chapter Two, provides a review of the ways in which homelessness has been approached by research teams over recent years. Drawing on quantitative and qualitative studies of homelessness in urban and rural areas, it sets the context for the research on which much of this book is based. In this chapter we also provide a wide-ranging discussion of our research on rural homelessness which not only includes details of the objectives, methods and products of the study, but also provides a reflexive account of the research process and the ethical issues bound up with research on homelessness.

In Chapter Three we set out the cultural context of homelessness in rural areas. Drawing on recent writings from sociology and cultural geography, it is argued that important socio-spatialisations of homelessness and rurality not only cast a cloak of invisibility over the existence of homelessness in rural spaces, but also construct homelessness as out of place in the purified spaces of rurality. Chapter Four switches attention on to the policy context of homelessness and rural homelessness. Here we provide a comprehensive and critical review of the development of homelessness policy in Britain, and connect these homelessness policies to the shifting housing and social welfare policy context of rural areas.

We examine the spaces of rural homelessness in Chapter Five, beginning by setting out new statistical findings on the overall picture of the extent and nature of homelessness in rural areas, and comparing the profile of rural homelessness with its urban counterpart. The chapter then moves on to provide an in-depth account of the local spaces of rural homelessness by drawing on research findings in the case-study areas. In Chapter Six we bring together key themes introduced in the two previous chapters by examining the shifting local governance of homelessness. Here we consider the ways in which the delivery of centralised homelessness policy in Britain is characterised by considerable spatial unevenness and we explore the emergence of complex networks of homelessness support in local rural spaces.

Chapter Seven is concerned with experiences of homelessness in rural areas. We begin by emphasising the circumstances of life crisis which render people vulnerable to homelessness in rural areas just as in the city. We then recount some of the narratives told to us by people who are or who have experienced rural homelessness, emphasising both the embodied experience of different forms of homelessness and the moral codes by which homeless people become 'known'.

The final chapter of the book provides a critical overview of the key academic themes that emerge from the preceding seven chapters. It also extends these themes into the realms of homelessness policy and practice. By drawing on key conclusions from a recent national policy and practitioner conference organised by the authors, this chapter sets out key obstacles impeding existing attempts to deal with rural homelessness. It also outlines a range of policy solutions that should be considered by different agencies with an interest in homelessness and social welfare issues in rural areas.

Note

[1] The study utilised a four-fold categorisation of areas – consisting of deep rural areas, mixed rural areas, non-rural areas (which we term urban within the remainder of this book), and London – derived from a combination of six previous classifications of local authority areas based on socioeconomic variables and population density.

TWO

Researching rural homelessness

Having set out the context of rural homelessness in Chapter One, we now want to discuss some key methodological issues bound up with researching homelessness in rural areas. This chapter is divided into three sections. In the first, we provide a critical review of the methodologies associated with recent academic studies of homelessness, drawing on research conducted both in Britain and in the US. The second focuses more specifically on rural homelessness and considers the ways in which the small number of studies undertaken have approached the subject. We also set out here the approach taken by the authors in their recently completed study of homelessness in rural England, and provide details of the main objectives, methodologies and products of this research. In the final section, we present a reflexive account of a range of ethical issues associated with researching rural homelessness, based on diary notes and research summaries provided by each member of the research team.

Researching homelessness

Any review of the large number of academic books and journal articles written on homelessness will reveal that the subject does not lend itself to easy research. In many ways, the complexities of definition discussed in Chapter One carry through into the process of researching homelessness. For example, a narrow definition of homelessness as rooflessness will tend to be associated with a research methodology that is different from one that would be utilised if a broader definition – encompassing a range of different housing situations – were to be adopted. Similarly, a normative definition of homelessness based on official statistical categorisations may necessitate a different methodological approach to one that relies on a definition of homelessness produced by homeless people themselves.

   In this section we want to review the ways in which the subject of homelessness has been researched in Britain and the US over recent years. In doing this, we consider that it is useful to point to two main approaches that have been taken within homelessness research. The first is heavily quantitative in nature, and bound up with the collection and analysis of primary and secondary data sets on the extent and nature of homelessness.

By contrast, the second approach has utilised qualitative techniques, involving ethnographic research, in-depth interviewing, and discourse analysis. In reviewing the methodological underpinnings of recent homelessness research we are struck by two observations: that the vast majority of studies have taken either a predominantly quantitative or qualitative approach, rather than adopting multi-method techniques and that, as with other research subjects in the social sciences, the study of homelessness has been dominated by quantitative methods of enquiry[1].

Quantitative assessments of homelessness

Quantitative assessments of homelessness have been dominated by statistical counts of rough sleepers. Figures on the scale of rough sleeping in Britain and the US have been made available by government based on counts undertaken as part of the decennial Censuses of population. However, it is widely recognised that these official statistics underestimate the real scale of rough sleeping as the techniques employed to measure street homelessness basically consist of 'clipboard counts' conducted over a single night period and focused on sites of known concentration of rough sleepers in urban spaces. Census estimates of the extent of rough sleeping have been supplemented over recent years by two other sources of statistical information. The first has been generated by agencies working with homeless groups that have organised their own counts of people sleeping rough in urban spaces. However, while these counts have uncovered higher levels of street homelessness, they have tended to utilise different methods of data collection and their spatial coverage has been extremely limited. Furthermore, it has been suggested that the political interests of these agencies in publicising homelessness issues can sometimes influence the ways in which counts are organised and data presented.

A second source of additional data on the incidence of street homelessness has emerged in Britain as a consequence of the Rough Sleepers Initiative (RSI), a central government scheme aimed at reducing levels of rough sleeping in a number of cities and large towns[2]. Enumeration has been fundamental to gaining access to central government resources linked to the RSI, with funding only awarded to local authorities that are able to demonstrate a 'significant rough sleeping problem' through a single night headcount of rough sleepers[3]. However, while having a clear-cut definition of homelessness as rough sleeping, enumeration has proved to be far from unproblematic.

There have been a series of initial reviews of the RSI in Britain. For example, Randall and Brown (1996, 1999) have evaluated it in England, beginning with a study of rooflessness in London but later widening their focus as the RSI itself was extended to other areas, while Yannetta et al (1999) have presented an interim evaluation of the first round of the RSI in Scotland. These reviews have highlighted problems associated with the standardised 'snapshot' methodology provided by central government. Randall and Brown (1999) provide an indication of the scale of undercounting of rough sleeping in London produced by the snapshot approach:

> In central London in 1997/8 around 2,600 people slept rough, of whom 1,900 were new to street homelessness. This is around ten times the figure found on a single night. (p 2)

Three main reasons can be advanced for this level of undercount. First, it can be difficult to locate some rough sleepers during the count process. As Crane (1997) suggests, "one of the main problems of counting people sleeping rough is finding them. For safety reasons, enumerators tend not to search in dangerous or inaccessible places" (p 17). Yet it is in these types of 'dangerous and inaccessible places' that rough sleepers, who are often anxious to avoid being harassed by members of the public or moved on by the police, are often found. The Simon Community, which conducts regular counts of rough sleepers in London, tries to circumvent this difficulty by involving ex-homeless people as enumerators – they know the various 'haunts'. Here, we believe, is an excellent example of how qualitative 'insider knowledge' derived from ethnographic or auto-ethnographic experience of rough sleeping provides a very necessary contextualisation for enumeration techniques.

Second, there is evidence that in smaller places rough sleepers will not wish to be encountered by enumerators. It can be suggested that a fear of being moved on from their sleeping-place (especially in the context of 'strong policing' of on-street homelessness), or of abuse or harassment, and a general mistrust of officialdom may lead to rough sleepers who have prior knowledge of a headcount absenting themselves from their normal 'bivvies' for the night of the count.

A third reason for the undercounting of rough sleepers through the single night headcount concerns the essentially fluid and transient nature of this form of homelessness. As Randall and Brown (1996) suggest from their evaluation of the RSI:

> Most rough sleepers had stayed in some form of accommodation recently, but often only for a short time. A quarter had found somewhere

they thought of as a permanent home since their first episode of sleeping rough, but had lost it again. Nearly three quarters had tried to find a new permanent home since they started sleeping rough, and two thirds had been offered help with finding accommodation in the past six months. (p 2)

In addition to these counts of the incidence of street homelessness, another valuable source of quantitative material in Britain is provided by official statistics on statutorily defined homelessness. Unlike the situation in the US and in other European countries, detailed statistical information on the incidence of particular forms of homelessness is published for England, Wales and Scotland by government. Beginning with the 1977 Housing (Homeless Persons) Act and withstanding several reforms of the housing system (most notably, the 1996 Housing Act), local authorities in England and Wales have been legally obliged to rehouse specific groups of homeless households defined as being in priority need. A key part of this obligation has been the recording of quantitative information about the scale and nature of homelessness approaches and acceptances. Bramley (1992) suggests that this "policy framework has actually generated over time a large and relatively consistent set of data on homelessness in Britain" (pp 128-9), while Burrows (1997) estimates that statutory statistics include around three quarters of all homeless cases. However, as with the rough sleeper counts, these official statistics underestimate the overall scale of homelessness and also represent a less than consistent source of data.

In relation to the former criticism, it is possible to point to three areas of potential underestimation. The first concerns the reactive nature of the collection of data on statutory homelessness; there is a reliance on homeless persons to make an approach to their local authority, and, as a number of studies indicate, certain individuals and groups experiencing homelessness may not, for a variety of reasons, approach statutory agencies with their problems (see Lambert et al, 1992; Thomas and Niner, 1989).

A second area of undercounting is bound up with the restrictive definitions of homeless groups and situations set out in recent homelessness legislation. Non-priority groups such as (young) single persons and childless couples are effectively barred from being accepted as homeless and in priority need, and even those considered as priority cases may be refused rehousing if they are deemed to be intentionally homeless. In fact, Hutson and Liddiard (1994) calculate that of those households making contact with English local authorities about homelessness in the early 1990s, an average of around two thirds were not accepted as priority-need homelessness cases. Third, Pleace et al (1997) suggest that statutory assessments of homelessness can be seen as undercounting actual levels through their focus on households rather than individuals within households.

The question concerning the consistency of statistics on statutory homelessness arises over the ways in which individual local authorities interpret central government legislation and other policy guidance. Studies by Evans and Duncan (1988), Niner (1989) and Hoggart (1995b) highlight widespread localised variations in the implementation of homelessness policy between local authorities, particularly in terms of interpretations of the vulnerability of homeless people and the intentionality of their homelessness. Consequently, Hutson and Liddiard (1994) argue that statutory homelessness statistics should be viewed more as 'social constructs' than 'empirical measurements' (p 33), reflecting different local policy and practice frameworks, which themselves are bound up with a complex mix of political, socioeconomic and housing factors in different locales (see also Watson and Austerberry, 1986; Hoggart, 1995b).

A final area of quantitative research on homelessness, and one that is dwarfed by statistical analyses of rough sleeping and statutory homelessness, concerns surveys of homeless people and agencies dealing with homelessness. There have been attempts to survey different groups of homeless people, usually in places and spaces of known concentration – shelters and hostels located in urban spaces. For example, Anderson et al (1993) conducted a survey of around 1,300 homeless people living in hostels, night shelters and bed and breakfast hotels, and those sleeping rough in five boroughs of London and five other English cities. Others have undertaken surveys of service providers, such as local authorities, in an effort to ascertain the nature of homelessness and agency responses to it (Evans and Duncan, 1988; Niner, 1989), while still others have analysed other official data sets that contain information on homelessness. Burrows (1997), for example, has analysed the Survey of English Housing – a continuous government annual survey since 1993 based on interviews with around 20,000 households – which provides a limited amount of information on the number and nature of surveyed households who had experienced a period of homelessness over recent years.

Qualitative homelessness research

While, numerically speaking, statistics have come to dominate recent research on homelessness in Britain and the US, qualitative studies have contributed much to the ways in which homelessness and homeless people are understood. This work has tended to be undertaken by social anthropologists, sociologists and cultural geographers, particularly those based in the US. However, while researchers may be drawn from different areas of the social sciences than those engaged in quantitative studies of homelessness, the focus of their research has been fixed on the same spaces; those of the city. Qualitative research has usually been based around local ethnographies of homeless individuals and groups. A key aim is to generate a detailed insider perspective of homelessness through prolonged periods of observation of and contact with homeless people. According to Glasser and Bridgman (1999), the ethnographic approach to homelessness has much to offer:

> Through the utilization of extended fieldwork, a holistic approach, and cross-cultural perspectives, anthropologists attempt to understand what drives individuals to life on the streets and to shelters, and what prevents them from gaining permanent and secure housing.... The insider's approach attempts to avoid a priori categories of other disciplines and therefore enables us to see the world through the eyes of the homeless themselves. (pp 6-7)

For Rowe and Wolch (1990), participant observation of the lives of homeless women in Los Angeles between 1986 and 1988 provided a great deal of familiarisation with their life-styles and "allowed for a depth of mutual revelation and understanding between field researcher and informants that would have been difficult to achieve through other means" (p 188).

We can point to a number of studies of homeless people in the US that have adopted an ethnographic approach. The lives of homeless people on 'skid rows' in different cities have been explored by, among others, Spradley (1970) and Wolch and Rowe (1992); connections between deinstitutionalisation and homelessness have been studied by Dear and Wolch (1987); and the everyday lives of homeless youth in Hollywood have been described by Ruddick (1996). In Britain, ethnographic studies of homelessness are less common. Wardhaugh (1996) has provided an ethnographic account of street homelessness in an English city, but there are few other such studies on which the researcher of homelessness can draw.

In addition to a desire to see homelessness through the eyes of homeless people, certain qualitative researchers have also attempted to explore social constructions of 'home and 'homeless'. Drawing on in-depth interviews with groups of 'homeless' people, researchers such as Veness (1993) and Watson and Austerberry (1986) have sought to question dominant categorisations of homelessness and, in so doing, have raised important methodological issues for researchers. Veness, for example, has argued that the 'homeless' people she interviewed saw themselves as living in what she describes as situations of 'un-home' rather than being homeless.

Several of these qualitative accounts of homelessness have sought to consider the situations of homeless people within a wider context of structural exclusion and regulatory frameworks. In so doing, they have moved beyond the stories of the homeless and brought into their research strategies more powerful groups of actors. For some, this has meant exploring the processes through which local space is controlled by agencies of the state and business (for example, Mitchell, 1997); others have focused on particular sites of conflict between the local state and homeless groups (see Smith, 1993); while still others have considered sets of tactics employed by homeless people to cope with or subvert a range of strategies used by more powerful actors to regulate local space (see Ruddick, 1996; Wardhaugh, 1996). Discourse analysis has also been used by a handful of homelessness researchers to examine the ways in which homelessness and homeless people are socially constructed within media and policy discourse (see Hutson and Liddiard, 1994; Takahashi, 1998a).

Having provided a review of the key features of qualitative research on homelessness, we want to finish this section of the chapter by pointing to some absent issues within this work. We want to discuss three issues in particular. First, writing this review has proved rather problematic owing to the limited amount of coverage that authors of published material on homelessness dedicate to the methods associated with their studies. We feel that there is a need for a broader and more open discussion of methodology within such published accounts of homelessness. A second problematic area which, in many ways, is linked to the previous one, concerns the issue of ethics within homelessness research. From this brief review of recent homelessness research, we would conclude that very rarely are ethical considerations brought into published work on homelessness (although see Cloke et al, 2000c). Third, while the qualitative accounts of homelessness reviewed here show a great deal of sensitivity towards the situations of homeless people, they also carry with them unhelpful assumptions about the spatialities of homelessness. In short, almost all research in Britain and the US has been undertaken in local spaces of the city, leading to a neglect of homelessness research in smaller towns and rural areas.

Researching rural homelessness

As we discussed in Chapter One, there has been relatively little attention given to rural homelessness by those within the academic and policy communities. While rural researchers have focused on issues of rural poverty and other welfare issues (see Cloke et al, 1997a, 1997b; Duncan, 1999), and rural housing (see Milbourne 1997; Shucksmith, 1990), research on homelessness in rural areas has been conspicuous only through its absence. Further, the small number of rural homelessness studies have largely been conducted in the US.

As with the urban studies, research on homelessness in rural areas has been dominated by quantitative modes of investigation. For example, Davenport et al (1990) have provided a comparative analysis of homelessness in rural and urban areas in the US, and First et al (1990) have examined the causes and patterns of rural homelessness using official statistics. It has only been through the work of Fitchen (1991, 1992) that any in-depth account of homelessness in rural areas emerges. Through qualitative research on homelessness in upstate New York, Fitchen not only outlines some of the key features of rural homelessness but discusses the methodological difficulties associated with researching a group that tends to remain hidden within small and scattered rural settlements that are not well served by homeless services and facilities (see also Aron and Fitchen, 1996).

The situation regarding rural homelessness research in Britain is less favourable than that in the US. In fact, as discussed in the previous chapter, there has been only one academic study of homelessness in rural areas and this was commissioned by a central government agency. The study, by Lambert et al (1992), is highly quantitative in nature and comprises a detailed spatial analysis of official homelessness statistics and a small number case studies of local policy responses to homelessness in different rural areas. It is within this context of a limited base of knowledge on rural homelessness that our study and this book need to be positioned.

The research on which this book is largely based has its origins in the mid-1990s when two of the authors – Paul Cloke and Paul Milbourne – became involved in small-scale qualitative studies of rural homelessness in South West England. While this work was focused mainly on local agency understandings of the nature of rural homelessness, emerging findings pointed to a need for a broader project on homelessness in rural areas. An application for such a research project was submitted to the Economic and Social Research Council in June 1995, which resulted in the award of a research grant for a period of two years. The research project commenced in January 1996 and was completed in December 1998. Three researchers were employed on the project: Rebekah Widdowfield, who acted as principal researcher; and Phil Cooke and Jenny Cursons, who were employed as ethnographic placements.

There were four main objectives associated with our research:

1. To develop theorisations of home, homelessness and rurality (see Chapter Three).
2. To examine the spatialities of rural homelessness (Chapter Five).
3. To explore the experiences of different types of homelessness in rural areas (Chapter Seven).
4. To consider the governance of rural homelessness at national and local spatial scales (Chapters Four, Six and Eight).

A methodological strategy involving three phases of research was undertaken to explore these objectives:

Extensive research

The first phase of research aimed to provide some indicative information about those aspects of rural homelessness which are conducive to national level research. We were able to access central government statistical evidence (1992 and 1996/97) on homelessness (P1E returns from the DETR), and we have used this data at a national level and in two study counties – Gloucestershire and Somerset – to present analyses of the nature, incidence and geographies of statutory homelessness in rural areas. As we suggested earlier, such data is important, but only presents a limited overview of homelessness, and therefore needs to be carefully critiqued. In addition we undertook a postal questionnaire survey of all local authority homelessness officers. With strenuous reminders and telephone prompts, this survey received 231 responses (61%; 154 from urban and 77 from rural authorities). Further information was gained via direct contact with officers in a number of authorities (notably Monmouth, Bristol, Caradon, Oxford, Warwick, Cambridgeshire), and 18 of the 30 Rural Community Councils contacted provided contextual information for rural authority areas. We interviewed representatives from 14 national homeless (including Shelter, Crisis, and Centrepoint) and rural organisations (for example, the Rural Development Commission [now the Countryside Agency]). We also monitored media outputs representing 'home' and 'homelessness' in the rural context.

Intensive research

The intention of this phase of the research was to understand the work carried out by the network of statutory and voluntary agencies dealing with homelessness in two 'rural' counties – Somerset and Gloucestershire (see Figure 2.1) – and to establish the opportunities to undertake unstructured interviews with homeless people from different points in the spectrum of homelessness in rural areas. The following interviews were undertaken in our Somerset and Gloucestershire case studies:

- local authority homelessness officers (10)
- representatives from voluntary agencies (44)
- homeless people (40)

Interviews with homeless people were partly conducted during the ethnographic placements, partly at key facilities for the homeless (such as hostels and drop-in centres) and partly through direct referral from various advice agencies. In this way 'roofless' and temporarily sheltered people formed the main body of these interviewees. However, people experiencing other, more 'grey area' forms of homelessness, were less easy to contact for interview (although advice centre referrals helped us to gain some valuable interviews here). We used press releases and widely scattered 'story to tell' adverts, to try to make freepost or free-phone contact with these other homeless people, and some interesting conversations arose. But it was in gaining access to anonymised case notes (from local authorities, voluntary organisations and advice centres) that we made contact with the circumstances and life histories of homeless people who could not easily otherwise be contacted for interview. As a result we conducted 40 face to face interviews (32 taped and transcribed, 8 noted) and we accessed 44 sets of case notes, meaning that qualitative information was gathered relating to 84 homeless people in the study areas. This research proved to be extremely time-consuming and challenging ethically but was thoroughly rewarding and provided the basis for many of our findings.

Ethnographic placements

The final phase of research sought to place researchers in two rural towns for an entire year to carry out ethnographic studies of homelessness in the surrounding areas. The placement of Phil Cooke (in Taunton) and Jenny Cursons (working out from Cheltenham to Cinderford/Cirencester)

Figure 2.1: The Gloucestershire and Somerset case study counties

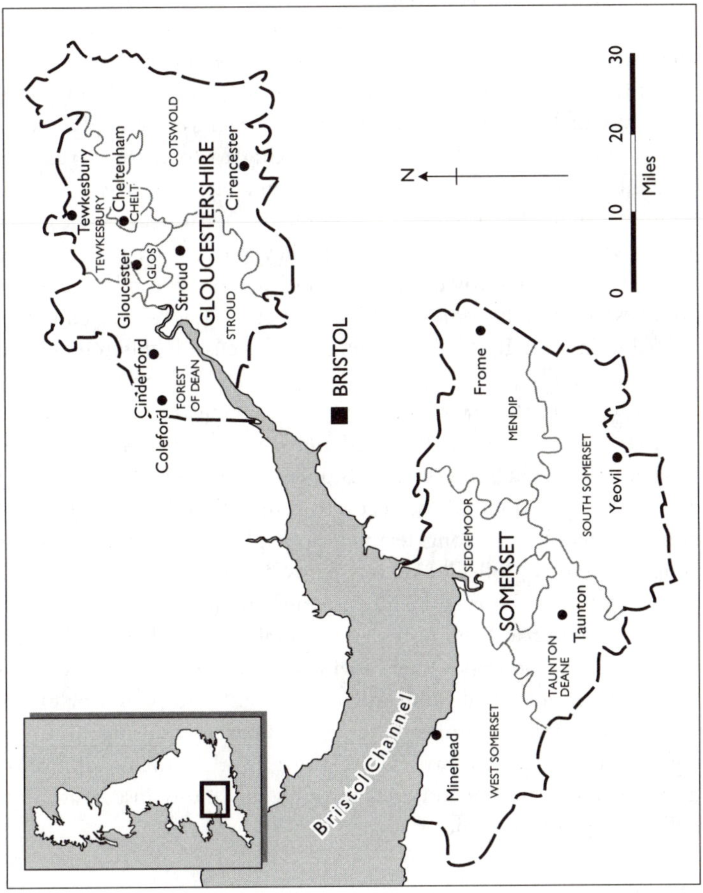

was seen as an innovative method of developing 'thick descriptions' of rural homelessness and homeless people by a mix of participant observation (in key facilities for the homeless), interviews, and association. Each placement necessarily involved a painstakingly slow start while the researchers became familiarised with particular agency and spatial contexts. They adopted overt rather than covert positionalities, and were unwilling to use tactics of persuasion or reward to gain interviews or to prolong them in cases of emotional stress. Nevertheless, key informants were 'got to know' longitudinally through these processes, and very valuable narratives of life history, experience of homelessness, coping strategies and so on emerged. We began by seeking to focus on a rurality that equated with small villages and open countryside. Indeed, very interesting findings emerged relating to these contexts. Yet it became clear that the 'towns' which served these areas are also key to issues of rural homelessness, for it is here that lowest-order facilities are provided, and where homelessness first becomes 'visible'. The ethnographic placements, then, contributed strongly to this widening of focus on different senses and scales of 'rurality'.

A key part of our strategy was to 'place' the two researchers ethnographically within localised networks of voluntary services for homeless people in Somerset and Gloucestershire. These placements were designed to gain appropriate access to some of the least visible groups of homeless people. The long-term ethnographic commitment to homeless people given by Phil Cooke and Jenny Cursons yielded very valuable ethnographic accounts of the life histories, circumstances and experiences of people who had been homeless in rural areas, and especially of those who had been roofless. Other 'obvious' points of access (hostels, drop-in centres, local authority files) provided us with interviews or case notes which extended our understanding of different housing histories and coping strategies. Some of the most hidden forms of domiciled homelessness were encountered through the anonymised case notes of different voluntary agencies.

The products of the research

The publication pathways emphasised by evaluators of academic research performance are refereed international texts, and so the production of papers and books for academic audiences (of which this is one) is a necessary fulfilment of the expectations of both the institutions in which we work and the sponsors of the research. However, were this to be the only channel of dissemination then clear ethical objections could and should be raised.

Recently one of us has commented that the growing sensitivity to a 'polyphony of voices' within social science has failed to consider fully multiple audiences (Milbourne, 2000). New words and new worlds have not really travelled to new ears and eyes, as research and writings on 'others' have been produced by and for academics. Within this project we have attempted to take our work into a variety of discursive environments. We certainly gain a great deal of fulfilment from contextualising our findings within wider bodies of theoretical literature relating to society, space, homelessness and rurality; as we attempt to make more visible an issue (rural homelessness) and group (homeless people in rural spaces) that remain marginalised within academic discourse. However, we also feel obliged to do something else with this material – to enter into the discursive environments of national and local policy so that rural homelessness becomes at least accepted, if not dealt with by policy makers. It is probably our interventions in these policy environments that will have a greater chance of improving the quality of life of those homeless people who have given their time to our project. We also spent much time discussing how best to disseminate findings from the project to these homeless people. Our uneasy conclusion is that, for a number of practical issues, this probably has to be done through agencies and organisations.

In our research we have taken steps to write extensively for professional and popular audiences and to participate in a wide range of conferences and broadcasting. We have provided agencies with which we have worked suitably anonymised and confidential summaries of our findings. We have arranged briefings for policy makers at national and local levels. We have organised a two-day national conference to publicise issues relating to rural homelessness which was attended by 70 delegates representing the main homeless and rural agencies in Britain. We have issued press releases about our research and been interviewed on radio programmes and by a range of newspapers and magazines. In many ways this is now a standard dissemination package adopted in much contemporary research. But is it sufficient to constitute 'giving something back' and therefore to ensure the validity of the research? Our disagreements over the answer to this question point right back to the reflexive and dialogic underpinnings of our research. We have argued with resignation (or realism) about whether it is possible to do more. We have also wearily argued over the inaccessibility of much of academic literature, alongside an excitement and fascination with the theoretical ideas and debates therein.

In the final evaluation we want to ensure that we have given sufficient back to persuade ourselves – and perhaps others – that we are not research tourists. We have needed to go further than just looking and collecting interviews in order both to capture the experience and to provide mementoes of the trip. More than this, though, we want to argue that the research has been part of, or has instigated, a long-term engagement for each of us in homelessness politics. In part, such involvement, whether through volunteering, further research, or other action will be the litmus test of 'giving something back'.

Ethics, reflexivity and research encounters with homeless people

We want to complete this chapter on researching homelessness with a detailed discussion of ethical issues bound up with our research on rural homelessness. Here we use personal diary accounts, both of specific ethical dilemmas which occurred during the interviews, ethnographic placements, and other encounters with homeless people, and of more generalised ethical strands that were woven into the research. What follows is an account of a range of ethical considerations which arose during the research as noted in our individual diaries or research summaries. Where common themes emerge, we agree to speak as a 'team' recognising, however, that each is subject to different positionalities and power relations within that team. Indeed the idea of 'teamwork' is acknowledged by us all to involve a complex and shifting mix of public and private identities. These include both *collective* identities associated with our commitment to share ideas and to co-author publications, presentations and other external forms of communication about the research, and *private* contributions, involving disagreements and tensions about the nature and direction of the project, the execution of particular research methods, and so on. Thus, individual contributions also reflect the contested and personalised nature of ethical responses within the research. For this reason, passages from particular diary summaries are introduced in the text, so that our individual voices can be heard where appropriate. We have structured our discussion into two main parts, dealing with issues of validity and practice of the research, although the two are interconnected, especially in terms of how the selves of our research encountered the otherness of homeless people.

The ethical validity of the research

One of the overriding considerations of our work on rural homelessness has been a questioning of the ethical validity of our research. Such an admission may elicit a response from some parts of the academic and policy communities to the effect that if this is the case then we should not be entrusted with such research. However, to suggest an unshakeable confidence that research is entirely valid and worthwhile, and can be explained as such unambiguously to a variety of different individuals and agencies, is to whitewash over a series of critical issues especially for self-reflexive research with marginalised individuals and groups. There are a number of contexts to be held in tension here: the academic imperative of 'grantsmanship' (sic), whereby the winning of research monies has become a crucial indicator of performance; the professional goals of researchers in terms of reputation, influence, career development; the ideological commitment of researchers to issues (often bridging between professional and other voluntary commitments); the topical, structural and political importance of the issue being researched; the degree of partnership with non-academic agencies and individuals that is built into the research; and the likely outcomes of the research in the public sphere. To some extent each of these contexts has its own discursive equipment which is used to provide different emphases at different stages of the research. For example, considerable confidence tends to be transmitted by researchers when completing grant application forms. We know what we want to do, why we want to do it, what significant findings will emerge, and the importance of those findings to 'end-users'. However, when faced with the everyday predicaments of (in our case) homeless people, it is difficult to maintain this same air of confidence, and pre-established ideas about the validity of the research will often undergo significant transformation.

Both as individuals and as a group of researchers, we had some ethical difficulties in explaining the purpose and value of the research accurately and unambiguously. Composing purposive statements for written communications about our intentions proved relatively problem-free. Yet when faced as individual researchers with the demystifying experience of explaining the validity of our research to those in need, considerable ethical turbulence occurred:

> "It was difficult explaining and justifying the project to the homeless people with whom I spoke. I heard myself sounding unconvincing when I informed interviewees that rural homelessness is an under-

researched topic and that the findings may impact positively on subsequent policies." (Jenny)

"Another issue with which I often found myself grappling was a real sense of impotence and inadequacy at not being able to do much, if anything, of immediate material benefit for some of the homeless individuals to whom I spoke. As one individual put it: 'What's the point? No one's going to change anything'. Often was the time when I found myself asking: Just what difference will this work I'm doing make to the people who are sharing their lives with me?" (Phil)

Jenny's "sounding unconvincing" and Phil's "what's the point?" reflect the dilemma of research validity when faced with 'othered' research subjects. Does it "console them to know they are part of a polyphony?" (Thrift, 1991, p 145). How can research values at a macro-policy and political level be justified to the people whose stories will be used to attempt to influence policy, opinion and provision which is so far removed from their personal situation and experience? During these encounters the resolve of the research team to ensure that their attempt would 'make a difference' seemed far away and somehow hollow when dealing face to face with the stark reality of an embodied person. As Phil noted:

"The simple fact of the matter (and it was one I found difficult to swallow) was that I could effectively do nothing there and then; I wanted to be able to promise more, but it all felt very much like a one-sided contract."

We all, at different times, questioned the ethics of this apparently one-sided contract, especially in view of our previous (and we reckoned) serious contemplation of the dangers of research tourism. The potential hypocrisy between what we write in abstract terms about how research *should* be, and how we *practise* research with other individuals was evident in these deliberations:

"I had written recently about the dangers of exploitative research tourism, and the unethical nature of 'flip' ethnographies in which academics flip in and flip out of the lives of other people staying just long enough to collect juicy stories. Yet I found myself doing just that in a particular village. Staying for just a weekend I had a chance encounter with two homeless men, and their stories have become integral to our findings. My commitment to them was so small, and the fact that I have a more regular commitment to homeless people in Bristol seemed at the time to be a disconnected excuse for flip ethnography." (Paul C)

Such seeming hypocrisy is not, we would argue, due to brazen disregard of ethical and moral imaginations. Rather, in specific research contexts, ethical decisions (in this case to seek out and interview two people) become not only detached from abstract guidelines, but also represent a negotiation about the positive impact that might accrue from the 'greater good' of the research at a national level. In any case, our experience was that many of the homeless people we met were, in fact, far less troubled by the idea of a one-sided contract than we were:

> "It was enough that their story might contribute something towards helping somebody, somewhere, sometime. This was actually a particularly humbling experience – not least because it showed that, while there were clearly ethical issues at stake (Had I been totally honest about the project's inevitable limitations? Had I been careful not to raise false expectations?), some of my tortuous deliberations were as much to do with my own patronising attitudes towards others, and the fact that maybe I was simply trying to salve my own conscience." (Phil)

The second ethical issue about validity, then, is for researchers to explain to *themselves* why they are doing the research. In part, such explanations are demanded by the very encounters with homeless people described above:

> "Throughout the research, I found myself becoming distanced from the project, even though my role was involved at a very practical level. I often lost sight of what the project was setting out to achieve and in what ways it could be useful for those being researched. In fact, I became quite disillusioned with research itself as I was coming face to face with 'real' problems being encountered by 'real' people in their everyday lives." (Jenny)

Just as often, however, disillusionment arises from the sheer difficulty of holding in tension the very different roles and discourses demanded of an academic researcher dealing with marginalised others:

> "A lot of the time I do not feel that what I do is worthwhile. In some senses, this is exacerbated by the nature of the topics in which I am

engaged (and the environment in which my research is being conducted, ie, in the academic rather than the policy sphere). In studying a social issue such as homelessness, there would seem to be more of an implicit responsibility for that research to be geared towards 'making a difference'." (Rebekah)

Such tensions over the value and validity of research do not occur in some vacuous abstract space. As Rebekah points out, 'without homelessness, I wouldn't have a job', and as Paul M notes, research money is integral to the notions of performance and reputation in the academic workplace:

> "I, like many other academics, have discovered that the generation of research income, from various sources, has come to play an increasingly significant part of my academic life in the Research Assessment Exercise era. In my brief academic 'career' I have been involved in 10 projects of funded research. All but one of these have been funded substantially by government agencies and their quangos. Most have concerned poverty and marginalisation with which I have a deep moral and academic attachment. Some though, quite unashamedly, have been undertaken to generate profit so that the academic unit within which I currently work can continue to meet its ever increasing income targets."

Nevertheless, researchers often face the dilemma that the funds supporting their research (in this case over £100,000) could be used to pay for tangible facilities which would bring benefit in this case to homeless people. The fact that the precise funds are not transferable in this way does little to mitigate feelings of guilt. We have often mused over the practical policy steps we would take if given £1m to deal with local homelessness issues. The thought that by scrapping 10 research projects such as ours these monies could become available, brings with it an obligation to use the research to make a positive difference towards the tackling of homelessness. This obligation has to be tempered with realism:

> "Realism demands an acceptance that it is unlikely that one particular piece of research will bring about any revolutionary change. As time has gone along I have had to become more realistic about what, if anything, my research can achieve, in order to avoid succumbing to a pervading sense of frustration and disillusionment." (Rebekah)

Different individuals in our team coped with these ethical dilemmas differently. Our personalities are different, as is the duration of our experience in coping with these issues. Some were content to throw small pebbles into large ponds without knowing where the ripples would end. Others, having experienced the possibilities (and disappointments) of attempting to connect research findings into policy and media networks through previous projects, have by now become persuaded of potential short- and long-term benefits of research. For us all, these motivations cannot be divorced from research being integral to our livelihoods, and from the heightened focus on performance and evaluation, which themselves provide validity (but hardly ethical validity) to the process of research. No wonder, then, that honest and unambiguous accounts of what the research entails – what is its purpose and its value – are made extremely complex by reflexive and dialogical approaches.

Carrying out the research

Ethical issues surrounding the purpose and value of our research occurred throughout the project, and have continued afterwards. A related series of issues are, however, traceable to the nature of the specific encounters between the selves of researchers and the otherness of homeless people. Here, the standard ethical prompts for research had to be set against the complexities arising from the shifting multiple identities of the researchers, the multi-functional roles and positions we found ourselves in, and the varying circumstances in which 'we' related to 'them' and vice versa. The interviews with homeless people – who are frequently excluded from direct involvement in the study of homelessness – were positively motivated by the desire to give them a 'voice' within the research process. From the start we were aware of issues relating to power and positionality, the potential negative impact on respondents, and possible interviewee dependency. As Rebekah noted:

> "The research team was well aware from the outset of the potential problems and ethical dilemmas which the project was likely to raise, and indeed those were clearly set out in the original proposal. I was guided in all aspects of the research by the belief that researchers should be as open and honest as possible about what they are doing and why, and should set clear boundaries as to what is and what is not acceptable. There was a common recognition of the need to adopt a reflexive approach, continually querying and reflecting on the *purposes* of each

of our questions – particularly in relation to personal and possibly distressing enquiries."

However, notions of honesty, openness, and clear boundary setting are in practice made complex in self–other encounters such as those which form the basis of this part of our research. For example, in each case informed consent was sought from potential interviewees. Here, obvious abuse of the ethics of consent, such as in the case of a German magazine reporter in our study area who had been offering street homeless people 'a fiver for their story, with photos' is easily recognisable. Yet permission in other cases is integrally interconnected with the risk of exploiting the potential interviewee:

> "Gaining permission for an interview is not a cut and dried event at the start. Even with agreement to conduct an interview, it seems as though the interviewee doesn't really release their permission until they begin to trust you. Equally, their responses are generally more interesting when permissive trust has been established. I certainly encountered instances of Punch's *mutual deceit*, where I was on my best ethical behaviour, often asking questions which were peripheral to my main interest, *until* I was being trusted, and effectively given permission to be more personal and directive. There is no doubt that I was more prone to exaggeration, concealment and other trust-seeking devices during the early part of interviews. This is a really distressing, though not perhaps uncommon, conclusion to reach." (Paul C – see Punch, 1986)

Any such exploitation is hardly a deliberate tactic, but nevertheless must influence the intertextual narrative that results from the interview. Another complication in the ethical evaluation of 'them' and 'us' encounters, is the realisation that the self is not a stable concept, but rather a shifting collection of identities which refuses to be subjugated to the identity of researcher or researched. Our diaries offer considerable evidence of how certain identities come to the fore during interview encounters. Jenny, for example, found her position vis-à-vis her interviewees to be strongly influenced by attributes that go beyond research training and experience:

> "The stronger part of my self-identity is that of a single parent, and my own struggle with the negative representations of my 'group' in the media and wider society. While I have never been homeless, I have on occasion had difficulty (as many people do) with trying to maintain my rent payments and provide for my family. These experiences allowed

for a certain degree of identification with my interviewees but, in certain situations, this proved problematic — at times it felt as if I was at once the researcher and the researched, perhaps too much of an 'insider' in some ways."

Both Rebekah and Paul C found that their identification as volunteers in (different) homeless peoples' shelters in Bristol impinged on their role as researchers into the problem of homelessness, although with different outcomes:

"I was anxious not to be seen as using this group as a means of accessing homeless people and the network of agencies directly or indirectly engaged in dealing with homelessness." (Rebekah)

"It was inevitable that my regular involvement at the shelter meant that I got to know some of the homeless people there pretty well. After all, conversation is one of the few 'luxuries' that people can choose to accept there. These conversations were times when a very grey space between research and volunteering was (re)produced. Indeed I heard much from people at the shelter which opened up broad lines of inquiry for the research, and while I told people what my job was, and of my research interests, I was never sure that they got much beyond the 'liberal do-gooder' tag that was so often voiced. I did, with permission, tape two interviewees at the shelter, but it was a somewhat uncomfortable mix of concerned volunteerism and permitted research encounter." (Paul C)

Another dimension of multiple identity occurred within the category of 'researcher'. Our diaries show that hierarchical positioning within the research team led to particular responsibilities being discharged during interviews. Paul M discusses his 'feelings of awkwardness' and 'subsequently frustration' when encountering homeless people in unexpected situations:

"How can I turn off this project when the subjects of the research are all around me? When 'out of the office' I pass homeless people, persons begging and *Big Issue* sellers on the high street and read articles in my local newspaper about campaigns to remove their visibilities from these spaces. I have even encountered a homeless man sleeping under a bush in my own back garden. If anything, the project has complicated my interactions with these homeless people. I find myself thinking carefully before striking up conversations with them during my 'out of work' hours as I attempt to separate the concerned citizen/academic researcher components of my ever-shifting identities. I feel awkward with many of the homeless people that I encounter on a regular basis, and such feelings result from the situations in which these encounters have taken place; their unexpected natures, the awkward environments, the crumbling of any public (work)/private (home) divide, and the multiple identities of myself as (interfering) researcher, writer and concerned citizen."

Much of Paul M's interviewing effort has been with representatives of housing agencies, but his 'distancing' poses interesting questions about the initial personal hurdles of talking to homeless people. Phil on the other hand reflects on his identity as a paid employee of the research team:

"I can't help but wonder whether my increased sense of ethical dilemma was not also partly due to the fact that, as an employee and part of a team, I felt somehow more beholden to my employers and colleagues to do a particularly good job of work and come up with the stories I was charged with collecting. This is not to say that I experienced any pressure from my colleagues to stretch ethical boundaries. I most certainly did not. But it is to make a somewhat obvious comment that the 'status' and 'role' of any researcher in a team is bound to affect the different ethical dilemmas and political 'conflicts of loyalty' they are likely to experience."

These and other instances of multiple identities problematise the category 'researcher' so far as ethical issues are concerned. They suggest different (in)abilities to 'leave the field' (Katz, 1994) by separating work from home, and they reflect different senses of mission which characterises interviews. We do not suggest essentialist connections between particular identity collectives and particular outcomes in terms of research style or technique, but we do suggest that multiple identities in researchers will impinge on the ethical decisions made during research encounters.

We illustrate this point further by reference to three very different research roles apparent in our diaries. Each of these roles reflects ethical decisions embedded within the process. The first example identifies researchers in different ways as *embodied and politicised outsiders*. Most of the interviews were carried out in an atmosphere of emotional discomfort. Not even year-long ethnographic placements overcame this sensitivity. Often, discomfort stemmed from an acute realisation of the difference between our powerful, (variously) affluent and problem-free life-styles (but see Jenny's earlier comment) and the plight of our interviewees. Sometimes, not unexpectedly, it was due to our ideological support for homeless people not being recognised by the individuals we met. Not only did we encounter people whose anger and frustration was sometimes exacerbated by use of alcohol or other substances, but more generally our positive inclinations towards homeless people were hard to convey to those whose life experiences lead them to believe that the world does not care about them. Almost everything about us marked us out as outsiders to the worlds of homelessness. Even our casual clothes marked us out as different, as if we were wearing business suits. With the exception sometimes of Jenny and Phil, who by dint of prolonged placement, and some experience of analogous life-issues, did achieve some familiarity, the research relationship was one of powerful outsider and powerless other.

Power in such situations is not, however, unidimensional. Two illustrations serve to demonstrate occasions when the 'powerful' researcher experienced fear rather than discomfort during the research. First, Jenny was visiting a drop-in centre, and was alarmed by a man shouting personal questions across the room at her. She was even more alarmed to hear from a worker at the centre that the man was a 'notorious flasher with a rumoured unhealthy interest in children':

> "Although I was equipped with a mobile phone, there were some situations in which I felt I was putting myself in danger and this restricted my ability to do some of the research. There were some places I just wasn't able to visit, where 'hanging-out' was not really an option. Thus, there were missed opportunities which resulted from my position as a lone female researcher who lacked experience in handling certain situations." (Jenny)

Gender and age in this case were crucial to the encounters and non-encounters, and issues of safety which were agreed before the commencement of the research had to be applied in a context-specific way in its practice. The second example comes from the oldest (male) participant in the team:

> "I was doing an overnight stint at the shelter, and one of the guys was being threatening with a used needle. This wasn't scaremongering, this was the real thing, and since then I have carried with me a slightly irrational AIDS-fear from the threat of needles as weapons." (Paul C)

These examples of fear and discomfort merely reflect that it is not possible to enter other people's worlds in a sanitised fashion, however much we would try to do so. The very process of inviting ourselves in as outsiders carries with it inherent discomfort and fears, which demand safe research practices, but also erode just a little the protective socio-positional armour with which we often surround ourselves.

The above complexity of relations involving power, discomfort and fear, often set the context for the second researcher-role, which is *researcher as sympathetic listener*. To begin with, different researchers are likely to feel more or less sympathetic towards different individuals, with same-gender interviews, for example, proving to be the most successful format. The narratives collected in our research are those where the homeless person concerned was willing to be listened to, and several interviews were stopped and discarded either when the patience of the interviewee with the process ran out, or when telling the story became too distressing for him or her. Ethical issues of privacy were differentially situated in these interviews. On occasions, we steered clear of particular areas for fear of delving into the privacy of the interviewee. However, we were often surprised by a willingness to relate intensively sensitive information:

> "Young people, some only 16 or 17, were confiding to me very personal and distressing stories. They didn't seems to care who they told; they had often had to tell so many people their stories in order to secure assistance from agencies.... I often wondered whether they would regret and feel exposed by the giving of these stories at some later time." (Jenny)

It is easy to suggest that the use of anonymity provides clear ethical ground for researchers in these cases. However, the decision about how far to prompt in interviews, and later choices of what parts of transcripts to use in publications, are also key decisions in maintaining ethics of privacy.

It is also the case that 'successful' sympathetic listening can produce 'results' for the research, and here again there are choices to be made, as in the case of 'James', interviewed by Phil:

> "I had been quite keen to talk to James, and in the course of a number of fairly superficial conversations, he did express a willingness (even desire) to tell me his story and to put it to tape. In the end, it took three or four different 'attempts' to actually sit down and talk with James, because each time things had worked out such that this would have been rather inappropriate. On one occasion, anxiety over an impending

court appearance had just got too much; on another James was struggling over the anniversary of a friend's untimely death; and on two others, I came to the conclusion that had I gone ahead it could have jeopardised James' efforts at the time to quit alcohol. I would not want to pretend that these were necessarily easy decisions to take, nor that the whole process was not extremely frustrating; for in the end it could have meant 'losing' James' story (and there were others that I did lose in this way)." (Phil)

Here, then, there is tension between the ethics of sympathetic listening and a third researcher-role, that of *researcher as story-gatherer*. Phil's sense of 'losing' stories is an important prompt here towards the sense of mission and motivation that underpins the research process. For it is these stories, particularly novel or sensational ones, with which the outputs of the research can be made effective and significant. There is no doubt therefore that during interviews we not only experienced senses of power being attributed to us as academic researchers, but also detected in ourselves times when we got excited at the prospect of taping a good story. Inevitably, the feeling that an interview will yield a 'crop of great quotes' is often accompanied by a wish to push the interviewee as far as they could reasonably go to ensure that the story is fully and appropriately spoken out. Moreover, these professional ambitions are sometimes linked with the interviewer's own curiosity:

"Isn't there also a part of us that wants at times to simply satisfy our own morbid curiosity? I constantly found myself having to ask 'Why am I interested in this? Is it relevant? What is it going to add to the project? And who, in the end, is this going to help?'." (Phil)

It is in the answering of these self-questions as the interview proceeds that situated ethics are decided on. Naturally, we would want to conclude that we made ethically sound decisions in these areas. However, there is no doubt that the power relations in interviews were stacked in our favour (despite discomfort and sometimes fear), and that the power to prevent exploitation lay largely in our own decisions. We *did* press for interesting narratives, certainly backing off when interviewees became distressed, but nevertheless fully making use of the permission that was granted to us. Providing honest and accurate descriptions of our research was difficult; suggesting any direct utility of the research to respondents was even more so.

Whether these encounters constitute unethical forms of exploitation is a difficult judgement to make. Outside of specific dilemmas, such as whether to tape an interview with a relative of one of the research team just as a local parish clerk was demonstrating a chronic lack of awareness of local homelessness (we did!), the general accusation of exploitation to some extent connects with our ability to use the information in the public (rather than academic) sphere. The ends do not *justify* the means. Exploitative research does have to be checked in the field, but within these bounds, the ends do have to be negotiated alongside the means.

Conclusion

In this chapter we have considered some key practical and ethical issues that are bound up with researching homelessness. It is clear that, whether occurring in urban or rural spaces, homelessness represents a challenging research subject. In terms of quantitative research, there exist relatively few reliable sources of statistical information on the incidence, profile and causes of homelessness. Further, the tactics employed by many rough sleepers in an attempt to maintain their invisibility from official gazes make the counting of homeless people an extremely problematic process. Clearly this process becomes more problematic in rural areas which generally lack spaces of concentration of homeless people – for example, hostels, shelters and drop-in centres – and any form of street homelessness. Consequently, qualitative methods of enquiry take on an added sense of importance in researching homelessness in rural areas. It is only by adopting such methods, with researchers spending extended periods seeking out and speaking with homeless people in rural spaces, that the nature and experiences of rural homelessness begin to emerge.

The research on which much of this book is based has followed a multi-method approach. It has provided a national (predominantly quantitative) picture of the scale, profile and causes of homelessness in rural areas by analysing unpublished official statistics on homelessness and by undertaking a national survey of all homelessness officers in England and Wales. It has also provided an in-depth (largely qualitative) consideration of rural homelessness through interviews with homelessness agencies and homeless people, and ethnographic studies of homelessness in two rural counties in England. In this chapter, we have set out the key features of the research process involved in our project. However, we have also gone further than this by providing an account of important ethical issues associated with the project and by setting out how we have striven to take findings from the research to a wide variety of academic, policy and lay audiences. In the remaining chapters of the book we set out key findings that emerge from our research on rural homelessness. We begin by considering the cultural context of homelessness in rural areas.

Notes

[1] However, the recent growth in the number of studies attempting to assess the statistical scale and composition of 'new' forms of homelessness can be said to have been triggered by social and political constructions of homelessness (see Gans, 1994; Daly, 1996; Glasser and Bridgman, 1999).

[2] Originally covering central London, in 1996 the RSI was extended to cover Bristol and has since been expanded to cover schemes in a number of other areas including Bath, Birmingham, Chester, Cambridge, Exeter, Leicester and Southampton.

[3] Section F of the HIPI form returned annually to the DETR asks local authorities whether they have any arrangements for monitoring/counting the number of people who sleep rough in the authority and to provide details if the answer is yes, to indicate their assessment of the typical number of people sleeping rough in the area on any given night. Where an authority has carried out a headcount on a specific night, it is asked to give the date and the number of people found.

THREE

The cultural context of rural homelessness

Discourses of rurality and homelessness

In this chapter we explore some of the difficulties in bringing together the concepts of rurality and homelessness, arguing that particular cultural constructs of what it is to be homeless, and what it is to live in the countryside, serve to resist, and sometimes deny the recognition of any material reality which might be called rural homelessness. The background to this discussion is formed by the existence of *privileged* constructs of rural space. It can be suggested that the most identifiable and accessible group of meanings constructed and circulated about rurality in England are bound up with notions of idyll. Although it is problematic to search for any notion of a single construction of the rural as idyll[1], Cloke and Milbourne (1992) have suggested a number of key meanings that have come to be associated with rurality – "a bucolic, problem-free, hidden world of peace, tranquillity and proximity to the natural" (p 361). Such constructs have become reproduced directly within the dominant imagination through a range of different cultural circulations. In other ways, notions of rural idyll, and particularly ideas of problem-free country spaces, have remained largely unchallenged within academic and policy discourses. Only a handful of academic studies have addressed issues of poverty and marginalisation in rural Britain (Cloke et al, 1994, 1997a, 1997b; Shucksmith et al, 1996; PSI, 1998), and these same issues have been conspicuous only by their absence within recent central policy documents on rural Britain (DoE, 1995; Welsh Office, 1996).

Such constructions of rurality have played a key role in reproducing dominant popular discourses on the British countryside. In one sense, a home in the country has become a much sought after commodity, with a recent national survey commissioned by the Countryside Commission (1997) highlighting that 54% of respondents in urban areas wish to reside in the countryside and that there is a more pronounced sense of contentment with place of residence among those living in rural areas than among those in urban and city environments. This combination of rural desires and urban discontentments has played a pivotal role in bringing about large-scale movements of new groups to the British countryside over recent years (for details of the scale of these movements, see Champion, 1994).

However, it is clear that such strong expressed desires for rural living are more easily realised by certain social groups than others. Writers such as Cloke et al (1998), Murdoch (1995), and Thrift (1989) have emphasised the prominence of middle-class, and more particularly service-class, groupings within these recent relocations to rural spaces, as the rural has become an important constituent of these groupings' dominant identity, which is able to be purchased through their considerable 'buying power' within local housing markets. Indeed, in this respect, Thrift (1989) has pointed to the role played by both economic capital (the ability to purchase properties in most rural housing markets) and cultural capital (the desire to purchase a rural life-style package). The scale of this in-movement by middle-class or service-class groups has also led to claims from Cloke et al (1998) and Murdoch (1995) that particular rural spaces now represent 'middle-class territories'.

Prominent within the types of constructions of rurality that are being imported by middle-class groupings are, first, the notion that the rural is a space that is non-urban – distant from the perceived threats posed by city living – and, second, the idea that it is distinctively rural – being able to conform to middle-class aspirations for idyllised life-styles bound up with close-knit and problem-free living, order, security, tradition, and so on. As such, 'rural' becomes (re)constructed as representative of 'prime', 'privileged', and 'purified' spaces (see Wardhaugh (1996), Takahashi (1998a), and Sibley (1995), respectively. It is viewed as the 'natural' space of home and community, allowing for the maintenance of a safe physical and social distancing of home from the perceived more marginal and stigmatised city spaces of crime, poverty, and homelessness. But once constructed in these terms rural space needs to be protected, so that its privileged and purified characteristics can be preserved. One key means of protection is through the expulsion from these spaces (either literally or in imaginary terms) of perceived marginal groups, and here we include homeless people (Sibley, 1995; Takahashi, 1998a).

In a city context, academic attention has been directed to the ways in which homeless groups have been excluded from particular prime spaces, through their physical redesigning to deter the presence of homelessness, the privatisation of prime spaces which allows for more effective policing, and the introduction of local anti-homeless legislation (see Davis, 1990;

Mitchell, 1997; Ruddick, 1996; Smith, 1993). Mitchell (1997, p 307) has commented that the aims of these local interventions have been:

> to control behaviour and space such that homeless people simply cannot do what they must do in order to survive without breaking laws. Survival itself is criminalized.... The hope is simply that if homeless people can be made to disappear, nothing will stand in the way of realizing the dream of prosperity, social harmony and perpetual economic growth.

However, such interventions are rarely required within the types of prime and privileged spaces of rurality being discussed here. With the possible exceptions of the mass trespasses of the 1930s (Hill, 1980) and the incursion of New Age travellers in the 1990s (Davis, 1997), the exclusivity of many parts of the countryside has been reinforced through the operation of planning systems and private housing markets that prevent or make more difficult the existence of poor or homeless groups in these rural spaces[2]. So the domination of private housing markets in rural areas, the restricted supply of new rural properties in smaller settlements, and the transposition of cultural capital into higher rural property prices have acted to problematise life on a low income in the countryside[3]. As such, we can employ Cresswell's (1996) idea of a 'doxic mode of experience' (that is, the construction of what is orthodox) in our discussion of homelessness in these privileged rural spaces, as the local housing fabric leads to situations in which it is 'taken for granted', if not 'natural', that low-income people experiencing housing problems in rural areas come to accept the inevitability of their housing circumstances and their 'out-of-place' position in these types of gentrified local housing markets.

Against this backcloth of 'privileged' rural space, consider the following statements:

> "The sight of a rough sleeper bedding down for the night in a shop doorway or on a park bench is one of the most potent symbols of social exclusion in Britain today." (Tony Blair, SEU, 1998, Foreword)

> "... youth homelessness is rising faster in rural areas. There are no cardboard boxes, or young people sleeping in doorways. They are in barns, under hedges or on friends' floors – but they are still there." (Close and Benson, 1996, p 36)

Here in a nutshell is the key difficulty to acknowledging rural homelessness – constructs of homelessness and rurality are all too often anathema to one another, and there has been a failure to couple these two discursive constructs into a recognisable and acceptable problem that demands political and policy responses. Thus Tony Blair's evocation of the rough sleeper as signifying social exclusion carries with it the symbolisms of urban spatiality – the shop doorway and the park bench. These seemingly instinctive connections between homelessness and urban places not only provide powerful images of a serious social problem, but also set that problem in a particular landscape. They thereby often serve, by implication, to exclude other spaces from consideration, including the barns, hedges and friends' floors and rural areas, referred to by Close and Benson.

Our concern, then, is to investigate this discursive non-coupling of 'rurality' and 'homelessness' – and vice versa – and in so doing to recognise the obstacles which lie in the way of any coupling of these constructs, both conceptually and in more grounded policy terms. In so doing we also seek a definition of homelessness that extends beyond rooflessness, and an understanding of rurality that extends beyond the idea of problem-free space. Until recently, discourses on homelessness from governments, voluntary agencies, academics and news media have presented the impression that the spatiality of homeless people is entirely encompassed by city limits. Here, homelessness is visible on the street; here facilities for homeless people are concentrated; here is the 'inevitable' focus for the migration of homeless people wherever they come from. Everyday experience has assimilated homelessness in city sites/sights and has begun to conflate the phenomenon with other adjacent 'urban' issues such as the street 'criminalities' of drunkenness, vagrancy and begging.

There are clearly very understandable reasons for this urban emphasis. Initially, most discursive scripting of homelessness in Britain was concentrated on issues in London, where concentrations of homeless people were most visible to the largest numbers of people[4]. Despite a widening of this horizon to other British cities, London continues to dominate policy and news discussions. Thus the government's 1998 announcement that £177m is to be spent on reducing rough sleeping over the period 1999-2002, carried an in-built emphasis on London, where £145m is to be spent, leaving only £32m for 'the regions' (mostly other big cities). And when the homeless charity Crisis recently published research on homelessness and suicide, news media were quick to headline the implications of that research in London:

> ... the homeless charity, Crisis, has suggested that people sleeping rough *in London* and dying of natural causes live to an average age of 46 –

that's 30 years younger than the national norm. (Meikle, 1997, emphasis
in the original)

Moreover, the widening of the spatial horizons of homelessness has
predominantly led to the incorporation of other cities. For example,
Henley's 1998 article on "a rash of homeless deaths" in Paris is accompanied
by pocket guides to "how other cities (Rome, New York, Johannesburg
and Geneva) handle people sleeping rough".
   It is equally the case that voluntary agencies have only recently turned
their attention to rural areas – Shelter's first conference on rural
homelessness was in 1995 – and that their attempts to promote issues
relating to homeless people have thereby inevitably reinforced the ways
in which constructs of homelessness and urbanism have become conjoined.
Academic discourses on homelessness follow a similar pattern. A who's
who of authors on homelessness (for example, Watson and Austerberry,
1986; Dear and Wolch, 1987; Barak, 1991; Veness, 1992; Daly, 1996; Ruddick,
1996; Burrows et al, 1997) have based their research and subsequent writings
on homelessness in cities. Daly's 293-page book *Homeless* (1996), for
example, which reports on a study of homelessness in Britain, the US and
Canada, devotes less than one page of discussion specifically to rural
homelessness (p 147) and makes no mention at all of Britain in this context!
   Discourses on rurality, by contrast, mostly steer well clear of explicit
connections between homelessness and rural areas. Rural policy invariably
focuses on 'housing' rather than homelessness, and recent research by the
Rural Development Commission (RDC, 1996) has revealed that over
half of the housing strategy statements prepared by local authorities did
not identify specific rural housing needs, and that 95% had not undertaken
a separate rural housing needs survey. Newspaper attention to rural
housing, moreover, is usually confined to the property pages where, for
example, a headline of 'A window on the countryside is opened' leads to
a story about the excellent value of the houses available to buyers with
£170,000 to £370,000 to spend in the country (Spackman, 1997) rather
than to an exposé of rural homelessness. And where rural homelessness
is made explicit, it tends to be in ways that are laced with signs of rurality
which reinforce mythologies of rural living:

   At a car park on the upper reaches of the Thames, though it could be in
   the Lake District or a Cotsworld (sic) village, the heart of the New
   Forest or somewhere near Glyndebourne or Ascot at the height of the
   season, a camper van has been parked, at a bottom corner, off and on
   for several weeks. It has been noticed, of course, but almost no one has

complained, not even the Nimby Brigade. This is probably because the vehicle is at a 'decent' distance from the wisteria that marks the boundary of the nearest adjoining house, the home of a local GP. The tattered and rusting former taxi which turns up from time to time causes more offence; its silencer doesn't seem to work. Rented accommodation in such an area being almost impossible to find, Mary and John live in the camper van, while Laura and Steve stay in the taxi. (Simmons, 1993)

The list of 'anywhere' places in the story consists of landmark countryside sites of cultural distinction, readily identifiable by urban consumers of the rural in Britain. The wisteria boundary suggests living spaces that reflect enviable nature–culture relations, and the very mention of 'causing offence' reflects the unusual nature of this transgression of the peaceful, problem-free tranquillity of rural life. Into this elaborately constructed setting is placed the homelessness experienced by four human beings. The 'issue' is newsworthy precisely because it counterpoints popular constructions of rural life. Like the vicar who sins, a 'problem' in the countryside or village provides a 'remarkable' exception to the supposed rule.

As we have detailed in Chapter One, there have been a number of significant attempts to draw attention to the fact and nature of rural homelessness, both in Britain and in the US. However, in broad terms we would argue that discourses of homelessness and rurality have so far only been brought together in a very preliminary way, and it is our contention that in Britain at least there are very significant elements of discursive non-coupling at work here. As a consequence, the sketchy indications that homelessness *does* occur in rural areas have not led to an acceptance of rural homelessness as an appropriate label. This in turn has hindered the answering of questions about where, with what intensity and with what outcomes does homelessness occur in rural areas, and about how homelessness is understood both by local domiciled populations and by homeless people staying in or passing through the rural localities concerned. In this chapter we suggest three lines of reasoning which help to explain the conceptual and then discursive non-coupling of homelessness and rurality: *morphological* characteristics of the countryside, which render homeless people less visible than in the city; *socio-cultural* constructs of rural life, which present barriers to the acceptance of homelessness as a problem; and *conceptual* constructs of homelessness and rurality, by which homeless people can be regarded as 'out of place' in the 'purified space' of rural areas. We discuss each of these in turn, giving particular emphasis to how normalised conceptualisations about rurality and homelessness serve to make each repellent to the other.

Spatial morphologies and homelessness

The first line of enquiry about how homelessness and rurality have become non-coupled discursively concerns a range of physical and material reasons why rural and urban spaces have varying qualities for hiding or revealing homeless people, and why the embodied experiences of homelessness have varying geographies. The morphological characteristics of the city render homeless people visible in a number of different ways. First, and perhaps most obviously, the provision of hostels, shelters, drop-in centres, soup runs, and so on occurs in urban centres. Such facilities represent points of congregation for homeless people, for whom they provide strategic landmarks on the map of where to obtain basic life requirements such as food, shelter, health and washing facilities. Equally, these facilities represent the 'obvious' places in which to encounter, identify, count and acknowledge homeless people (Veness, 1994). Equally obvious in terms of the visibility of homeless people is that the kinds of places and spaces they occupy in the city are usually open to public view. Although not all homeless people engage in these activities, the earning potential of begging, busking or selling the *Big Issue* (Murdoch, 1994) will involve some homeless people in colonising very public on-street places for long periods of the day. In addition, living 'on the streets' involves endless iterations of walking, waiting, dossing down, in what is often a public manner. Urban hiding places are not only competitively contested, but also often not very hidden, as this account from a homeless person in Toronto suggests:

> "Several weeks ago, I was too late to get a bed in any of the downtown hostels. I made a tour of the all-night coffee shops. Walking around, I noticed that the bus shelters I passed on Queen Street were occupied, as were many doorways. Around 3 a.m. I ran out of coffee money, so I headed for a quiet park to lie down. Of course it started to rain. Well, in the course of the next hour, I scrambled alleyways, fire escapes, across warehouse roofs – and without exception, every little hiding hole was filled with some unfortunate person like myself. Finally I saw some piles of cardboard by some tractor-trailers. I pulled the first pile aside. Someone was sleeping underneath. The same thing with the second pile. And the third had two people under it. All this within fifty feet of trendy Queen West. (*Rumours*, Toronto, 1986; quoted in Daly, 1996, p 128)

Although there are many more hidden forms of homelessness in urban places, it is these embodied experiences of the concrete landscape of the city that are further highlighted by local newspaper coverage which is often antagonistic to the homeless people concerned. For example, the *Bristol Evening Post*, using headlines such as 'Beggar Off' (29 October 1998) and 'We'll Kick Out Beggar Menaces' (10 December 1998), has, over the last three years, run sustained editorial campaigns to 'clean up' the streets of Bristol (by removing homeless people from them) and to expose the 'cheats' who are begging on these streets (some of whom were found, by reporters, not to be 'homeless').

Given the high visibility of often-considerable numbers of homeless people in urban places, it is unsurprising that constructs of 'urban' and 'homeless' are mutually inclusive. By contrast, rural places contain few, if any, points of concentration and visibility for homeless people. The provision of hostels and other dedicated facilities is usually restricted to large market towns, where the scale of voluntary activity can, in some cases, just sustain such ventures, and outside of which characteristics of scale, and cultural expectation, usually render them untenable or unsuitable[5]. Rural areas do not provide accessible services for homeless people, nor do they offer on-street earning potential:

> "It's only a tiny village, so you can't busk in it. There's no point. You
> can't earn money there." ('Jim', interviewed in Taunton, talking about
> the village where he had currently pitched his tent)[6]

Rural places, therefore, present two polarised options for homeless people. First, they can be places where the small scale of the built environment, and the often-restricted nature of housing and employment opportunities, throw a very public spotlight onto the experience of homelessness. This visibility can be illustrated by reference to comments made by 'Peter', a rural vicar who works closely with homeless groups in rural Somerset. Here we witness the difficulties faced by one homeless man in the local countryside resulting from what we might term 'cultures of rurality'. In the following extract from an interview, 'Peter' discusses problems concerning the limited employment opportunities available in local villages, but also the cultural difficulties associated with being homeless in rural spaces, concerning restricted anonymity, accentuation of difference, and active, informal policing of perceived deviance:

> *Peter:* "The jobs that are available to this guy that I'm talking about
> round here are far fewer than they might be for part-time odd-jobbing

around Taunton ... and because travel is expensive ... he hasn't got a car or motorbike, he's got to measure up whether it's worth going to Taunton or Chard to do a part-time job.... Whereas if he goes to Taunton [permanently], he can odd-job, he can sleep in odd places, get a place if he can get enough money together.... And also, if you're homeless or unemployed in [village A] it sticks out. In Taunton they wouldn't know you from Adam but if somebody's walking round the shops [here] every day, killing time, you know, he'll feel more obvious. And that must be hard to handle."

Interviewer: "You say 'obvious' and 'stick out', what sort of precisely do you mean by that?"

Peter: "Well, the smaller the community ... if someone's milling around and going round the same places ... it's more exposing for that person. It identifies and accentuates their sense of failure or sense of lack of worth ... I mean if you walk up the high street of [village B, nearby] where there's about a hundred people in the village and only about thirty of them during the daytime, they're likely to ring up the police and say 'Hey, there's a strange man walking up the street'. You can't live there unemployed and sort of roofless. You really would be actually frozen out."

A homeless woman who had been living in a different Devon village confirmed this visibility to us:

"When I lost my place, it was like my position in the village changed. I was one of them, like, but then everyone knew about me and I was like an outcast – sticking out like a sore thumb." ('Janice', interviewed in a Devon village)

This position of visibility for the homeless person is not counteracted by the urban notion of 'safety in numbers'[7]. Instead the specific problems of homelessness are compounded by the identifiable isolation of being known to be homeless in a rural place. The response to these issues is often to leave that place, pushed by a very visible form of disadvantage, and pulled by the availability of housing or shelter in other places. Recent studies by Button (1992), Davenport et al (1990) and Wright and Vermond (1990) have highlighted these migrations of rural homeless or near-homeless people to nearby towns and cities.

The second option for homeless people in rural areas is to choose invisibility. It is clear from the accounts given to us by homeless people of their journeys through and sojourns in rural areas, that the morphological characteristics of the places concerned lent themselves to tactics of invisibility. Country paths, open fields, isolated hedges, ditches and barns offer a territory in which homelessness can be relatively incognito. They are places of dispersal, where encounter and identification can be avoided if care is taken during the embodied practices of walking, sleeping, cooking, washing and so on. 'Jim', for example, told us of his invisible travels and stays in the Exmoor area:

> *Interviewer:* "Going back to this place at [village name] … your ideal sort of place to stay, what is it that makes it ideal?"
>
> *Jim:* "Countryside. Miles and miles of open countryside. And the fact that I'd rarely see anybody unless I wanted to. Unless I wanted to walk into the village and see people. And where this particular spot is, very few people go up there. It means a lot of climbing and stuff like steep hills and walking across fields … through woods."

Equally, for 'David', rural areas offered 'quiet' areas and the opportunity to 'do what you want out there' without 'people nosing about and seeing what you're up to'. However, in order to attain such isolation and anonymity in rural spaces 'David' needed to employ a number of tactics of invisibility that allowed him to blend into the local environment. He tended to avoid the visible, prime spaces of the village and instead sought a deeper, more marginal countryside of open fields and isolated buildings. He slept in a hay barn until discovered and 'kicked out' by the owner. 'David' then moved into a phase of literal homelessness over the warmer summer months in which he slept and poached in fields and woods. Again, movements and tactics of invisibility form an integral part of 'David's' existence in these spaces. He felt forced to move on if faced with the possibility of being discovered poaching or trespassing, he wore camouflaged clothes, utilised his survival training received in the armed forces, and also developed tactics that allowed him to cope if he became visible to rural landowners.

> *David:* "[I was] sleeping in fields because it was mainly like summer and it was hot. I was just like lying out in the ground … I'd wake and see a couple of deer walking past me…. [I was there for] a good five or six months, um, but I was just living. Like a couple of times I came close to actually getting caught poaching and then I had to do a runner …

but apart from that everything was all right. People didn't know me, I was walking like, I was just walking around with my gun in my case...."

Interviewer: "Did they know you were sleeping rough?"

David: "No, no because I had, um, camouflaged trousers, I had my boots on from the Navy and nobody thought any differently. I just blended right into the countryside because they didn't think that I was a town person. Because it was the way I dressed, so I just blended right in with the country. And sometimes I would walk onto people's private property and I'd just carry on walking. 'What you doing on my property?' 'Well, I'm going for a walk.' 'Can't you read?' 'Well no, not really, I'm not a very good reader.' They'd say, 'Oh, OK, fair enough, [do] you know where you are going?' I'd say, 'Well, I'm just going for a walk anywhere.' They'd say, 'Well, there's a nice place up there...'. So you know, off I go. I was just listening to what people, what advice people give me. When I got tired I just, mainly it'd be the night time I got tired, I'd just lie down, put my gun by the side of me and that was it, I was asleep.... I was going all over the place. Um, I'd walk round like 10, 15 miles a day in the countryside, just carry on walking, walk across main roads, dive through hedges and you know, just doing things like that. Um, if I seen a rabbit I'd shoot it and um, find somewhere that was nice and isolated and then start cooking it. And then once I'd eaten it, stay around for 5–10 minutes and then, um, destroy the fire, make sure it looked like no-one had had a fire and then disappear." ('David', interviewed in Minehead)

Such experiences, along with others of washing in rivers, sleeping in barns, meeting others 'on the road' and so on suggests embodied experiences in morphology dominated by nature, but although some of our interviewees did regard this proximity to nature as a positive aspect, such experiences should not be translated into romanticised stereotypes. 'Stu' emphasised this point:

"People think it's a lovely way of life – it's bloody horrendous! You get cold, you get frozen, you get soaking wet. You don't know where your next food is coming from. You don't know where your next bit of money's coming from. Your shoes wear out, you stink, you can't shave. It's not fun. Not fun." ('Stu', interviewed in Ilminster)

Although these sentiments could have been expressed regardless of place, they emphasise that invisible homelessness in the countryside has its costs, in terms of different levels of shelter and facilities to the morphology of the city[8].

We are not suggesting here that *all* people in rural areas who experience homelessness will adopt the same strategies of response merely because of the overriding characteristics of rurality. Clearly the precise tactics pursued by individuals and households will vary according to a range of different circumstances. What we do argue, however, is that these different tactics are to some extent normalised by the degree of social surveillance that occurs in many rural places, and that the morphology of many rural places lends itself to those who seek out invisibility for a period of time[9]. Equally, although 'urban' and 'rural' categories of homelessness represent only one of many ways of understanding experiences of homelessness, rurality does appear to be a salient distinction in the minds of homeless people we have interviewed.

We argue that both the stigmatic visibility of the homeless person in a rural place, and the tactics of invisibility employed in, and encouraged by, negotiating the countryside as a homeless person, are strongly connected with the non-coupling of rurality and homelessness. Where rural homelessness is visible, the problem is often labelled differently (usually as a 'housing problem') and may disappear through out-migration, or by the homeless person hiding their problem (for example, by finding other short-term insecure accommodation, such as a friend's floor, or by sleeping rough outside the village). Where rural homelessness occurs invisibly in the countryside, it can be ignored. Either way, rurality and homelessness tend not to be coupled together in the physical-material morphology of rural areas.

Socio-cultural barriers to recognising rural homelessness

The second line of thought about how rurality and homelessness are discursively non-coupled relates to the socio-cultural barriers that exist within the practices, thoughts and discourses of rural dwellers themselves, leading them to deny that homelessness exists in their place. This 'denial' of a serious social problem by rural residents has been widely discussed in the context of poverty and deprivation in rural areas (Bradley et al, 1986; Cloke, 1995; Cloke et al, 1995; Woodward, 1996). It has been argued that both within rural areas and beyond, cultural constructions of rurality which associate rural England with some form of arcadian and pastoral idyll tend to exert a pervasive yet obfuscatory influence over the ability of decision makers, urban residents and rural residents to recognise the existence of poverty in the midst of that idyll. Fabes et al (1983) make two important suggestions in this context. First, they argue that the rural idyll *exacerbates* poverty because it is the lack of housing, transport and employment opportunities in rural areas that makes those areas so attractive to urban-based visitors and immigrants. Second, they contend that the rural idyll *conceals* poverty:

> In this respect, the poor unwittingly conspire with the more affluent to hide their own poverty by denying its existence. Those values which are at the heart of the rural idyll result in the poor tolerating their material deprivation because of the priority given to those symbols of the rural idyll, the family, the work ethic and good health. And when that material deprivation becomes so chronic by the standard of the area that it has to be recognised by the poor themselves, shame forces secrecy and the management of that poverty within the smallest possible framework. The newcomers do not want to see poverty because it is anathema to the rural idyll which they are seeking to preserve. (pp 55-6)

Woodward (1996) further suggests that such concealment of poverty is embedded in discourses of rurality in a number of ways: by naming it as a historical problem not a contemporary one; by constructing it as a failure of the individual, so as to 'blame the victim'; by an in-built reluctance to admit to poverty where it exists; by a similar reluctance to seek assistance; and by naming it as an urban problem, thereby invoking an urban 'otherness' to the idyll of the rural.

We would argue that similar socio-cultural barriers exist to the recognition of homelessness in rural areas. The most ready acceptance of any form of rural homelessness often seems to relate to historical figures – tramps and hobos – whose presence in rural areas has subsequently been somewhat romanticised. Thus in the *News of the World* story, referred to in Chapter One (Johnson, 1997), in which a group of rural residents are said to be purchasing a piece of land so that a homeless man can settle there, the man concerned is variously labelled 'super-tramp', 'king of the road' and 'the happy hobo', but is not identified as homeless.

In addition to these romanticising and historicising discourses of rurality and homelessness, there is also evidence from our interviews of the other discursive manoeuvres suggested by Woodward. An illustration of these manoeuvres may be drawn from an interview with an elderly parish councillor – 'Louie' – about homelessness in her Devon village:

Interviewer: "Do you know of any problems of homelessness in the village?"

Louie: "There isn't any homelessness here. We have a good, helpful community. If folks are in trouble we help them.... All the undesirables keep themselves to themselves or move away. We've had some lovely people come to live here."

Interviewer: "What would you do if you saw a homeless person in the village?"

Louie: "Well I'd die of shock, I think. We just don't get that round here – in Exeter maybe, but not out here."

Here, the supposed 'failing' of some individuals is marked by the differentiation between "folks" (who are helped) and "undesirables", who are being blamed as victims. Louie's insistence that "there isn't any homelessness here" contrasts with her willingness to envisage problems of homelessness in the nearest city, thus invoking the urban other to her own "good helpful community". Even when homelessness is transposed as a 'housing' problem, she sees it as one that somehow just 'moves away' from her village.

This discursive construction of 'helpfulness' in rural settings presents significant and value-laden insights about the supposed spatiality of 'those who care' and 'those who do not'. It invokes implicitly idyllised and romantic notions of rural living and its urban other, as well as a class-ridden view of rural society. However, it also invokes the notion that homelessness cannot occur in caring rural communities, suggesting that where it does occur it can be put down to the individual concerned who is not part of the 'good community' (therefore 'bad') or who resists the ethos of that community (also 'bad'). The idea of a 'helpful' community, then, discursively constructs rural society, and problems such as homelessness within that society, in such a way that rurality and homelessness are further disconnected.

In these kinds of ways, many rural residents will refuse to acknowledge to themselves, let alone to the outside world, that their idyllic rural life-style could be tainted by the presence of homeless people in the vicinity. Equally, socio-cultural barriers serve to prevent homeless people from acknowledging their problem in terms of homelessness. A representative of a charitable agency working with young people in rural Somerset confirmed to us that homeless young people make different decisions about whether to declare themselves as homeless. He suggested that "people who have had a real crisis in their lives and have gone to the local authority for help ... are much more inclined to perceive themselves as homeless", whereas other people – those staying with friends, or living in caravans or in tents – "didn't want to be identified ... they just wanted to blend in, really, and not be spotted". He concluded that:

> "If they're attempting to sort things out themselves ... then they will tend *not* to declare themselves homeless. I mean, to be identified as homeless is a signal to yourself that you've lost control over your life."

Part of this 'signal' is, however, contextualised by the surrounding community. The practices of not being identified, wishing to blend in and not being spotted, suggests a deviant otherness about homelessness within rural space. Although some rural people clearly do present themselves to local authorities as 'homeless' this action too can encounter barriers to the acceptance of their homelessness. As Larkin (1978), Lidstone (1994) and Hoggart (1995a, 1997) have pointed out, local councils often seem to establish an environment in which rural people do not consider it worthwhile applying to be housed because they perceive little hope of success. 'Rural homelessness' is yet again both non-coupled discursively and translated into more comfortable 'rural housing' terms. In some cases rural local authorities might even use caravan sites as 'dumping grounds' for 'homeless families' (Larkin, 1978, p 16), thus denying the problem by ghettoising the people concerned into temporary and often unfit housing solutions, and helping them to 'blend back in' again. Such barriers within the very identities and practices of rural people feed more standardised discourses that further serve to emphasise the non-coupling of rurality and homelessness.

Conceptual separations of rurality and homelessness

Homelessness as rooflessness

The third strand of our discussion focuses on how 'standard' conceptualisations about both rurality and homelessness will often serve to separate the two concepts, and contribute to the assumption that homelessness is an urban phenomenon, which is rendered invisible in rural space. As we have discussed in Chapter One, a minimalist definition of homelessness as *rooflessness* continues to dominate the agenda within much political and some academic discourse. Hence, policy responses have tended to be directed to the emergencies of 'rough sleepers' and 'cold weather' sufferers. This understandable and in many ways important emphasis on the most visible forms of homelessness has the effect of ignoring the needs of those experiencing less extreme, yet still distressing and potentially destructive forms of homelessness, and has particular implications for the identification of *rural* homelessness, where the problem tends to exist in a more 'hidden' form. That homelessness is more complex than rooflessness has been widely debated elsewhere (see, for example, Watson, 1984; Watson and Austerberry, 1986; Blasi, 1990; Hutson and Liddiard, 1994). However, while there is a general consensus that those without any form of shelter are homeless, as the definition is extended to encompass people with recognisable but less extreme housing problems – for example, those living in insecure or overcrowded accommodation – it becomes increasingly difficult to draw a distinction between those with and without a home (Thomas, 1989; Johnson et al, 1991; Neale, 1997).

'Home' here clearly means more than a 'dwelling'. Indeed Watson (1984, p 70) argues that "in policy and research terms what is needed is a recognition that material conditions and standards, the need for space, privacy, control, safety, self-expression and physical and emotional well-being are all important aspects of a dwelling and have to be taken into account". These aspects in turn suggest the need to widen the currently accepted popular definition of homelessness so as to include more hidden forms. Some hiddenness occurs in relation to the processes by which individuals are, or are not 'captured' as *officially* homeless by local authorities. Thus, Bramley et al (1988) argue that the hidden homeless include: people whose objective circumstances are indistinguishable from those officially accepted as homeless, but who do not register under the formal system for whatever reason; people who are, or are about to become, homeless, but who are not prioritised in homelessness legislation; and people whose circumstances clearly put them 'at risk' of becoming homeless within a finite period. Other hiddennesses occur well beyond the ambit of local authority validation, including: people who sleep rough, but not regularly, or in known sites; those who live in some form of institution, primarily because there is nowhere else for them to live; those who want to live as a separate household, but who have to share with another household, irrespective of whether or not they can technically stay there; and, perhaps most controversially, those who describe their own situation as constituting homelessness or who say their present housing is not their home (Webb, 1994).

We argue that given the morphological and socio-cultural characteristics of rurality as previously discussed, these hiddennesses tend to militate against the recognition of homelessness in rural areas. It is not that the causal processes of homelessness somehow do not exist in rural areas. Indeed, political economic processes occurring in rural areas serve to exacerbate the disadvantages of a rural location. For example, reporting on a conference on youth homelessness in rural areas, Button (1992) notes:

> Whatever the local infra-structure or individual reasons for wanting to leave home, when they do leave, young people inevitably find themselves in competition with people who are more affluent, can afford to buy available local housing, and who are not necessarily dependent on local services for their existence or for maintaining their lifestyle. As more people like this move into an area, buying up housing once available for local people to rent, all local people and services suffer. Shops close, public transport dwindles and villages become museums rather than thriving communities made up of a range of age groups and types of people. The dilemma for young people in these areas occurs when they leave home to be independent, but lack the resources to realistically achieve this. 'Young people can not simply compete with the yuppies' was how one conference delegate expressed it. (p 7)

It is rather that homelessness exists predominantly in forms which are at odds with the conventional definition and associated images of homelessness as people living on the streets or in hostels in major urban centres. The resulting false impression that rural homelessness is limited or non-existent, and the lack of attention paid to this issue is consequently at least in part due to the tendency to equate homelessness with rooflessness, rather than applying a more generous definition which takes into account less visible forms of homelessness including, for example, 'concealed' households; people living in short-term, insecure accommodation, such as short-hold tenancies and seasonal lets, or in other forms of temporary accommodation, such as mobile homes and caravans; victims of domestic violence; and households living in unfit accommodation (Lambert et al, 1992).

Socio-spatial dialectics

A less obvious but perhaps equally important standardisation in the non-coupling of rurality and homelessness relates to how the standard *conceptualisations* of rurality (as space) and homelessness (as social 'problem') have become internalised by wider society and which have served to drive the two constructs apart. We refer here less to the conceptualisations of rural dwellers themselves and more to the ways in which the public at large, policy makers, news media, politicians and academics imagine, picture, envisage and assume the relationship between rural space and the problem of homelessness. Our interest, then, is in how problems and spaces are socially constructed, and how social issues are influenced by space and vice versa. Accordingly, we turn to ideas from socio-spatial dialectics to inform our discussion of the spacing and placing of homelessness.

Philo's (1986) work on the outsider status of people with mental health problems is most helpful in this respect. He noted that social construction of mental illness has been attributed many meanings, ranging from how the pressures of urban industrial living actually induce problematic psychological conditions, to the view that mental illness is simply an 'empty' space which has many different and cultural meanings constructed onto it. His discussion suggested that 'from the outside looking in', both impersonal forces of political economy and more cultural forces of community and professional norms were active in producing and sustaining the marginalised positions and identities of people with mental health problems. This view posits space as a 'resource' over which are waged both conscious and non-conscious conflicts, but also as a 'resource' which repeatedly enters into these conflicts, being integrally involved in the transactions between core and marginalised members of society. The production of marginalisation occurs through space rather than just within it, and different places will provide different and complex spatial contextualisations for this marginalisation.

Philo's study of mental illness offers a rich seam of socio-spatiality for our concern with homelessness, steering a middle course between political–economic structures and cultural construction, and implicating the different places of space as active agents in the production of social marginalisation. To this strand of socio-spatial thought we can add that certain spatial arrangements and cultural forms can, together, produce some accepted codes of what are, or are not, acceptable practices in particular places. The work of Shields (1991) is instructive here, particularly his notion of 'social spatialisation', in which the coming together of culture and space will often be illustrated in the ways particular places become 'actualised and endowed with meaning' and acquire 'connotations and symbolic meanings'. They thus become labelled in terms of dominant 'place-images' that collectively form overall 'place-myths' based on widely understood core representations and practices. While dynamic in nature, social spatialisation creates conditions in which people coordinate their activities and activity-sites, as well as their attitudes to other people's activities and activity-sites, in response to the question 'what to do, when and where?' (Shields, 1991, p 64). The answers to these questions transform imaginary geographies into everyday practices and actions. Clearly variation in social spatialisations that recognise homelessness as part (or otherwise) of place-images and place-myths, redolent (or otherwise) in what is accepted as everyday practice, will be powerful mechanisms in the spatial differentiation of homelessness as an issue or problem.

Shields' social spatialisation inculcates space into cultural differentiation, but might be thought to overemphasise culture in the recognition of places at the margin. Cresswell (1996) draws on, and adds to, the writings of Bourdieu (1979, 1989) in his discussion of how uses of spaces are constructed as *appropriate* or *inappropriate*. Although Bourdieu tends to treat 'social' struggle as 'class' struggle (thereby rendering gender, ethnicity, age, sexuality and so on, invisible as specific identities of differentiation), he usefully argues that an established social order is reproduced by a naturalisation of common sense. What is natural and common sense will lead to the erection of boundaries between common sense notions of appropriate or inappropriate behaviour in particular places. There is thus a taken-for-granted nature (a 'doxa') of practices and events in places, and places themselves will display different doxa, or senses of the obvious. Where transgressions occur, things will seem 'out-of-place' because of a lack of doxa-conformity:

> The occurrence of 'out-of-place' phenomena leads people to question behaviour and define what is and is not appropriate for a particular setting ... although 'out-of-place' is logically secondary to 'in-place', it may come first existentially. That is to say, we may have to experience some geographical transgression before we realise that a boundary even existed. (Cresswell, 1996, p 22)

Cresswell concludes that place is essentially implicated in the creation and maintenance of ideological beliefs, and that the taken-for-granted meanings of place are not natural, but have been socially and historically constructed.

These contentions intersect with Sibley's (1995) writings on geographies of exclusion. Sibley argues that spatial purification is a key feature in the organisation of social space:

> The anatomy of the purified environment is an expression of the values associated with strong feelings of abjection, a heightened consciousness

of difference and, thus, a fear of mixing at the disintegration of boundaries. (p 78)

Here, there is not only the taken-for-grantedness about what is 'in-place' or 'out-of-place', but also a sense in which the built environment assumes a symbolic importance which reinforces a desire for order where the environment itself is ordered and purified:

> In this way, space is implicated in the construction of deviancy. Pure spaces expose difference and facilitate the policing of boundaries ... the exclusionary practices of the institutions of the capitalist state are supported by individual preferences for purity and order.... A rejection of difference is embedded in the social system. (pp 86-7)

These arguments relating to social spatialisation, out-of-placeness, and purification of space suggest to us the strong possibility that rurality and homelessness have been normalised conceptually in relation to each other. First, homelessness has been assumed in many key discourses to be spatialised and in place in certain urban settings. This point is confirmed by the work of Dear and Wolch in the US (Dear and Taylor, 1982; Wolch and Gabriel, 1984; Dear and Wolch, 1987) who report three processes – spatial filtering of individuals, locations decisions of institutions, and processes of urbanisation – working together to produce service-dependent ghettos in inner cities. As Ruddick (1996, p 36) concludes:

> When Dear and Wolch analyse the de-institutionalisation and the concentration of homeless mentally ill in the service-dependent ghetto, they are describing a process wherein space only reaffirms the marginality of the subject in question: in a quite literal sense *these people occupy a space of difference 'already prepared for them'*. (author's italics)[10]

Second, homelessness is assumed to be out-of-place in certain kinds of rural spaces. Rural homelessness, therefore, represents a transgression where the doxa does not conform to the weight of socio-spatial expectations. Moreover, rural homelessness as transgression, marks the boundary of in-place and out-of-place homelessness. Following Sibley, we can identify the countryside as a purified space whose boundaries are policed and where the rejection of difference is embedded in the social system. Here, homeless people may be forced to employ 'tactics' of invisibility in order not to challenge their excluded position from the purified socio-spatial boundaries which currently suggest rather tight culturally constructed constraints on the in-placeness of homelessness in rural areas.

Conceptual non-coupling of rurality and homelessness

These suggestions that imaginary geographies of rurality and homelessness become transformed into the everyday practices and actions relating to what people actually do *in* and *about* rural places, can further be supported with reference both to discourses relating to rurality, and to those of home. The broad assertion that rurality represents a purified space where social problems such as homelessness are out-of-place mirrors that made by other researchers. For example, Sibley (1995, 1997) in his discussion of British government legislation which attacked New Age travellers but supported hunting in the countryside, suggests:

> ... the countryside, it seems, belongs to the middle class, to landowners and to people who engage in blood sports.... This case suggests how a group, like New Age Travellers, can be denied a place in society through a particular construction of place. A rigid stereotype of place, the English countryside, throws up discrepant others.... These groups are other, they are folk-devils, and they transgress only because the countryside is defined as a stereotypical pure space which cannot accommodate difference. (Sibley, 1995, pp 107-8)

Sibley here refers to the socio-cultural constructions of place in the countryside, and it is important to confirm that many contemporary academic discourses do not view rurality as any kind of naturalistic or self-defining spatial category. A vigorous and useful debate has gone on over recent years (Mormont, 1990; Cloke and Milbourne, 1992; Cloke and Goodwin, 1992, 1993; Philo, 1992, 1993, 1997; Halfacree, 1993; Murdoch and Pratt, 1993, 1994, 1997; Pratt, 1996; Lawrence, 1997) which has served to differentiate between geographical spaces and social spaces of rurality. Given the near-universal spread of urban cultures through urban-based media, the increases in commuting from 'rural' areas into metropolitan centres, the opposite flows of tourists and leisure seekers, and the movements 'out-of-town' of the housing, shopping malls and other architectures of suburbia, traditional distinctions between rural and urban geographical spaces have been significantly blurred (Wilson, 1992). There are enormous international and intra-national spatial variations in this blurring with, for example, marginal areas in large continental nations continuing to be dominated economically by primary sector activities (usually agriculture or forestry), while in other rural areas agriculture continues to dominate the landscape, but not the economy. Moreover, there remains a strong sense of identity around the idea of the village in the city, with the rural enclaves of Hampstead, for example, representing 'real' rurality just as strongly as small villages remote from cities. It is no longer possible therefore to attach an uncomplicated label of 'rural' to many geographical spaces, and it is insufficient to regard urban and rural as dichotomous spaces, and new ways have been sought to chart and represent their interconnections (see Lawrence, 1996).

One potential outcome of these changing conceptualisations of rurality is further to problematise the constitution of spatialities and cultural practices, and the ways in which these are labelled discursively as 'urban' and 'rural'. In so doing, the rural/urban framework could itself be transgressed – as indeed has been variously suggested elsewhere (Hoggart, 1990; Murdoch and Pratt, 1997) – in favour of a focus on different mappings of the socio-spatial construction of identity, exclusion and mobility. Alternatively, further emphasis can be given to the continuing importance of rurality as a series of socio-cultural constructs. From this perspective, it is important to recognise that the rural referent has become detached from its geographical moorings with two significant results. First, iconographic representations of rurality have now spread, often via powerful advertising media, throughout the consumption of our everyday life, as illustrated by 'country' clothing, fabrics and furnishings, four-wheel drive vehicles, and numerous spatialised representations of the 'natural' in countryside places. Second, the distinctiveness of rurality is increasingly to be found in the meanings, ideologies and moralities attached to it. Although there are many discursive versions of these, varying over time and space and among individuals, considerable common consent is given to more communal representations of rurality in social space. In rural England, it has been possible to trace common imagined geographies of idyllistic rural life-styles, which present rural life as close to nature, enjoying the benefits of close-built community and free from the pollution, criminality and social problems of the city.

We argue, here, that socio-cultural constructs of idyllised rurality are embedded in a range of important discursive materials which serve to position rural areas as purified spaces where both the issue of homelessness and homeless people themselves, are cast as out-of-place. Three brief examples from different discursive arenas may be used to illustrate this point. First, in addition to the kinds of national newspaper stories outlined in the Introduction, *local* press coverage of homelessness issues often reinforces the apparent wish to purify rural spaces and to render unwelcome any outsiders whose wandering, transience or simple mobility may threaten the settled and localised nature of rural life[11]. For example, the *Somerset County Gazette* over recent years has become a mouthpiece for those who would clear the streets of Taunton of beggars and vagrants (Cloke et al, 2000a). Thus the managing director of a local hotel argues in its pages that:

> "Beggars and vagrants do nothing to enhance the area for people who come here to use business facilities and spend money." (*Somerset County Gazette*, 14 March 1997)

The then Conservative MP argues that selling the *Big Issue* in Taunton is the start of a downward spiral into (even) less desirable activities:

> "Once it is established that you can solicit money by playing music or selling the *Big Issue*, then it's only a matter of time before people sit there and ask for your money." (*Somerset County Gazette*, 13 September 1996)

And a Conservative town councillor (and local business owner) suggests the clearance of beggars from the town centre:

> "... so the people of Taunton can shop in the town centre without feeling a sense of potential danger." (*Somerset County Gazette*, 30 August 1997)

The overarching message is that homelessness can be conflated with begging and vagrancy and does not, or should not, exist in what is seen as a rural centre. These clear, popular discourses mirror the assumptions which so often underlie the speeches and policy documents of politicians. A second example here may be drawn from the government White Paper *Rural England: A nation committed to a living countryside* (DoE, 1995). Outlining a housing strategy that seeks to "encourage a wide range of housing options to maintain balanced, living communities, serving all aspects of housing need" (p 68), the White Paper outlines (among other things) measures to secure the provision of affordable housing, to ensure that the planning system releases an adequate supply of land for housing, and ultimately to relieve pressure on the countryside by making cities more attractive places in which to live. The issue of homelessness is neither recognised as a problem in rural areas nor addressed in policy strategies. It seems merely to be subsumed in discourses of housing. A very similar story is recorded in the case of rural Wales (Cloke et al, 1997a).

It is unsurprising that these discursive traits are also reflected in radio and television programming, by which cultural constructions of rurality are so readily circulated. To give a third example, the long-running radio drama *The Archers*, which since 1950 has mapped out a kind of 'official' version of rural life in England, has featured storylines which deal with issues relating to rural homelessness. Perhaps the two best-known relate to the squatters (unnamed) who turn up in one of the Home Farm cottages in 1985 and to the story of Sharon Richards (in 1989) who is given temporary shelter by the vicar – Jerry Buckle – and then found an old caravan to live in by Pat Archer. Although the term 'homelessness' *is* used in Sharon's case, both storylines highlight stereotypical reactions of widespread disapproval and blaming of the victims by most of the villagers of Ambridge, who make it quite clear that the doxa of village life are being transgressed both by the homeless people themselves (who are the subject of rumours about 'drug-taking' and described as 'spongers on society') and indeed by the people who come to their aid (Whitburn, 1996).

In combinations these discursive constructs from print journalism, government and broadcasting tend to be mutually reinforcing. Moreover, academic accounts of the blurring of urban–rural distinctions, and the uneasy fit between the geographical spaces and various social spaces of rurality, have themselves highlighted the idyllised myth-making power of rurality in the cultural realm. It is almost as if the entrenched academic discourses which insisted on a rural–urban dichotomy (see Tonnies, 1957) or continuum (see Redfield, 1941), and which transposed ideas of *Gemeinschaft* and *Gesellschaft* onto rural and urban categories respectively, have not been argued away, but simply regenerated in the imagined socio-cultural spaces of rurality. These transposed academic discourses, too, have created common social spaces of the rural which connect to the issues of purified space, the making and keeping of social boundaries, and the appropriation of 'appropriate' behaviour.

Although the English rural idyll should not be regarded as transferable to other rural geographical spaces, the importance of distinctive imagined geographies based on particular socio-cultural constructs of rurality should not be underemphasised. In his study of rural homelessness in Iowa, Lawrence (1995) notes that the rural is commonly constructed as perhaps the 'quintessential geographic site' of representations of nature. This role, he argues, raises very significant barriers to the coupling of 'rural' and 'homelessness' at a socio-cultural level. In particular, the representations of rural space tend to valorise matters of privacy, property and independence, while homeless people are positioned in social space in such a way as to challenge these representations. Homelessness, then, is both institutive of and transgressive of the imagined geographies of rural society, not least because it violates representations of self-sufficiency, propertied and privately constituted individualism. As Lawrence points out:

> The homeless person is defined (1) simultaneously by public scrutiny and public effort to dissimulate about her existence, (2) by expectation of property ownership and vilification because she does not possess, and perhaps most problematic of all (3) by the tension between the assumption on the one hand that work insures protection from falling into a state of being defined as homeless and the realisation on the other hand that many of the new homeless are employed. (pp 305-6)

The production of rural space in the socio-cultural arena is thereby threatened by any kind of recognition of such a challenging other. Homelessness is thus out-of-place in the countryside in those places where cultural doxa (and these can vary – rural England is not the cultural equivalent of rural Iowa) establish a weight of socio-cultural expectations which cannot be met by the transgressive homeless person, and the transgressive homeless 'issue'. Rural homelessness occupies spaces for which it was unintended, and thus becomes a challenge to the boundaries of geographic expression of rural social space.

Thus far, the purity of rural space has been linked with broad cultural constructs of rurality involving 'naturalness' as a setting for idyllic or individualistic life-styles. Homeless people (along with others) are constructed as 'not belonging' in this purified space, and this being out-of-place, or not belonging, is a major cultural prompt – to rural residents and to those whose agency jurisdiction covers these geographical areas – not to acknowledge homelessness as a legitimate part of their discourses on rurality. There is, however, another significant cultural prompt in relation to rural social space that has a direct antithetical impact on the issue of homelessness. As well as transgressions relating to being out-of-place, there are also transgressions relating to an inability on the part of homeless people to be 'at home' in the countryside. Like the term homelessness, home is a 'multivariate concept with meanings varying across individuals, culture and time' (Moore et al, 1995, p 10; see also Veness, 1992, 1993). As Neale (1997, pp 54-5) points out, meanings of home:

change according to the households involved, according to the individuals within it and according to the prevailing economic, social and political climate. No single definition of the home can be considered absolute, because meaning is relative and varies historically across different regions and/or societies.

These variations highlight the importance of the *context* in which meanings are formed, yet this is something which is frequently overlooked. This omission is noted by Despres (1991, p 98) who criticises studies examining the meaning of home for what she refers to as their 'interpretative bias', neglecting the "impact of societal forces and the material properties of the built environment on individuals' perceptions, judgements and behaviours, and the experience of and about the home" and giving "little indication of the socio-political context of the settings under the investigation".

We can, therefore, suggest two areas of importance about the 'home' in homelessness. First, it is possible to identify a number of common signifiers of home, which seem to traverse differences over time and space and between individuals (Somerville, 1992). Second, we would suggest that the construct of home is equally susceptible to the production of different social spaces, which when intersecting with the social spaces of rurality, for example, can produce distinctive imagined geographies of home. There is some evidence, both in rural places colonised by new middle classes (Cloke and Thrift, 1990) and in more remote areas (Hughes, 1997) that the so-called rural idyll carries with it particular forms of domesticity and familism, and that the rural 'home' is very much part of the purity of rural space (see also Little and Austin, 1996). Once again, commonly circulated discursive sources – from *The Archers*; to government policies to ensure decent housing; to glossy but tasteful design features on country cottages that are so prevalent in the weekend newspapers – serve to reinforce the cultural significance of the rural home, somehow promising "old-fashioned decencies and good homely sentiment ... [and] a sense of rootedness" (Barnett and Scruton, 1998, p xvi) to rural dwellers. Being without a home, then, in geographic space where the *imagined* geography is one where the home is valorised to this extent, is once again to transgress the socio-cultural meanings and moralities which lie at the heart of rural life.

Conclusion

In this chapter we have discussed three areas of reasoning which help to indicate why homelessness and rurality have become anathema in terms of conceptual and discursive non-coupling. Together, these arguments about the morphological, socio-cultural and conceptual characteristics of rurality and homelessness suggest that *urban* areas and homelessness are strongly equated in the imaginations of many people, whereas any equivalent complimentarity between rural areas and homelessness is usually unimaginable. Rurality is subject to imaginings that are often dominated by idyllised places and life-styles, in which the benefits of close-knit communities and closeness to nature are themselves closely associated with traditional moral values asserting the importance of home and settlement. The imagined purity of such places and life-styles is easily threatened by contradistinctive phenomena, be these poverty, crime, drug-taking – or homelessness. Accordingly, rural spaces can be (re)purified against out-of-place people and practices, either by strenuous denial of the very existence of phenomena such as homelessness, or by purposeful exclusionary practices, designed to move the people, and the troublesome issue, on into its 'proper' urban place.

These arguments have been supported by evidence of tangible examples of particular discourses that emphasise both the boundaries between what is, or is not, in-place in rural areas, and the naturalness of urban sites/ sights of homelessness. Moreover, we have begun to offer other evidence that suggests that rurality and homelessness *do* mesh together in a way which is neither expected by, or accommodated in, conventional discourses. To the limited statistical evidence of homelessness in rural areas can be added the testimonies of interviewees who have been in the past, or are currently, homeless in rural areas. Such evidence encompasses both local people who have become homeless in their local rural area, and more mobile non-local people who have chosen to live out their homelessness in rural settings. In these cases, the lack of home and the refusal to be settled respectively transgress imagined and practised conventions of appropriate behaviour, and therefore fail to conform to the doxa of purified rural space. The usual response is to adopt tactics of invisibility, involving either hiddenness or migration.

Any attempts to bring about a coupling of rurality and homelessness will, therefore, face very significant discursive, political and practical hurdles, and will necessitate a very considerable shift in the ways in which notions of space and social problems are combined in the understandings and actions of policy makers and rural residents. It would be easy to be pessimistic about this prospect, especially in view of the woefully inadequate response to the injustices of homelessness more generally. However, there may be two grounds for some limited optimism. First, there has been a long history of interest in rural housing issues, and more recently the issue of affordable housing has gained momentum as a problem requiring policy response (albeit rarely a radical response). Currently, housing discourses tend to subsume and render invisible homelessness issues in the countryside. However, if 'homelessness' can be discursively decoupled from 'housing', then anti-homelessness strategies could emerge. Something similar is beginning to occur with the stirring of interest in *antipoverty* strategies in rural areas now that poverty has (to some extent at least) begun to be accepted discursively as an issue that needs to be dealt with outside of the cities.

Second, there is some scope for optimism in the traditions of voluntarism and beneficence that historically (and almost certainly currently) are present in rural areas. Much of the work with homeless people in the cities is done by volunteers. Although the scale of potential volunteers in rural areas will be much smaller, it could be that the voluntaristic spirit of rural people could be awakened to the needs of homeless people in their areas. Donohue's (1996) *In the open: Diary of a homeless alcoholic* adds some credence to this suggestion. Although for much of the diary, he is based in US urban centres, staying in missions or in his tent, Donohue describes a short stay in the small town of Henderson, where someone has just given him a brand new 20-dollar bill:

> I have to admit that the people of Henderson have been extraordinarily kind and giving. Nowhere else in the country have people approached me with such frequency to offer food, clothes, and even money. This might have something to do with the fact that there are not *too* many homeless here. A surplus of that kind will turn people sour after a while. This seems to me to be a general precept of human behaviour that is ignored by the homeless population at their own peril. Why do they concentrate themselves into specific areas, provoking the contempt of the local population, and depriving themselves of the goodwill and benevolence that can be evoked only when they are seen on a less frequent basis? (p 184)

To some extent, Donohue evaluates rural Henderson as resource rich – a good place to be homeless in, at least for a while; a place where the very unfamiliarity of his presence, his out-of-placeness, engenders generosity rather than marginalisation from residents. Homelessness and rurality are at least temporarily coupled in this instance, at least until other homeless people begin to 'colonise' Henderson and reduce the levels of goodwill and benevolence on offer.

Nevertheless, whether pessimism and optimism are in order, it must be a continuing priority to provide critical deconstruction of how and why key social issues such as homelessness become, and remain, non-coupled with rurality. Anything less merely reinforces academic and other discourses which emphasise incompatibility between rural areas and responses to key social issues.

Notes

[1] We will critique social constructs of the 'rural' as idyll and discuss other meanings attached to rurality by homeless people later in this chapter.

[2] We do not wish to imply here that there exists either a unity of rural space or privilege but that particular rural spaces are awarded different levels of privilege according to their constructed proximity to dominant national discourses of rural idyll.

[3] In a historical context, Sibley (1995, p 59) has discussed how the 1947 Town and Country Planning Act, which has dominated patterns of new housing provision in the countryside for more than 50 years, was viewed by its many postwar supporters as capable of controlling the 'spread of disorderly development' and, by extension, of excluding 'working-class people from middle-class space'.

[4] Analysis of the 1996 DoE statistics of the numbers of households accepted by local authorities in England as homeless shows that 20.6% of such acceptances were in London, 14.4% in rural areas and the remaining 65% in 'other urban' areas. The focus on London, therefore, responds to the greatest spatial concentration of homeless people, but by no means the bulk of homelessness in national terms.

[5] This point is developed in Chapters Five and Six.

[6] It should be noted, however, that some rural areas do attract migrant homeless people because of the availability of seasonal work. For example, Butlins holiday centre at Minehead in Somerset was found to exert just such a drawing power.

[7] 'Safety in numbers' is a relative concept in the urban experience of homelessness. Many interviewees told us of how they were subjected to abuse and violence in city streets.

[8] As indicated by our reference to interviews with men in this section, it may be that most rural 'rough sleepers' and 'journeyers' are men. It was suggested by many of our interviewees that women find it easier to secure alternative

accommodation (either from the local authority, or more informally), although more evidence is required to substantiate this.

[9] This discussion of invisibility is developed at greater length elsewhere (see Cloke et al, 2000b).

[10] Such locational filtering is often made transparent by anti-homeless laws where legal boundaries are erected between homeless spaces and non-homeless spaces by the barring of homeless people from key public sites (see Mitchell, 1997).

[11] As noted earlier, local press coverage is also often hostile to urban homelessness, and also campaigns for the purification of urban space.

FOUR

The policy context of
rural homelessness

Discussion of rural homelessness needs to be set within the relevant policy context. The first thing to note, however, is that there is no policy which specifically addresses the issue of rural homelessness. Consequently, in this chapter we focus on general homelessness policies and then on those rural policies which have a bearing on preventing and tackling homelessness in rural areas (see Table 4.1 for a timeline of key policy reports and developments).

In the first part, we trace the development of the homelessness legislation over the past 25 years. We begin with a brief review of the 1977 Housing (Homeless Persons) Act, before looking in more detail at the events leading up to the implementation of the 1996 Housing Act – under which homelessness is currently dealt with. We then turn our attention to developments since the election of the New Labour government in May 1997, examining the proposed reforms to the homelessness legislation as set out in the Housing Green Paper (published in April 2000) and Part II of the subsequent Homes Bill, introduced into the House of Commons later that year.

These documents make little or no reference to the particular needs of rural areas. Instead, it is left to the Rural White Paper (published in November 2000) to set out the government's policy in relation to housing and homelessness in these areas. In the second part of this chapter we provide a comprehensive account of this policy, looking in particular at government initiatives to increase the amount of affordable accommodation in rural areas. We also highlight the potentially positive contribution that non-housing policies can make both to preventing and dealing with homelessness in rural areas.

In the third part of the chapter we look at government efforts to tackle rough sleeping. To date, the homelessness legislation has been primarily geared towards addressing the needs of homeless families and a number of other selected groups deemed to be in priority need of accommodation. Priority cases are dominated by households with or expecting children who consistently account for two thirds of homeless households in this category[1]. The single homeless have, for the most part, been left to make their own arrangements with the exception of one particular subset of this population – rough sleepers. This group has been the focus of a considerable amount of attention and has received substantial resources under the Rough Sleepers Initiative. We provide a brief overview of this and subsequent initiatives to reduce the number of people sleeping rough. While the policy towards tackling rough sleeping has been predominantly focused on London and other urban areas – particularly in its earlier phases – as the public face of central government's response to homelessness, it is important to set out the key features of this policy.

The chapter ends with an examination of agency responses to the Housing Green Paper and Rural White Paper, providing an illustration of the way in which the issue of rural homelessness can fall through the gap between homelessness and rural policies.

Table 4.1: A homelessness and rural policy timeline

July 1998	Social Exclusion Unit report on *Rough sleeping*
February 1999	*Rural England: A discussion document*
April 1999	Homelessness Action Programme launched; Rough Sleepers Unit (RSU) set up.
August 1999	*Annual report on rough sleeping*
November 1999	*Rural England: Summary of responses*
December 1999	Government launches *Coming in from the cold: The government's strategy on rough sleeping*
January 2000	*Coming in from the cold: Delivering the strategy*
April 2000	Housing Green Paper: *Quality and choice: A decent home for all*
May 2000	Select Committee on Environment, Transport and Regional Affairs publishes its Seventh Report on the proposed Rural White Paper
July 2000	Housing Minister Nick Raynsford announces details of the Spending Review 2000 settlement for housing
Summer 2000	RSU publishes progress report on government's strategy on rough sleeping
November 2000	Rural White Paper: *Our countryside: The future – A fair deal for rural England*
December 2000	Homes Bill introduced into the House of Commons; Housing Policy Statement published
January 2001	*Quality and choice: A decent home for all: Summary of responses*
February 2001	Homes Bill passed to the House of Lords
March 2001	*Rural White Paper Implementation Plan*
June 2001	Homelessness Bill published

The 1977 Housing (Homeless Persons) Act

Prior to 1977, homelessness was treated as a welfare problem. Under the 1948 National Assistance Act, county authorities were obliged to provide temporary accommodation for persons in urgent or unforeseen need. However, although a Ministry of Health circular, released the same year, emphasised that the Act was intended to assist people made homeless through an emergency such as fire or flood rather than those who were 'inadequately housed', the Act was unable to cope with the number of people seeking help. The majority of these people were victims not of an emergency but of the general housing shortage and needed permanent homes that welfare departments were quite simply not in a position to provide (Richards, 1992, p 129). Yet housing departments were reluctant to rehouse these households, considering them undeserving and irresponsible and their application as contrary to waiting list principles. As a result, with neither welfare nor housing departments willing or able to take responsibility, the needs of many homeless households went unmet.

Despite an apparent awareness of the problem, however, homelessness in the 1950s and 1960s was a subject "on which government expressed concern, commissioned research, set up working parties and issued guidance and advisory circulars, but did not legislate" (Raynsford, 1986, p 44). Pressure for legislative reform mounted in the 1960s and 1970s as growing public concern and media interest in the plight of homeless families, particularly following the televising of the drama *Cathy come home* in 1966, brought homelessness into the public eye and to the forefront of political debate. A number of charities including Shelter, the Catholic Housing Aid Society and the Child Poverty Action Group joined together to form the Joint Charities Group to press the case for reform and finally in 1977 – after much disagreement and prevarication – the Housing (Homeless Persons) Act was passed.

Although criticised for its restrictive definition of homelessness and weakened during its passage through Parliament, the Act represented "an important landmark in housing policy" (Malpass and Murie, 1990, p 82). For the first time, housing authorities were statutorily obliged to accept responsibility for households in urgent need of accommodation. Yet, while undoubtedly a notable achievement which improved access to housing for many homeless households, the Act only dealt with homeless households in priority need – namely families with children, pregnant women, or anyone deemed 'vulnerable' as a result of old age, mental or physical disability or other special reason – and left the needs of a large number of homeless people essentially unaddressed. At the time of its introduction, proponents of the 1977 Act hoped for a gradual extension of its remit to statutorily provide for all homeless people rather than only those in priority need, but in practice the Act was interpreted in the narrowest possible terms and the subsequent 20 years witnessed, if anything, a toughening up of the homelessness legislation (Blake, 1993; Watchman in McCarthy and Simpson, 1991). This was demonstrated most recently and most clearly in the 1996 Housing Act (Parts VI and VII) which abolished the priority on the waiting list (now more commonly referred to as the housing register) formerly accorded to homeless households and removed their entitlement to *permanent* accommodation.

In 1989, a government review of the homelessness legislation concluded that it "has worked reasonably well and should remain in place as a 'long-stop' to help those who through no fault of their own have become homeless" (DoE, 1989, p 21). The legislation was seen as having struck "a reasonable balance between the interests of the genuinely homeless and others in housing need". Yet despite such independent endorsement and a general conclusion that there was no need for change, the Conservative administration of the time was determined to press ahead with reform.

Reforming the homelessness legislation: motivations and responses

The 1996 Housing Act for England and Wales was the first major revision of the allocation of council housing (to homeless people) since the 1977 Housing (Homeless Persons) Act, which had first placed a statutory duty on local authorities to house homeless people in priority need. (For an account of debates surrounding the introduction of the 1977 Act see Raynsford, 1986.) While primarily promoted as part of a package of measures "to improve fairness in the allocation of social housing" (DoE, 1997), reforms to the homelessness legislation were also motivated by the practical necessity to restrict access to a limited resource and by broader ideological concerns to limit the power of local authorities and move further along the road towards a privatised, market-dominated housing system.

The preceding Consultation Paper (CP) – *Access to local authority and housing association tenancies* (DoE, 1994a) – setting out the proposed reforms sought to recast homelessness and homeless people in a number of different ways.

In the first place the government suggested that applicants were not really homeless, arguing that, "In the great majority of cases, someone accepted as homeless is in fact occupying accommodation of some sort at the time he or she approaches the authority" (DoE, 1994a, para 2.8). This reflects the ambiguity of the term. By positioning itself at one extreme of the homelessness continuum (referred to in Chapter One) and adopting a minimalist definition which equates homelessness with rooflessness, the government effectively challenged the 'legitimacy' of claims to homelessness among households in less extreme, but still highly inadequate housing situations.

Second, references to 'genuine' homeless applicants and 'real' housing need, which peppered the government's case for reform, suggested that some applicants were 'bogus' and their claims of homelessness fraudulent. The Consultation Paper referred to applicants abusing the system, seeing the homelessness legislation "as a 'fast track' into social housing and so *contriving* to fall within its provisions" (para 2.9; emphasis added).

Third, in criticising present methods of allocating housing which give priority access to homeless households as "unfair because they do not always ensure that it goes to the people with the best claim to it" (para 2.4), the government implied that homeless people were *less deserving* than other households in housing need (see also Fitzpatrick and Stephens, 1999). With the loss of council housing (through the sale and transfer of property) having progressively undermined the ability of local authorities to meet need, this labelling process served as a useful mechanism for rationing access to the limited stock that remained.

By constructing unmet need and housing shortages as a result of certain households (such as homeless families) 'jumping' the housing queue – in other words, the 'wrong' people gaining access to housing – the government was able to detract attention from the central issue, namely the inadequacy of supply. At the same time, setting homeless households and people on the waiting list against each other in this way fragmented potential opposition to reforms and helped disguise the fact that both these groups "are equally victims of a situation in which there is a basic shortage of housing to rent" (Thompson, 1988, p 85).

Thus, employing key discourses focusing on the (un)deservability of certain households provided the government with a way of justifying reforms to the homelessness legislation and ensuring that they gained public acceptance.

The reforms were perhaps driven less by an overwhelming 'sense of fairness' than by practical concerns to limit demand for an over-subscribed resource and the proposals were widely opposed. The Consultation Paper generated more than 10,000 responses, the majority of which were overwhelmingly critical. Some concessions were made – for example, proposals not to begin the duty to house until after investigations had been completed were dropped – but the tone and substance of the proposals were essentially unchanged. Instead, George Young (the then Housing Minister) in an address to Parliament in July 1994, dismissed much of the criticism, claiming that "many of the responses did not address the actual proposals but responded to misleading claims by lobby organisations" and he condemned the "alarmist propaganda" put about by "vested interests" (DoE, 1994b). Yet, in contrast to what this might suggest, opposition was not confined to a small number of minority or extremist groups. A survey by *Housing* magazine (September 1995, pp 26-31), for example, found substantial opposition to the proposed changes to the homelessness legislation among a range of professional organisations – including the Local Government Association, Shelter, the Council of Mortgage Lenders and the National Federation of Housing Associations.

The reforms were condemned as both unnecessary and as detrimental to the health and welfare of homeless families. Despite such widespread opposition the government proceeded (essentially unswayed) along the course it had set itself and on 31 October the 1996 Housing Act received Royal Assent.

The homelessness provisions of the 1996 Housing Act

In line with the government's desire to exercise greater control over what housing is allocated and to whom, the 1996 Housing Act introduced new restrictions regarding which homeless households are entitled to rehousing by the local authority and in what circumstances. Under the Act a number of households are considered ineligible for assistance including certain persons from abroad (principally those who are unable to claim social security benefits), asylum seekers with any accommodation – however temporary – available in the UK (or elsewhere), along with anyone else deemed ineligible by the Secretary of State.

Eligibility and homelessness in themselves, however, are not sufficient to secure rehousing. As under the earlier legislation it replaced, the Act restricts entitlement to certain groups of homeless people. Local authorities are only obliged to rehouse households who are unintentionally homeless and in priority need of accommodation (namely families with children, pregnant women, or anyone deemed 'vulnerable' as a result of old age, mental or physical disability or other special reason). In addition, the Act introduced a further restriction on access to housing for homeless households. Where an authority considers there is 'other suitable accommodation' available in the district, its duty is limited to providing sufficient advice and assistance to enable the applicant to gain access to that accommodation.

For those homeless households who *are* deemed eligible for rehousing, reforms to the homelessness legislation have significantly affected their security of tenure. The 1996 Act reduced the duty of councils to homeless households in priority need to securing accommodation for a minimum of two years with local authorities obliged to allocate secure tenancies through the housing register. (The Act also provides for local authorities to fulfil their obligations by rehousing homeless households in the private rented sector.)

While the duty to provide temporary accommodation can recur if homelessness and eligibility for assistance continues beyond two years, the expectation is that households in long-term need will be granted a permanent tenancy through the housing register at some point during this period. By solving the immediate problem of their homelessness, temporary rehousing places homeless households on a waiting list for permanent accommodation from the housing register, so fulfilling the government's aim for homeless households to be considered for permanent accommodation "alongside other applicants on the basis of their *underlying needs*" (DoE, 1997) (emphasis added).

Despite these proscriptions, local authorities have considerable freedom to draw up their own system of allocation. Although Section 167(2) requires that the allocation process gives 'reasonable preference' to a number of different groups (including people occupying insanitary or overcrowded housing, families with dependent children and households with limited opportunities to secure settled accommodation), local authorities are free to add any number of other groups of households to this list in response to the local situation. In addition, it is up to the individual authority to decide how to prioritise *between* these groups such that – in effect – some households have more of a reasonable preference than others.

The provisions set out in the Act cannot therefore be seen as a blueprint of how housing is allocated to homeless households. Local authorities retain considerable autonomy in allocation decisions and, as we shall see in the following chapter, outcomes for homeless households are likely to continue to rest on the way in which the homelessness legislation is interpreted and implemented by individual authorities.

New Labour and homelessness

During the passage of the 1996 Housing Act through Parliament, the Labour opposition ensured that some of the more draconian and restrictive measures proposed – such as a one-year limit on help for homeless people – were dropped. Elected to government in May 1997, the Party acted promptly to withdraw some of the sting from the Act. Secondary legislation was introduced requiring local authorities to ensure that accommodation in the private rented sector is available for a minimum of two years and homeless households were added to the list of groups accorded a 'reasonable preference' in the allocation of housing.

These and other proposed reforms to the homelessness legislation were set out in the Housing Green Paper – *Quality and choice: A decent home for all* (DETR, 2000a). Published in April 2000, this was the first comprehensive review of housing for 23 years and set out the government's strategy for achieving 'a decent home for all'. The Green Paper generated substantial discussion with some 1,099 individuals and organisations taking the opportunity to respond during the subsequent consultation period (DETR, 2000b). Following on from this, on 13 December 2000, the government released the *Housing policy statement: The way forward for housing* (DETR, 2000c), detailing its ideas in the light of the comments received in response to the Housing Green Paper.

The proposed reforms to the homelessness legislation (outlined in Chapter Nine of the Housing Green Paper and confirmed in Chapter Seven of the *Housing policy statement*) are already receiving parliamentary attention within a new Homelessness Bill which was published in June 2001. This Bill includes all the homelessness provisions of Part II of the Homes Bill that was introduced into the House of Commons in December 2000 (DETR, 2001a) but ran out of parliamentary time with the calling of a general election for June 2001. According to the government, the earlier Homes Bill represented "an important part of the Government's strategy to ensure that everyone has the opportunity and choice of a decent home" (DETR, 2000d). In particular, the Bill (DETR, 2000e) sought to:

- ensure that unintentionally homeless people in priority need are provided with suitable temporary accommodation until they can obtain a permanent home;
- enable local authorities to use their own housing stock to provide temporary accommodation for homeless people until a long-term home becomes available;
- allow local authorities greater flexibility to provide accommodation to non-priority homeless households;
- encourage a more strategic approach to the prevention of homelessness.

Both the Homes Bill and Homelessness Bill have received a ringing endorsement from Shelter. In relation to the former Bill, a Shelter policy briefing headlined, 'Homeless people get *their* Bill' (emphasis added) stated:

> Shelter strongly welcomes the publication of the Bill. The measures it contains will create a modern framework for reducing homelessness which shifts the emphasis from crisis-driven intervention to a strategic approach which focuses on prevention. It will provide the statutory framework necessary to help reduce all forms of homelessness and will play an important role in meeting the Government's long term objective of tackling social exclusion. (Shelter, 2000a, p 3)

The charity, particularly praised the fact that:

> rather than simply repeal the more draconian provisions in the 1996 Act, in the Homes Bill, the Government has identified, and seeks to tackle, the shortcomings of the previous legislation such as the lack of attention to prevention and support and limitations within the current priority need categories. (p 3)

Part II of the Homes Bill (now incorporated into the new Homelessness Bill) is effectively in three sections. The first places a requirement on local authorities to carry out a review of homelessness in their area and formulate a strategy for dealing with the problem. In reviewing homelessness, local authorities will be required to outline current and likely future levels of homelessness, the activities carried out in relation to tackling it and the resources available for these purposes. This review will provide the necessary basis for formulating a strategy on homelessness that should cover its prevention, securing accommodation, and the provision of support for homeless people and those at risk of homelessness. While the housing authority is envisaged as the lead player in reviewing homelessness and drawing up a strategy, the Bill specifically requires social services authorities to assist the housing authority in exercising these functions. In addition, both authorities are required to take the strategy into account when carrying out their normal activities.

There is much that is positive about this section of the Bill. In particular, the emphasis on prevention represents a move away from a purely reactive response – *dealing* with homelessness – to a more proactive and long-term approach that seeks to prevent it from occurring in the first place. The requirement on social services and housing authorities to work more closely together in responding to homelessness, while perhaps difficult to ensure on the ground, is an important statement of principle and intent. It has long been recognised that tensions between these two authorities and disagreements over responsibilities can lead to certain vulnerable individuals falling through the net.

Also welcome, are the references in the Bill to the need to provide support to homeless people and those at risk of homelessness. This demonstrates a valuable recognition that tackling homelessness involves more than providing someone with a roof over their head.

However, the Bill makes no further stipulations as to the nature or level of support to be provided or to whom. The Green Paper is similarly lacking in detail, merely stating that many homeless people need additional support services and that "housing authorities, in liaison with other agencies, will be required to provide advice and assistance to help them to access these support services" (DETR, 2000a, para 9.62).

Furthermore, providing support is not just a question of joined-up working, or simply a question of helping people gain access to support services. Often these services do not exist (this may be particularly the case in rural areas) or are already heavily oversubscribed. A general lack of resources restricts who can receive support (often only 'crisis' cases are dealt with), the level of support available, and the period of time over which it is provided. In addition, support for homeless households is often provided through voluntary sector organisations relying on time-limited and/or insecure funding which hinders the development of effective and strategic services.

Without more specific obligations on local authorities backed up by additional resources, significant variations in the provision of support across the country are likely to develop, reflecting the importance individual authorities attach to making such provision and the resources at their disposal. There is a danger that in many localities support will remain merely a rhetorical, paper commitment with little material consequence for homeless people on the ground.

The second section of Part II of the Homes Bill amends the duties on local authorities to provide assistance to unintentionally homeless people. It will allow local authorities to provide accommodation to non-priority homeless people who are not intentionally homeless. According to Shelter, "this places a stronger emphasis on local authorities to house non-priority homeless people where they have capacity within their housing stock, but does not impose a duty on them to do so" (Shelter, 2000a, p 4). However, there is nothing to prevent local authorities from housing non-priority homeless households at present and while the measure may improve the position for people in areas where there is a surplus of housing available, it is unlikely to have much impact in areas where demand is high. The needs of homeless households continue to remain secondary to the resources available. Whether so-called non-priority homeless households get accommodation continues to be determined less by need than by the availability of resources.

The Bill repeals the two-year restriction on the use of local authority stock to provide housing. Under the terms of the Bill, the duty to provide temporary accommodation for unintentionally homeless people in priority need is only brought to an end when the applicant has been provided with settled accommodation. In practice, at present, most authorities provide settled accommodation within the two-year period stipulated in the 1996 Housing Act or continue to provide temporary accommodation where this is not possible. However, repeal of the two-year restriction will, in the words of Shelter, "bring to an end the insecurity faced by homeless applicants and restore the recognition that homeless people need long-term solutions" (Shelter, 2000a, p 4). Section 197 of the 1996 Housing Act, which requires local authorities to consider whether other suitable alternative accommodation is available before letting its own property to a homeless household, is also repealed. In practice, this provision is rarely used. However, its repeal suggests an important point of principle, setting up social housing, rather than the private rented sector, as the first port of call for those in need.

The Homes Bill also includes measures to prevent priority homeless households from being housed in inappropriate private rented sector accommodation. In particular, it prevents local authorities from discharging the main homelessness duty through the use of assured shorthold tenancies in the private rented sector without an applicant's agreement. If such a tenancy is not appropriate to the needs and circumstances of the applicant, they can reject the offer, without this affecting their entitlement to rehousing.

Clauses included within the Bill amend the current statutory framework relating to the allocation of social housing in line with the government's objectives (set out in the Housing Green Paper) of giving local authorities greater flexibility to introduce lettings policies that offer more choice to homeless people and others in housing need. While most of the provisions in this section of the Bill relate to the general allocations process, a number have implications for homelessness and the rehousing of homeless households. In particular, although councils will have to consider *all* applications for housing (except those from ineligible people), Shelter remains concerned that local authorities will be able to continue to exercise discretion to deny people access to housing. This fear is heightened by the removal of an applicants statutory right (under the 1996 Housing

Act) to review an authority's decision to exclude them from the housing register. This is of particular concern to Shelter, which has collected a substantial body of evidence highlighting the way in which certain individuals and groups are excluded from local authority waiting lists and hence prevented from gaining access to social housing (see, for example, Niner 1997; Bacon, 1998). Indeed, Shelter research suggests that in England as a whole over the two-year period of 1996-98, around 200,000 households may have been excluded from the housing register (Butler, 1998). Shelter is concerned that the Homes Bill will allow exclusionary practices to continue and has called for the Bill to be amended to build in safeguards (including a right of appeal) to ensure that exclusions and suspensions from both local authority and registered social landlord housing registers should only occur in exceptional circumstances.

Outstanding policy issues

Suitability of accommodation

Part II of the Homes Bill (now included within the Homelessness Bill) leaves outstanding a number of issues in relation to the homelessness provisions of the 1996 Housing Act. In particular, reservations remain as to the adequacy of accommodation in which homeless households are rehoused. Section 210 of the 1996 Act stipulates that accommodation provided by local authorities in discharging the main homelessness duty must be 'suitable'. As highlighted earlier, this is a subjective term, but evidence suggests that homeless households are often placed in accommodation that is inappropriate to their needs. Particular concerns relate to the increasing use of bed and breakfast accommodation, which has risen sharply in recent years. At the end of December 2000, in a total of 72,440 homeless households accommodated in temporary accommodation by local authorities, 9,860 were living in bed and breakfast accommodation – an increase of 22% on the previous year (Shelter, 2001). The detrimental impact of living in such accommodation is well known (Murie and Jeffers, 1987; Carter, 1997) and although bed and breakfast can provide an important stopgap, it is important to ensure that such provision is not used routinely to accommodate homeless households. Nor should it be used to house homeless households for sustained periods of time.

There are also concerns as to whether accommodation is suitable in terms of location. This has been raised by Shelter particularly in relation to 'hard pressed London boroughs', but also has a resonance in rural areas where the limited availability of emergency accommodation and social housing more generally can lead to homeless households being rehoused a substantial distance from their previous area of residence with subsequent impacts on children's schooling and access to support networks. In reflection of such concerns, Shelter has called (in its response to the Housing Green Paper) for current definitions of 'suitability' of temporary and settled housing to be expanded to cover "location, minimum standards of accommodation, stability, sustainability, and the use of bed and breakfast hotels" (Shelter, 2001, p 10).

Priority need

As noted earlier, under the 1996 Housing Act, local authorities are only obliged to provide accommodation for homeless households deemed to be in priority need of accommodation – namely, families with children, pregnant women, or anyone deemed 'vulnerable' as a result of old age, mental or physical disability or other special reason. This definition is unchanged from that included in the 1977 Housing (Homeless Persons) Act and has arguably left other vulnerable individuals ineligible for support. The Housing Green Paper stated the government's intention to extend the groups of people who are considered to have a priority need for housing to include homeless 16- and 17-year-olds, care-leavers aged 18-21, and people that the council considers to be vulnerable as a result of fleeing domestic violence or harassment or as a result of an institutionalised background (for example, those leaving prison or the armed forces). The *Housing policy statement* confirms that these changes will be made 'shortly' by order under Section 189 of the 1996 Housing Act[2].

This is an important and welcome reform and one that has been lobbied for strongly by the main national homeless charities. Research shows that the groups to which priority need is being extended are extremely vulnerable to becoming homeless. The government's report on rough sleeping, for example, noted that: between a quarter and a third of rough sleepers have been looked after by local authorities as children; around half have been in prison or a remand centre at some time in their life; and between a quarter and a fifth have served in the armed forces (SEU, 1998, paras 1.12-1.16). The proposals to extend priority need received near-universal approval from respondents to the Housing Green Paper, although a number of these respondents pressed for a more generous upper age limit for young people defined as vulnerable – with 18, 21 and 24 variously suggested as a more appropriate cut-off age.

However, for these reforms to make a difference on the ground, adequate resources must back them up. Broadening the definition of priority need will have a financial impact on local authorities that must be addressed. As Crisis, the national charity for single homeless people, has commented, "There is no point in extending priority need if it is simply a paper commitment" (Crisis, 2000, p 4). Resources are required not only to guarantee that sufficient accommodation is available to house these additional priority need cases, but to ensure that the necessary mechanisms are in place to provide these vulnerable households with the support they require to maintain a tenancy. The Chartered Institute of Housing in particular has questioned whether there are sufficient resources available in this regard stating: "Funding for these proposals is vital to ensure that vulnerable households receive the support they need.... There is a real danger of overloading local authorities with high priority cases without the resources to house them and provide them with the support they need" (CIH, 2000).

The government has gone some way towards meeting these and related concerns raised by respondents to the Green Paper about the need for additional resources to put reforms into practice. In December 2000, the government used its *Housing policy statement* (DETR, 2000c, para 7.10) to announce that local authorities will receive additional revenue funding of £8m a year to meet the extra costs incurred in implementing the proposed changes to the homelessness legislation and in adopting a strategic approach to homelessness.

Single room rent

Another issue not addressed in the Homes Bill but with important bearings on the extent and nature of homelessness is the Single Room Rent (SRR) which restricts the amount of Housing Benefit payable to people under the age of 25. In response to concerns that this restriction is making it difficult for young single people to access and maintain accommodation, the Housing Green Paper suggests broadening the definition of the SRR to include a range of rents for shared accommodation (for example, shared houses, flats and bedsits) instead of the current restrictive one room non-self-contained accommodation definition. "By doing this the rent that Housing Benefit would pay might", in the words of the Green Paper, "better reflect the type of shared accommodation which is available for rent in the private sector" and "help young people obtain and maintain accommodation" (DETR, 2000a, para 11.48).

The SRR has been identified in a number of research reports as a significant contributory factor to youth homelessness (see, for example,

Griffiths, 1997; Niner, 1997; Allison, 1998) and is undoubtedly a major source of concern. Of the 495 responses received to the Green Paper's chapter on 'Improving Housing Benefit' (within which the SRR is discussed), almost three quarters (73%) commented on the SRR, with 62% of these respondents calling for its abolition (although this was not an option proposed). Abolitionists included not just homelessness charities and other interest groups but arguably more 'objective' commentators such as local authorities and registered social landlords.

While there was support for reform, this was generally regarded as second best to outright abolition. For example, while welcoming the proposal to extend the SRR as a 'step in the right direction', Victor Adebowale, Chief Executive of Centrepoint, argued that it would be much more constructive to end discrimination against young people by scrapping the restriction altogether (Centrepoint, 2000). Other charities were more forceful in their criticism and less prepared to countenance reform as an acceptable alternative. Shelter, for example, in its final response to the Housing Green Paper, stated unequivocally: "The single room rent should be abolished. Proposals to redefine it will not tackle the hardship and misery currently caused by the restriction" (Shelter, 2000c, p 12).

The government, however, remains (after 'careful consideration') committed merely to broadening the definition arguing, in its *Housing policy statement*, that "it would be wrong for the benefit system to provide unemployed young adults with better housing than their working peers could afford" (DETR, 2000c, para 10.37). This has echoes of the deserving/ undeserving poor distinction apparent in earlier legislation and introduces a moralistic element which is arguably out of place in determining policy.

Affordable housing

As the government itself has recognised, alongside changes to the homelessness legislation, combating homelessness also involves looking at the wider issues, such as the supply and affordability of accommodation. Some progress has been made since 1997. The government started well, announcing the release of £5 billion of capital receipts to fund the renovation of some 250,000 council dwellings. Subsequent years have seen further investment in housing such that by 2001/2, spending on housing is set to be more than double the level Labour inherited on coming to power in 1997 (DETR, 2000f). Yet access to social housing is likely to remain in short supply. The Right-to-Buy scheme (accepted by Labour since the mid-1980s) remains in place and although changes reducing the current maximum discount may result in a reduction in the number of sales, and increases in the Housing Corporation's Approved Development Programme should increase the amount of social housing being built, the New Labour government has some way to go if it is to reverse 18 years of decline and under-investment which have seen the social housing sector shrink from some 5.5 million dwellings (31% of stock) in December 1979, to 4.2 million (20% of stock) in March 2001 (DETR, 2002).

In rural areas, the stock of social housing is estimated to have fallen from some 711,000 properties in 1990 to 684,000 in 1999. This represents a fall of 3.8% which, although lower than the 4.7% fall recorded for England as a whole, adds to the pressure on an already inadequate supply of affordable accommodation (Cabinet Office, 2000, p 62). This is undoubtedly a matter of paramount importance to people living in rural areas. Indeed, over a quarter (27%) of the individuals and organisations responding to Chapter Eight of the Housing Green Paper, 'Providing new affordable housing', specifically drew attention to the importance of recognising and acting on the needs of rural communities. Yet, while the Housing Green Paper emphasises that local housing strategies must recognise the needs of rural communities (para 8.32), it has little to say about rural housing and nothing at all to say about rural homelessness. Most chapters do not mention the word 'rural' or only refer to it in terms of 'rural and urban areas' and in the context of bland statements – for example, "Our vision for social housing in the 21st Century is of homes that support balanced, thriving communities and a high quality of life for all in urban and rural areas" (para 1.10) – rather than in relation to specific initiatives.

Although the Green Paper does devote a specific section to 'Rural housing' (paras 8.32-8.37), it merits only 386 words (in a chapter of more than 3,200). Furthermore, this section simply outlines current policies and programmes – referring for example, to the Housing Corporation's Rural Programme, restrictions on the Right to Acquire, resale restrictions on Right-To-Buy properties, and the rural exceptions policy – rather than introducing any new proposals. Instead, it is left to the Rural White Paper to set out the government's policies for housing in rural areas (para 8.37) and it is to this document we now turn.

Rural social policy

The Rural White Paper (RWP), *Our countryside: The future - A fair deal for rural England*, was finally published on 28 November 2000 (DETR, 2000g)[3]. It had been a long time coming to fruition, making its appearance two

years and a day from Deputy Prime Minister John Prescott's announcement
of the government's plans to draw up a new RWP and 21 months from
publication of *Rural England:A discussion document* (DETR, 1999a), which
sought public and agency views on the needs of rural areas. Despite the
long gestation period and frustration at the delays in its publication[4] the
RWP was, according to the Countryside Agency, 'worth the wait'.

The Countryside Agency announced that "England's countryside and
rural communities stand to gain enormously from new proposals in the
Government's Rural White Paper" (Countryside Agency, 2000a), and it
was welcomed by a wide range of organisations. Moira Constable, Chief
Executive of the Rural Housing Trust, awarded it "about eight out of ten
for ambition and commitment" (Rural Housing Trust, 2000a); Chris
Holmes, Director of Shelter, proclaimed it "a real opportunity ... to achieve
lasting regeneration in rural areas" (Shelter, 2000b); and even the frequently
confrontational Countryside Alliance, heralded it as an "important step
forward in ensuring a future for Britain's countryside and its people"
(Countryside Alliance, 2000).

The RWP represents something of a paradigm shift, moving away from
the traditional focus on agriculture and countryside issues, which has
dominated rural policy for more than 50 years, to consider social needs
in rural areas and economic needs which go beyond those of the
agricultural community.

The issue of housing is dealt with as one of five chapters in a section
entitled 'The living countryside'. Of particular note, is the title of this
chapter. It is not just about housing but about 'An *affordable* home'
(emphasis added). Discussions about housing in rural areas are often
dominated by concerns to protect the countryside from unwanted
development (manifest, most overtly, by the impassioned debate which
greets each new set of household projections, predicting an ever greater
demand for housing). It is therefore refreshing to find that although
issues of development and design are dealt with in the chapter (and
elsewhere in the RWP), the focus remains firmly on ensuring an adequate
provision of affordable housing. This suggests a level of cognisance with
the housing difficulties faced by many young people and other low-
income households living in rural areas that was previously largely absent
from government rural policy[5]. Furthermore, the inclusion of a specific
section on 'Rural homelessness', while limited in scope, represents the
first explicit recognition of the problem in official policy documentation
of this kind.

The chapter begins by setting out the government's vision for the
future of rural housing. This includes the wish to see:"A high proportion

of affordable and decent housing, both for rent and sale, in market towns and villages to support a living, working countryside with inclusive rural communities which help young people to remain in the area where they grew up" (DETR, 2000g, p 45).

Perhaps somewhat surprisingly, and in contrast to other areas of government policy, this vision is backed up by additional resources. Not only will rural areas benefit, alongside urban areas, from a virtual doubling of the Housing Corporation's Approved Development Programme (ADP) (which provides funds for the provision of social housing by registered social landlords), but they will also gain more particularly from a doubling of the size of the Corporation's Rural Development Programme (RDP) which provides social housing in small rural settlements (those with fewer than 3,000 inhabitants).

The increase in funding for the Housing Corporation's ADP had been revealed four months earlier in the government's Spending Review 2000[6] and attention therefore focused on the new announcement of additional funding for the RDP. While this increase in resources received widespread support, there was a general consensus that the initiative did not go far enough. Margaret Clark, Director of the Countryside Agency, for example, while welcoming the commitment to increasing the provision of affordable accommodation, stated that she was "disappointed not to see more" (*Countryside Focus*, 2000, p ii).

There is some justification for Clark's disappointment. In the first place, the rural programme produces relatively few houses a year. Doubling current production will still only result in the building of some 1,600 homes a year. Second, such an increase in production merely restores output to former levels. Figures from the Countryside Agency's *State of the countryside 2000* report, demonstrate the substantial decrease that has befallen rural housing provision from the mid-1990s. Between 1993/94 and 1999/2000, for example, the number of units approved through the Housing Corporation's RDP fell from 1,618 to 800 (Countryside Agency, 2000b, p 29). Doubling production will actually do little more than ensure the continuation of the rate of building which has been achieved since the Housing Corporation began its special housing programme for England's smallest villages in 1989[7].

Furthermore, while the projected increase in production represents a significant rise in the *proportion* of dwellings in small settlements approved by the Corporation from a target of 3.4% of the ADP in 2000/01 to a new target of 6.4%, this, as with the *number* of units built, simply constitutes a return to the levels pertaining prior to the savage cuts of the mid- to late-1990s. Although it should be noted that – given the significant increase in the Housing Corporation's ADP – there is now a bigger cake to share, the proportion of development in rural areas falls well short of the 15% called for by The Rural Group of Labour MPs (2000) in their *Manifesto for rural Britain*.

According to the RWP (Select Committee on Environment, Transport and Regional Affairs, 2000), the government expects further affordable housing in small rural settlements to be provided by local authorities who will be *encouraged* to provide more new affordable housing in areas of high demand through use of the Local Authority Social Housing Grant (financed partly from allocations from central government and partly from authorities' own resources). This, together with 'the judicious use of planning powers' is expected to bring some 1,500 new social homes a year to small rural settlements. As with other measures throughout the RWP, however, the government provides no indication of *how* local authorities will be encouraged to spend the social housing grant in this way. Unless there is a specific requirement on local authorities and a means of enforcing compliance there is no guarantee that the provision of affordable housing by local authorities will reach the desired (or 'expected') levels.

Even assuming, perhaps somewhat optimistically, that the Housing Corporation successfully doubles its provision in smaller rural settlements to 1,600 dwellings a year and local authorities use the Social Housing Grant to provide a further 1,500 properties, the combined total of 3,100 expected to be built annually by 2003/04 – while a welcome improvement on current levels of production – is inadequate to meet demand and "falls well short of the Countryside Agency's analysis which shows that the increasing rural population requires 5000 new affordable homes a year" (*Countryside Focus*, 2000, p ii).

The size of the shortfall is even greater from the perspective of the Rural Housing Trust who argue that, "providing even as many as 3,000 new affordable homes by 2004 is barely significant when compared to a current estimated need of around 50,000 homes in small settlements for people on modest incomes" (Rural Housing Trust, 2000a). On the basis of the Trust's figures, even at the increased rate of provision envisaged, it will take some 17 years to meet existing need, let alone respond to any further need that arises in the meantime.

However, while recognising the importance of providing new affordable homes in small rural settlements, the government envisages that most new affordable housing will be provided in market towns which account for roughly half the rural population (DETR, 2000g, p 48). Directing development in this way fits in with the government's wider strategy, which sees market towns as the lynchpin in the regeneration of rural areas. To this end, the RWP announces £37m of funds over three years to support the rejuvenation of England's market towns "as service centres and hubs for the surrounding hinterland" (DETR, 2000g, p 73).

While it is obviously important to ensure that affordable housing continues to be provided in smaller rural settlements, focusing development in market towns in this way may have a particularly positive contribution to make in terms of both tackling and preventing rural homelessness. As has been highlighted in earlier chapters, rural homelessness is often not just about a lack of housing but is intricately bound up with other difficulties such as an absence of support services, inadequate transport networks and limited employment opportunities. By building housing where such services and opportunities are more readily accessible, it should be possible to provide a more holistic and sustainable response to the problem of rural homelessness.

The RWP notes that some 6,300 affordable homes – 3,800 Housing Corporation and 2,500 local authority dwellings – were approved in rural districts in 1999/2000. This figure is expected to rise in light of the increased resources flowing to both the Housing Corporation and local authorities[8]. Again, however, there are no mechanisms for ensuring that levels of affordable housing provision in rural areas are sustained, let alone increased.

Even if the government's expectation that its measures will deliver around 9,000 affordable homes annually in rural districts by 2003/04 is achieved, this projected level of new-build would seem to fall short of what is required, particularly in light of the existing backlog of need. As the Select Committee on Environment, Transport and Regional Affairs (2000) pointed out in its Seventh Report, while there was an estimated need to provide 80,000 additional affordable homes in rural areas between 1990 and 1995, fewer than 18,000 such properties have been built since 1990. Indeed, there has been a net loss of affordable property in rural areas over this period. Government figures show that between 1990 and 1999 the number of social housing units in rural areas fell by 3,000 in deep rural areas and 24,000 in mixed rural areas (Cabinet Office, 2000, p 62). Furthermore, an ever-increasing rural population suggests a greater rather than lesser demand for housing in rural areas in future years[9].

At present, it is difficult to provide any accurate assessment of the extent of housing need in rural areas. National estimates vary, depending on whether current or future needs are being assessed. For example, the Rural Housing Trust (2000b) estimates that between 50,000 and 80,000 affordable homes are needed throughout rural England, while the

Countryside Agency estimates that more than 10,000 affordable homes a year are required to meet the needs of low-income households in rural areas. At a local level, the government is keen to encourage a better identification of rural housing needs. To this end, the RWP notes that all authorities with rural areas are being asked to make a specific assessment of the rural housing needs in their district. The resulting figures could be used to produce a more informed and reliable estimate of rural housing needs for the country as a whole and provide a yardstick against which to evaluate the adequacy of proposed levels of provision.

Alongside increasing the provision of new affordable housing, there are somewhat half-hearted attempts to prevent further depletion of the existing stock in rural areas through restrictions on the resale of Right-to-Buy homes. Present policy allows local authorities in a national park, an area of outstanding natural beauty, or any one of the 24 areas designated by the Secretary of State as a rural for resale restriction area since 1980, to impose one of two restrictions (DETR, 2000g, pp 51-2). Either they can require a former tenant, reselling within 10 years, to offer them the first chance to buy back the property (thereby bringing it back into their stock of affordable homes for rent), or they can require the tenant to resell only to someone who has lived or worked locally for at least three years – a requirement which binds all subsequent buyers of the property.

Applications to become a rural for resale restriction area can be made to the DETR. However, while the RWP notes that the government "will remind authorities in rural areas where there is a significant demand for affordable housing to consider the possibility of applying for designation" (DETR, 2000g, p 52), the government makes no commitment to increasing the number of areas designated or imposing its own zones.

The RWP also sets out a number of measures for 'Making housing available for local people'. This includes (DETR, 2000g, p 52):

• promoting more flexible lettings policies by local authorities, so as to take more account of specific rural needs in their area;
• funding the Empty Homes Agency to work with local authorities to bring more empty rural property back into use;
• encouraging additional conversion of properties for residential use by cutting the VAT rate to 5% for residential conversions.

However, the measure which received particular attention and featured prominently in the media's coverage of the RWP, was the government's proposal (subject to consultation) to give councils the power to levy full Council Tax on second homes (as opposed to the statutory 50% discount which exists at present). The issue of second and holiday homes has become significant in recent years. Although few commentators would identify second homes as the primary cause of rural homelessness, the ownership of such homes undoubtedly impacts negatively on the availability of housing for local rural residents.

According to the Countryside Agency, in 1991 some 58% (46,932) of England's second homes were located in rural districts (Countryside Agency, 2000b, p 28). This represents less than 1% of homes in rural areas across the country, but there is substantial variation between areas, with much higher than average proportions of second homes in popular holiday areas such as Cornwall and the Lake District and in particular settlements within these areas. In the village of Troutbeck, in Lakeland, for example, a recent survey found that 40 of the 105 houses in the village were either second homes or holiday lets. Moreover, of the three properties on the market in November 2000, the cheapest was priced at £340,000 – this in an area where annual incomes are often around £15,000 (P. Hetherington, 2000). In such circumstances, it is unsurprising that local people in Cumbria are moving out to larger towns in search of somewhere to live, particularly in light of the limited availability of social housing.

In this context, the proposal to allow local authorities to charge the full Council Tax on second homes and use the revenues to alleviate local housing shortage, would seem particularly progressive on two levels. In the first place, the cost of having to pay the full rate of Council Tax may act as a deterrent to those buying second/holiday homes, leaving that property available for local people and easing the upward pressure on house prices in rural areas stimulated or exacerbated by the demand for second homes[10]. Secondly, where property continues to be sold as second homes charging the full rate of Council Tax will provide additional funds for the provision of replacement (affordable) housing.

According to the Rural Housing Trust, subsidising second home owners through the 50% Council Tax discount costs £150m annually. The Trust estimates that collecting the full tax – worth an annual £700 to its well-off beneficiaries – would subsidise an extra 5,700 affordable homes every year (Rural Housing Trust, 2000b). There was consequently disappointment that not only would implementation be delayed by what some critics (such as the Countryside Alliance) considered an unnecessary period of consultation, but that it would be left to local authorities to decide whether or not to implement the full charge. The government argued against a blanket imposition of the full tax on the grounds that "pressure on housing varies from one area to another and some authorities might wish to encourage second home owners who can bring a useful input to the local economy" (DETR, 2000g, p 52). However, this discretionary approach was denounced by a number of rural groups. The Rural Housing Trust (2000a) for example, described the proposal as 'a fudge', complaining that local authorities would not increase the charge unless directed to do so. Similarly, Ewen Cameron, Chairman of the Countryside Agency, called for the government to force councils to charge the full tax on second homes, rather than leaving it up to an individual authority's discretion.

Rural homelessness

Of course, as we have highlighted in this and earlier chapters, homelessness is often about much more than the provision of housing. While the initiatives relating to affordable housing detailed in the RWP have an important contribution to make in supplying the housing which provides the necessary basis for tackling homelessness, there is a danger that rural homelessness becomes subsumed within a wider discussion of rural housing which, while relevant, does not necessarily get to the heart of the problem. It is therefore encouraging to find that not only is the problem of rural homelessness mentioned in the RWP, but it is the subject of a dedicated section. This amounts to just one page of a 176-page document (and fewer than 500 words out of a chapter of more than 5,000) but it reflects a welcome recognition of the problem at a national level and an important entry into policy discourse.

Yet discussion of the problem is somewhat limited. The section simply highlights levels of homelessness in rural areas through a graph of statutory homeless acceptances, and outlines the work of two projects helping to tackle the problem rather than proposing any new initiatives or measures. Indeed, the only action proposed is the production of "good practice guidance for councils which will address the particular difficulty in ensuring access to housing advice and homelessness services in rural areas" (DETR, 2000g, p 53).

In addition, the RWP seems to adopt a rather narrow, stereotypical understanding which equates homelessness with rooflessness. Money for tackling homelessness in rural areas is seen as coming from existing schemes, namely the Homelessness Action Programme and the Special Innovation Fund, both of which are aimed at addressing rough sleeping. The RWP also suggests that the government sees rural homelessness as primarily, if not solely, a problem experienced by young single people. This reading is supported by the two examples chosen to illustrate agency responses: The Benjamin Foundation – a project providing specialist advice, counselling and accommodation for young homeless people in North Norfolk and Newark, and Sherwood Foyer – a project tackling homelessness and unemployment among young people.

In some respects, the section on rural homelessness is more notable for what is left out, than for what is included. There is, for example, nothing about the problems that homeless households face gaining access to housing in rural areas, nothing about the shortage of emergency 'direct access' accommodation and nothing about the lack of employment opportunities which trap households in the no job–no home cycle. However, to some extent this reflects the multi-dimensional nature of homelessness and a number of these (and related) issues are addressed elsewhere in the RWP – most obviously in the sections on affordable housing (discussed earlier) but also in those on transport, employment and access to services.

Furthermore, while we might have hoped for a fuller and franker discussion, that rural homelessness is deemed significant enough to merit a distinct section within the RWP reflects a valuable growing awareness of the problem and is an important further step towards the development of measures aimed at its prevention and resolution.

Wider issues

In light of the multi-dimensional nature of homelessness just referred to, there are a number of measures throughout the RWP which might impact positively on, and make a valuable contribution towards, preventing and tackling homelessness in rural areas. For example, the RWP announces an additional £240m over three years to support rural transport schemes including £132m to fund expansion of the Rural Bus Subsidy Grant, which allows local authorities to subsidise rural bus services that would otherwise be uneconomic to run. Such improvements in public transport could provide links to employment opportunities and thereby the level of income necessary to attain and maintain a home in rural areas. Improved transport could also facilitate access to housing advice and other services for homeless households and those at risk of becoming homeless.

Related to this, homeless households may also benefit from the government's emphasis on providing "access to high quality public services – services often delivered in new ways, and through new outlets" (DETR, 2000h). The RWP heralds the introduction of a Rural Services Standard setting out minimum standards and targets covering access to and the delivery of a range of public services in rural areas including health, education, employment and access to benefits.

Rural homelessness and related issues may also be more specifically addressed in the work of the Countryside Agency which, under the RWP, receives £4.5m over three years to fund additional community development work and help communities establish new projects to tackle social exclusion.

At the same time, initiatives within the RWP to ensure that the government takes account of the specific needs and circumstances of rural areas when developing and implementing policy (so-called 'rural proofing'), should lend a greater visibility to the problems (such as homelessness) experienced by people living in rural areas and help to prevent these from being overlooked in national and regional policy debate[11].

Rough sleeping

A chapter on the policy context surrounding rural homelessness would not be complete without some discussion of the government's efforts to tackle rough sleeping, although it is debatable how far this policy has brought benefits for homeless households and individuals in rural areas.

Rough sleeping first became a focus of significant government attention in 1990 when, in response to a growing population of visibly homeless people sleeping on the streets of London, the then Conservative government launched the Rough Sleepers Initiative (RSI). This initiative sought to end the need for anyone to sleep rough, bringing together key agencies in the voluntary sector, local authorities and government departments to provide accommodation, outreach, resettlement and other support services for people sleeping rough. Originally covering central London, in 1996 the RSI was extended to cover Bristol and subsequently expanded to a number of other parts of the country. Yet when Labour took over the government some seven years and £200m later, there were still an estimated 2,000 people sleeping rough in England on any given night and some 10,000 over the course of a year.

As a potent and highly visible example of the social exclusion it has vowed to tackle, the Labour government has made reducing the number of people sleeping on the streets a key priority. Rough sleeping was identified as one of the first topics to receive the attentions of the Social Exclusion Unit that was established in December 1997 to examine a number of specified issues which potentially cut across the remit and responsibility of a number of government departments. In July 1998, the Unit published its report into rough sleeping (SEU, 1998). Having first examined the causes behind the problem, the report set the target of a two thirds reduction in the number of people sleeping rough by 2002, and outlined a range of measures for achieving this goal. These included: a more integrated approach towards tackling rough sleeping at a national level, improved coordination of service delivery and moves towards preventing people ending up on the streets in the first place, with particular attention to the needs of those leaving care, prison or the armed forces (whom the report had shown to be disproportionately represented among the street homeless population).

One of the outcomes of the report was the creation, the following April, of the Rough Sleepers Unit (RSU). Originally established to tackle rough sleeping in London, in September 1999 its remit was extended to cover the whole of England. Two months later the Unit unveiled *Coming in from the cold: The government's strategy on rough sleeping* (RSU, 1999a). Building on the analysis and findings of the SEU report (and the progress made in the intervening 18 months) the strategy seeks to take forward many of the recommendations contained therein. Vaunted as "radical new plans to ensure that no-one is forced to sleep rough on the streets in the 21st Century" (RSU, 1999b), the strategy was widely welcomed. As with the earlier SEU report (1998), there was much to commend including: an increase in hostel beds, money to fund specialist workers to help rough sleepers with alcohol, drugs and mental health problems, support to rough sleepers in sustaining tenancies, greater support for people leaving the care system, prison and the armed services, and measures to prevent people becoming homeless.

Undoubtedly, the government's policy has had a considerable degree of success. Between June 1998 and June 2000, the number of rough sleepers fell by 36% – more than halfway towards the final target of a reduction of two thirds by 2002 (SEU, 2001). The strategy has also had wider benefits, helping rough sleepers to access not only accommodation but also drug and alcohol services, education resources and employment opportunities. Yet from the outset central government's response to rough sleeping has been essentially an urban programme and would seem to have provided little benefit to rural areas. For example, the extension of the Conservative's Rough Sleepers Initiative beyond London in 1996 saw money allocated initially to Bristol (March 1996) and subsequently (in October 1996) to Brighton, Bath, Bournemouth, Cambridge, Exeter, Leicester, Manchester and Nottingham.

This inattention to rough sleeping in non-urban areas has survived the change of government[12]. Not only does the Labour government's response to rough sleeping continue to focus on the larger urban areas, but it is overwhelmingly London-centric. Indeed, in many ways *Coming in from the cold* (RSU, 1999a) seems to represent a strategy for tackling rough sleeping in (central) London rather than across the country as a whole. For example, the Contact Assessment Teams, Tenancy Sustainment Teams, basic shelters, night centre and day centre for people with alcohol problems outlined in the strategy are all located in London.

References to rough sleeping in other locations are typically bland and non-committal such as, "we will review resettlement services in areas outside London" (RSU, 1999a). Even where London is not explicitly mentioned, comments and findings tend to pertain to the particular situation in the capital – for example, there is little or no evidence to suggest that the apparent proliferation of services such as soup runs – so castigated by Louise Casey, Director of the Rough Sleepers Unit, for allegedly helping to sustain street homelessness – occurs anywhere outside of (central) London.

Clearly the government's vision extends beyond London. The Homelessness Action Programme (announced in 1999) provides £34m over a three-year period for tackling rough sleeping in areas outside of London. However, not only does this level of resources compare somewhat unfavourably with the £145m allocated to the capital (which accounts for just a third of rough sleepers nationwide), but these funds are predominantly channelled towards those areas with the highest numbers of people sleeping rough (as identified in a single night street count). These are inevitably urban areas. In June 1998, there were seven areas with street counts of over 30 rough sleepers, all of which were cities (Birmingham, Brighton, Bournemouth, Bristol, Oxford, Manchester and Cambridge).

The government's emphasis on tackling street homelessness in London and those predominantly urban areas outside of the capital, identified as having the largest numbers of people sleeping rough, while understandable, inevitably results in an inattention to tackling rough sleeping in rural areas where the numbers are lower (although possibly representative of a higher *proportion* of the population than in some urban areas receiving assistance) and the incidence of rough sleeping is more dispersed.

In contrast to measures aimed at tackling rough sleeping, however, preventative measures – which have arisen at least partly in response to the government's emphasis on reducing rough sleeping – hold out the possibility of benefiting people living in rural and urban areas alike. There have been a number of progressive developments towards preventing rough sleeping including:

- Extension of priority need to homeless 16- and 17-year-olds, care leavers aged 18-21 and applicants who are vulnerable as a result of an institutionalised background or as a result of fleeing domestic violence or harassment (see p 97).
- The 2000 Children (Leaving Care) Act, which extends local authorities' responsibilities to include the provision of accommodation and support to 16- and 17-year-olds who have been in care for 13 weeks or more in the two years before their 16th birthday.
- Support for prisoners leaving prison. The government has sought to implement a number of the recommendations contained within the RSU (2000) report *Blocking the fast track from prison to rough sleeping*. Pilot schemes operating in seven prisons are providing pre-release housing advice to short-term offenders vulnerable to rough sleeping. In addition, following a successful scheme piloted by the RSU in London to distribute housing and benefits advice leaflets to prisoners at both arrival and release stage, these will now be produced nationally by the Prison Service.
- Support for servicemen and women leaving the armed forces. The RSU has funded English Churches Housing Group to run the SPACES (Single Persons' Accommodation for the Ex-Services) project based in Catterick. Set up in September 2000, this pilot project – run in partnership with the Ministry of Defence – aims to help armed forces personnel find a home and provide them with ongoing support while they make the transition back to civilian life. Following the success of the project, the RSU and Ministry of Defence plan to develop such services nationally by 2002.

Conclusion

As noted in Chapter One, there is a reluctance to acknowledge the existence of rural homelessness. At a national level, rural agencies tend to neglect the issue of homelessness and, more particularly, homelessness agencies tend to neglect the issue of rurality. This is highlighted by Table 4.2 which records agency responses to the Housing Green Paper – *Quality and choice: A decent home for all* (DETR, 2000a) – and its rural equivalent – *Rural England: A discussion document* (DETR, 1999a). As the table shows, the homelessness agencies responded predominantly to the former and the rural agencies to the latter with little crossover between the two. In such circumstances rural homelessness risks falling through the gap.

Similarly, all of the four main national homelessness charities

Table 4.2: Agency responses to central government consultations on housing and rural policy changes

	Housing Green Paper	Rural England: A discussion document
Rural agencies		
Action with Communities in Rural England	✓	✓
Countryside Agency	✓	✓
Countryside Alliance	X	✓
Council for the Protection of Rural England	X	✓
Homelessness agencies:		
Centrepoint	✓	X
Crisis	✓	X
National Homeless Alliance	✓	X
Shelter	✓	X

(Centrepoint, Crisis, National Homeless Alliance, Shelter) considered the Housing Green Paper of sufficient importance to merit a press release. In contrast, none of these charities responded to what could be seen as the rural equivalent and only Shelter commented on the publication of the RWP in the form of a press release. For rural agencies the reverse applied, with the Countryside Agency, Countryside Alliance and the Council for the Protection of Rural England (CPRE)[13] each issuing a press release on publication of the RWP but making no such comment on the Housing Green Paper.

That said, there are some signs that rural homelessness is beginning to enter official/policy discourse. The Countryside Agency's *The state of the countryside 2000* (Countryside Agency, 2000b) for example, which provides a compendium of information about rural areas and the people who live in them, includes a section on rural homelessness as, more importantly, does the RWP.

Yet while there is some evidence to suggest that rural agencies are beginning to recognise the problem of homelessness in rural areas, homelessness agencies have yet to develop a comparable awareness in respect of rurality. The notion of rural proofing, which is frequently talked about in terms of government policy, needs to be taken on board by these agencies, which continue largely to overlook the fact that homelessness also has a rural dimension. For example, the National Homeless Alliance is a membership organisation for those providing services to homeless people and claims to be 'the voice of 1,000 front line agencies'. Presumably, few of these are from rural areas. A search of what is otherwise a very comprehensive, up-to-date and informative website, records no hits either for the word 'rural' or 'countryside'.

That is not to say that the national homeless charities completely neglect the problem of rural homelessness. Centrepoint in particular has shown an active commitment to rural areas, often working with the Countryside Agency to tackle the problems associated with youth homelessness in these areas. Crisis meanwhile commissioned one of the few in-depth research projects on rural homelessness – later published as part of its 'Homeless Voices' series (Evans, 1999). However, for the most part, rural homelessness remains a peripheral concern.

The national homeless charities have an important role to play as respected organisations in raising awareness and campaigning for policy change. It is therefore crucial that rural homelessness becomes part of their mainstream agenda. Unless, or until this happens, it is unlikely that the government will give more than cursory attention to the problem. In such circumstances, we cannot realistically expect any significant advances in policy to be forthcoming and rural homelessness looks set to remain largely unacknowledged and unaddressed.

Notes

[1] Latest figures available at the time of writing reveal that 57% of households accepted as priority homeless during the final quarter of 2000 contained dependent children, and a further 10% included a pregnant woman (DETR, 2001b).

[2] At the time of writing (April 2001) this order has yet to be issued.

[3] The White Paper applies to England but some of the legislation and measures referred to are UK-wide or pertain to England and Wales.

[4] The original intention was to produce a Rural White Paper by the summer of 1999 (DETR, 1998).

[5] The 1995 Rural White Paper, *Rural England: A nation committed to a living countryside*, produced under the former Conservative administration (DoE, 1995) for example, dedicated just one page specifically to affordable housing.

[6] Outlined in July 2000, the Spending Review announced an extra £872m over three years for the Housing Corporation's ADP, almost doubling the Programme from planned expenditure of £691million in 2001/02 to £1,236million by 2003/04 (DETR, 2000i).

[7] Over the 11 years from 1989/90 to 1999/2000 the Corporation funded the development of 16,670 homes in the smallest settlements in rural England (Housing Corporation, 2000). This amounts to some 1,515 dwellings a year.

[8] According to the RWP, the resources allocated to local authorities for housing investment in 2000/01 are around twice the amount allocated for 1997/98 and are set to rise by a further 40% over the next three years (DETR, 2000g, p 48).

[9] Between 1984 and 1998, the population of districts with a predominantly rural character increased at almost twice the national rate (10.3% as opposed to 5.3%) (Countryside Agency, 2000b, p 19). This increase is set to continue, with the number of households in England's rural districts projected to increase by more than 1 million (that is, 19%) from 1996 to 2016 (Countryside Agency, 2000b, p 27).

[10] It is debatable whether someone who has sufficient income to buy a second property is likely to be deterred by what will, after all, represent a minimal additional expenditure in relation to the overall costs of purchase.

[11] These initiatives include: an annual report by the Countryside Agency on the rural aspects of government policies; a rural 'check-list' for government departments to ensure that they take account of the rural dimension in developing policy; and the establishment of National and Regional Rural Sounding Boards. Although a welcome recognition of the need for the government to 'think rural', these measures fall far short of calls for the creation of a Department for Rural Affairs and the appointment of a Minister for the Countryside.

[12] For example, in November 1997, the government announced £1m pump-priming funding to support six new rough sleeper strategies in Birmingham, Blackpool, Canterbury, Chester, Southampton and Tower Hamlets. In February 1998, a further tranche of money was allocated to support rough sleeping strategies in an additional 12 areas outside London namely: Bury, Gloucester, Great Yarmouth, Guildford, Northampton, Norwich, Plymouth, Portsmouth, Reading, Sheffield, Slough and Stoke-on-Trent.

[13] ACRE (Action with Communities in Rural England) does not currently retain a searchable archive of press releases.

FIVE

The spaces of rural homelessness

The previous two chapters have provided wide-ranging discussions of the cultural and policy contexts of rural homelessness. In this chapter we want to explore the complex geographies of homelessness in rural England. We want to do this in two main ways. First, we provide key findings on the scale and nature of homelessness in England by drawing on unpublished government homelessness statistics and a national survey of all local authorities in England. In this section of the chapter we not only compare the extent and profile of homelessness in rural and urban areas, but also consider the spatial unevenness of homelessness within rural areas. In the second main section of the chapter we explore the local spaces of rural homelessness in two districts located in the study county of Gloucestershire. Here we consider the ways in which local housing structures and cultures of rurality impact on the experiences of homelessness in these two rural districts.

The scale, profile and spatial unevenness of homelessness in rural England

An analysis of unpublished official homelessness statistics reveals that 15,950 households were accepted as priority homeless by local authorities in rural England in 1996[1]. This level of rural homelessness represents 14.4% of the total for England and is equivalent to 70% of the homelessness figure for London (Table 5.1). In relative terms, though, standardised levels of homelessness in rural England are lower than in London and urban authority areas. In 1996, homelessness accounted for only 3.5 per 1,000 households in rural areas, compared with standardised rates of 7.6 and 5.7 per 1,000 households in London and urban areas respectively. In fact, 19 of the 20 local authority areas recording the highest levels of standardised homelessness in England were located in either London (9) or urban areas (10), with only the mixed rural area of Redcar and Cleveland featuring in this list (Table 5.2). Nevertheless, 14 rural authority areas (equivalent to 17.5% of all rural areas) did record levels of standardised homelessness above the national mean (Table 5.2). The geographical distribution of homelessness in rural areas is provided in Figure 5.1. This

Table 5.1: Changing levels of homeless households in England, by area (1992-96)

	1992 Number of local authorities	1992 total	1992 % of national total	1996 total	1996 % of national total	1992-96 total change	1992-96 % change	1996 homelessness per thousand households
England	365	135,045	100.0	110,999	100.0	-24,046	-17.8	5.5
London	33	31,508	23.3	22,907	20.6	-8,601	-27.3	7.6
Urban	207	87,558	64.8	72,142	65.0	-15,416	-17.6	5.7
All rural	125	15,979	11.8	15,950	14.4	-29	-0.2	3.5
Mixed rural	96	13,402	9.9	13,061	11.8	-341	-2.5	3.5
Deep rural	29	2,577	1.9	2,889	2.6	+312	+12.1	3.7

Source: authors' analysis of unpublished DETR, PIE returns, 1992, 1996

Table 5.2: Homelessness per thousand households – top ranked authorities in England and rural England (1996)

Top 20 authorities	Area type	Homelessness per 1,000 households	Rank of all authorities	Rural authorities recording levels of homelessness above the English average	Area type	Region	Homelessness per 1,000 households	Rank of all authorities
Walsall	urban	27.3	1	Redcar and Cleveland	mixed	NE	11.5	12
Birmingham	urban	19.5	2	Tunbridge Wells	mixed	E	8.0	42
Manchester	urban	16.3	3	Isles of Scilly	deep	SW	7.1	60
Camden	London	15.9	4	Taunton Deane	mixed	SW	6.9	63
Westminster	London	13.4	5	Malvern Hills	deep	WM	6.8	65
Brent	London	13.2	6	Newark and Sherwood	mixed	EM	6.6	71
Hounslow	London	13.1	7	Salisbury	mixed	SW	6.6	72
Islington	London	13.1	8	East Lindsey	mixed	EM	6.5	74
Broxbourne	urban	12.7	9	South Somerset	mixed	SW	6.3	78
Redditch	urban	12.6	10	South Hams	deep	SW	6.2	82
Greenwich	London	12.3	11	Crewe and Nantwich	mixed	NW	6.0	87
Redcar and Cleveland	rural	11.5	12	South Derbyshire	mixed	EM	5.9	95
Ealing	London	11.3	13	Daventry	mixed	EM	5.7	99
Derby	urban	10.2	14	Carrick	mixed	SW	5.7	100
Trafford	urban	10.1	15					
Hackney	London	9.9	16					
Mansfield	urban	9.9	17	England average			5.5	
Bristol	London	9.9	18					
Leicester	urban	9.8	19					
Croydon	London	9.7	20					

Note: NE, North-East; E, East; SW, South-West; EM, East Midlands; WM, West Midlands
Source: authors' analysis of unpublished DETR, P1E returns, 1996

map highlights important regional variations in levels of homelessness in rural England, with highest homelessness rates evident in parts of the South-West, East Anglia and the East Midlands, and lowest levels present in northern regions. However, alongside these regional differences in homelessness, it should be stressed that considerable localised variations are evident. For example, both the North-East and South-West regions are characterised by local authority areas with lowest levels of homelessness (less than 2 per 1,000 households) sitting alongside areas with highest homelessness rates (of more than 5 per 1,000).

While the number of homeless households in rural areas may be small in both absolute and relative terms, rural homelessness levels have continued to rise in relation to urban and London authority areas over the decade. Table 5.1 demonstrates both a *proportional increase* in rural homelessness across the 1990s – with homelessness in rural areas increasing from 11.8 to 14.4% of the national total between 1992 and 1996 – and an *absolute rise* of 12.1% over this period in 'deep' rural areas compared with losses of 27.3% in London and 17.6% in urban authority areas. Indeed, rural local authorities, and particularly those in deep rural areas, feature prominently among those authorities recording highest increases in their homelessness totals over the 1990s. For example, 28.7% of all rural local authorities, and 41.4% of those categorised as 'deep' rural authorities, witnessed homelessness rises of at least 25% between 1992 and 1996, compared with only 10 and 18.4% of London and urban authorities respectively (Table 5.3)[2]. The geographies of recent homelessness change in England

Table 5.3: Changing levels of homelessness, by area (1992-96)

	Number of local authorities	Local authorities recording an increase of more than 25%		Local authorities recording an increase/ decrease of up to 25%		Local authorities recording a decrease of more than 25%	
		no	%	no	%	no	%
England	354*	76	21.4	183	51.7	95	26.8
London	30	3	10.0	18	60.0	9	30.0
Urban	202	38	18.4	106	52.5	58	28.7
All rural	122	35	28.7	59	48.4	28	23.0
Mixed rural	93	23	24.7	49	52.7	21	22.6
Deep rural	29	12	41.4	10	34.5	7	24.1

* information not available for 9 local authorities
Source: authors' analysis of unpublished DETR, PIE returns, 1992, 1996

Figure 5.1: Homelessness per thousand households in rural England, by local authority area (1996)

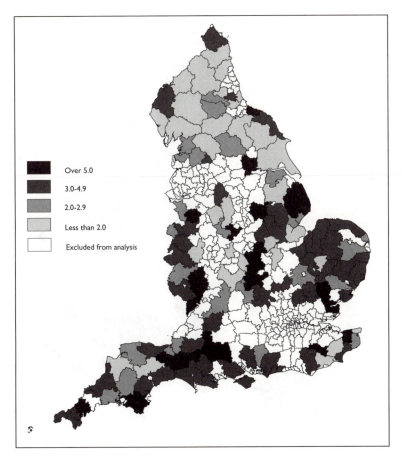

Over 5.0

3.0-4.9

2.0-2.9

Less than 2.0

Excluded from analysis

Figure 5.2: Changing levels of homelessness in England, by local authority area (1992-96)

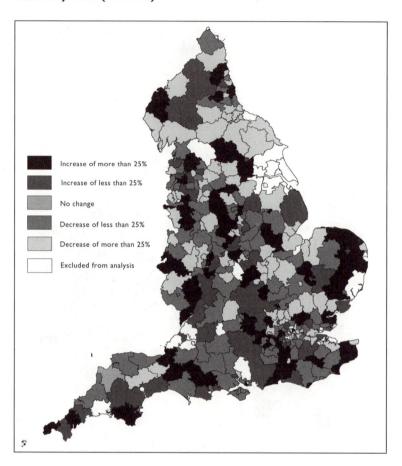

are highlighted in Figure 5.2. The picture that emerges is one in which increases in rural homelessness have been most pronounced in southern parts, particular in the South-East and Eastern regions. However, as was the case with the geographical distribution of homelessness levels in 1996, there exist considerable local variations in rates of change, with, for example, the South-West containing rural local authority areas falling in to each of the five categories of change over the 1990s. Indeed, care should be exercised when discussing general increases in rates of rural homelessness, given that Table 5.3 illustrates that 23.0% of rural authority areas also recorded reductions of more than 25% in their homelessness totals over the decade.

The profile of groups accepted as priority homeless by rural local authorities in the late 1990s remains dominated by families, comprising 63.3% of all homeless households in 1996, and considerably above the English average of 55.5% (Table 5.4). All other vulnerable groups, except elderly households, account for lower proportions of homelessness in rural than in London and urban local authority areas, and this is particularly the case among persons considered vulnerable as a result of domestic violence, where the rural level is almost half that recorded for England as a whole. Examining these homeless profiles over the 1990s, the most significant trend, evident in both rural and non-rural areas, has been a reduction in the proportion of families accepted as homeless by local authorities. Other less significant but nevertheless noteworthy changes in the profile of rural homelessness have been above-average rises in the proportion of households in the following categories of vulnerability – mental illness, young persons, domestic violence, and emergency homeless.

The aggregate figures, however, mask considerable localised variations in rural homelessness profiles. In Table 5.5 we present the highest and lowest proportions of different types of homeless groups accepted by rural local authorities in 1996. What emerges from this table is that only one homeless group – families – features in the homeless profile of *all* rural local authorities and, even here, there is a large differential evident between the highest (100% of all acceptances) and lowest (41.5%) scoring authority areas. Other vulnerable groups remain absent from significant minorities of rural local authority areas, including cases of domestic violence – not featuring in 30.4% of areas, compared with only 9.3% in urban areas – and young people who are absent from 36% of rural profiles but only 16.8% of those in urban authority areas.

Table 5.6 shows that almost 90% of the homelessness accepted by rural local authorities in 1996 resulted from one of four factors: a loss of rented or tied housing (33.2%); parents or relatives no longer being able to

Table 5.4: Types of households accepted as homeless by local authorities in England, by area (1996)

% priority need cases	England	London	Urban	All rural	Mixed rural	Deep rural	All rural 1992	England 1992
Households with dependent children	55.5	50.9	55.2	63.3	63.7	61.2	71.6	70.0
Pregnant woman	11.3	14.3	10.3	10.9	11.1	9.9	11.5	13.1
Vulnerable through old age	4.8	5.5	4.0	7.1	7.2	6.9	7.7	4.5
Vulnerable through physical disability	5.4	9.2	4.3	4.5	4.7	3.8	2.8	3.7
Vulnerable through mental illness	7.0	10.6	6.1	5.3	5.3	5.3	2.5	4.0
Vulnerable young people	3.1	1.5	3.8	2.1	2.0	2.4	1.2	3.2
Vulnerable through domestic violence	7.1	3.4	9.2	3.6	3.0	6.4	1.3	4.6
Vulnerable for other reasons	4.8	3.3	6.0	1.9	1.8	2.2	1.0	4.7
Emergency homelessness	1.0	0.5	1.0	1.4	1.3	1.7	0.4	0.9

Source: authors' analysis of unpublished DETR, PIE returns, 1992, 1996

Table 5.5: Highest and lowest acceptance rates among rural local authorities in England (1996)

	Highest % of accepted groups	Lowest % of accepted groups
Households with dependent children	100.0 (1 authority)	41.5 (1 authority)
Pregnant woman	23.5 (1 authority)	0.0 (2 authorities)
Vulnerable through old age	23.2 (1 authority)	0.0 (4.0% of authorities)
Vulnerable through physical disability	11.7 (1 authority)	0.0 (15.2% of authorities)
Vulnerable through mental illness	17.9 (1 authority)	0.0 (11.2% of authorities)
Vulnerable young people	15.0 (1 authority)	0.0 (36.0% of authorities)
Vulnerable through domestic violence	23.9 (1 authority)	0.0 (30.4% of authorities)
Vulnerable for other reasons	18.1 (1 authority)	0.0 (44.0% of authorities)
Emergency homelessness	11.5 (1 authority)	0.0 (31.2% of authorities)

Source: authors' analysis of unpublished DETR, PIE returns, 1996

accommodate a household (23%); a relationship breakdown (21.1%); and mortgage arrears (10.9%). Over the decade, though, it is possible to chart changes in the relative importance of these factors. In particular, we can point to fewer households becoming homeless as a result of mortgage arrears as interest rates have fallen dramatically since the early 1990s; increases in homelessness caused by the termination of private rental tenancies, as recent housing legislation has granted private landlords greater powers; and rises in the incidence of homelessness linked to relationship breakdowns.

While the same four factors accounted for the vast majority of accepted homelessness in London and urban authority areas in 1996, it is nevertheless possible to highlight four important rural–urban variations in factors contributing to homelessness in the late 1990s. First, a lower proportion of rural homelessness resulted from parents or relatives no longer being able to house the applicant than in urban areas. While Bramley (1992) explained this feature with reference to greater levels of 'social stress' in urban areas and variations in local authority homelessness policies, we will outline later how this feature may also be connected to the (often forced) reliance by groups of homeless households in rural areas on informal networks of kith and kin support.

A second rural–urban difference relates to the increased importance of losses of private rented or tied accommodation in rural areas[3], which may be linked to more limited pools of rental housing, seasonal lettings associated with the tourism sector, and reductions in numbers of properties

Table 5.6: Main factors contributing to officially accepted homelessness in England, by area (1996)

Percentage of households accepted as homeless	England	London	Urban	All rural	Mixed rural	Deep rural	All rural 1992	England 1992
Parents/relatives no longer able to accommodate	28.6	38.5	26.7	23.0	23.0	23.0	32.9	40.1
Breakdown of relationship with partner	24.0	15.4	27.4	21.1	21.1	21.1	14.1	16.7
Mortgage arrears	7.1	4.3	7.1	10.9	11.1	10.3	16.4	9.7
Rent arrears	1.9	2.5	1.8	1.8	1.9	1.1	2.0	2.1
Termination of assured shorthold tenancy	11.7	9.7	10.3	21.1	20.9	22.2	13.1	6.2
Other reason for loss of rented/tied accommodation	9.4	9.2	8.9	12.1	12.2	11.9	13.6	8.3
In institution or care	2.8	3.5	2.6	2.3	2.4	2.1	1.2	2.1
Newly formed or split households	0.6	0.5	0.6	0.6	0.5	0.8	0.9	1.8
Former asylum seeker	0.6	2.7	0.1	0.1	0.1	0.1	0.2	1.2
Other, including homeless in emergency, returned from abroad, sleeping rough, in hostel	13.1	12.9	14.5	7.0	6.9	7.4	5.6	9.9
Total	100.0	100.0	100.0	100.0	100.0	100.0	100.0	100.0

Source: authors' analysis of unpublished DETR, P I E returns, 1992, 1996

tied to the agricultural industry. Third, a higher level of mortgage arrears was present in rural authority areas connected to restricted rental opportunities, intense competition for local housing and above-average property prices in many rural housing markets, which mean that lower-income households can often only remain in their local areas through property purchase. Indeed, the highest levels of homelessness resulting from mortgage arrears were concentrated in accessible rural areas of high housing demand located close to major urban settlements in the South-East and East Government Office Regions (17 of the top 20 'mortgage arrears' rural authority areas were 'mixed rural' and 12 were situated in these two regions). Lastly, a lower proportion of households in rural areas fell into the 'other' category, which includes those previously sleeping rough and living in hostels. While Bramley viewed this as confirmation that these types of homelessness were less pronounced in rural areas, we would wish to qualify this by pointing to findings from other parts of our research that highlight both a presence of such groups in rural areas and the ways in which the limited provision of emergency homelessness support and advice facilities in these areas acts to push some homeless households into proximate towns and cities.

In 1996, 46,748 households were recorded as making approaches to rural local authorities about homelessness; a level equivalent to 12.5 per thousand households. Our survey of homelessness officers in England, though, indicates that the recording of approaches by homeless persons is subject to considerable local variation. It is evident in Table 5.7 that different methods of approach were recorded differently by local authorities, with 95% recording an interview with a housing officer as a statistical approach, but less than half formally recording telephone calls and letters to housing departments. Further, we will go on to highlight how low rates of recording of postal and telephone approaches may well be more problematic in a rural context than in London and urban authority areas.

The process of dealing with homelessness applications is also subject to considerable local variations, both *between* rural and urban authority areas, and *within* rural areas. For example, Table 5.8 indicates that intentional homelessness, while accounting for a relatively small number of decisions, was a more prominent feature of decisions made by rural authorities (2.1%) than those operating in urban areas (1.3%). Further variations are evident in the proportions of applicants not deemed homeless (19.5% in deep rural areas but 27.4% in London) and overall levels of acceptances (39.6% in deep rural areas and 32.8% in urban areas). Whether such variations are connected to different local compositions of homelessness,

Table 5.7: Recording procedures employed by local authorities in England, by area (1996)

Type of approach that leads to household being recorded as an enquiry	London	Urban	All rural	Mixed rural	Deep rural	All authorities
Face-to-face contact with housing officer	100.0	90.6	94.8	95.2	92.9	92.6
Telephone call to housing department	25.0	39.9	31.2	31.7	28.6	35.9
Letter to housing department	56.3	50.0	44.2	42.9	50.0	48.5
Referral from other department in authority	75.0	75.4	83.1	84.1	78.6	77.9
Referral from other agency	56.3	62.3	54.5	55.6	50.0	59.3

Source: authors' survey

varying local authority practices, or a combination of the two, it is clear that geography matters when it comes to interpreting statistical indicators of homelessness in England. This point is reinforced when we consider local differences in homelessness within rural areas. Here, we witness large-scale variations in levels of acceptances (ranging from 89.1% of all approaches in one 'mixed' rural authority to only 9.1% in another 'deep' rural area) and rates of intentional homelessness (accounting for no decisions in 15 rural authorities but 18.4% in one 'mixed' rural authority).

In an attempt to examine these spatial variations in the nature of rural homelessness in greater depth, we undertook a postal survey of homelessness officers in all 125 rural local authorities in England. Key findings from this survey correspond to those emerging from recent research in the US, in pointing to the hiddenness of homelessness in rural areas. While 62% of officers in the survey considered that rural homelessness represents a 'significant national problem', 90% felt that it remains hidden within dominant discourses of homelessness and rurality, and around half the officers pointed to the reduced physical visibility of homelessness in rural spaces resulting from dispersed settlement patterns and low numbers of rough sleepers. As one homelessness officer commented, the significance of rural homelessness is downplayed by "the relative scale of the problem, combined with people's impression of 'idyllic' rural areas and rundown deprived inner-city areas".

Our survey also indicates important spatial variations in the nature of rural homelessness and the ways in which complex local circumstances impact on the experiences of homelessness in rural spaces. To a large

Table 5.8: Homelessness approaches to and acceptances by local authorities in England, by area (1996)

	London	Urban	All rural	Mixed rural	Deep rural	England	All rural 1992	England 1992
Total approaches	65,482	220,667	46,748	39,450	7,298	332,497	47,933	344,995
Not dealt with under Section 64	15.1	25.4	27.2	28.0	22.8	23.6	25.5	15.8
Deemed not homeless	27.4	23.1	23.6	24.3	19.5	24.0	24.6	22.2
Deemed homeless but not in priority need	16.5	17.5	12.9	12.4	15.8	16.6	13.9	21.1
Deemed intentionally homeless	1.6	1.3	2.1	2.1	2.3	1.5	2.6	1.8
Asylum seeker	4.4	0.1	0.1	0.1	0.0	0.9	n/a	n/a
Total acceptances								
– number	9,886	55,858	12,713	11,051	1,662	78,467	15,979	135,045
– percentage of all approaches	35.0	32.8	34.1	33.1	39.6	33.4	33.3	39.1

Source: authors' analysis of unpublished DETR, P1E returns, 1996

extent, local housing markets were viewed by officers as underpinning this variation. In accessible rural districts, local homelessness was viewed as resulting from a combination of high levels of competition for private sector housing stock, leading to increased property prices and private rental levels, and increased pressures on a dwindling stock of social rental housing. As two of the responding homelessness officers commented:

> "The problem is that demand for housing throughout tenures in [the district] is extremely high, social housing lists are long ... [leading to] an affordability problem and homelessness as a significant problem." (North-East)

> "The town is at the centre of a comparatively affluent area with a chronic lack of affordable rented accommodation in the private sector." (West Midlands)

In other, predominantly remote, rural districts, such housing pressures were seen as connected with problems resulting from the local tourism sector:

> "Because the area attracts tourists, it is felt that we get more of the families fleeing [domestic] violence [and also] due to the fact landlords can charge [high] holiday rents during the summer season, there are a number of tenancies which expire every six months." (South-West)

However, the survey of rural officers reveals how the nature of rural homelessness is bound up with a wide range of more locally-specific factors, which can include the restrictive nature of the local planning system in spaces of natural beauty, particular types of homelessness resulting from the presence of military bases in the local areas, and the structure of local economies:

> "The district has designated areas of outstanding natural beauty or land that is in the ownership of the National Trust. This curtails the opportunity for new build by housing associations which obviously has a significant impact [on the way the authority can deal with homelessness]." (South-East)

> "[Homelessness is influenced by] Salisbury Plain army camps, with families separating or being discharged." (South-West)

"Homelessness is a problem [due to] poor wages and seasonal land work."
(East)

Given the scale of the spatial unevenness of homelessness in rural England uncovered by the DETR statistics and the importance of local circumstances emerging from this national survey of homelessness officers in rural areas, in the next section of this chapter we want to examine the local spaces of rural homelessness in greater depth.

The local spaces of rural homelessness

Our in-depth localised investigation of rural homelessness is focused on two rural districts – Cotswold and Forest of Dean – within the county of Gloucestershire (see Figure 5.3). In this second section of the chapter we draw on key findings from in-depth interviews conducted in 1998 with local authority homelessness officers and representatives of voluntary agencies dealing with homelessness in these two rural districts. We want to highlight three main findings relating to the local circumstances of rural homelessness that emerge from these interviews: connections between rural homelessness and the structures of local housing markets; the ways in which distinctive cultures of rurality impact on agency responses to local rural homelessness; and the experiences of being homeless in these local rural spaces. Before discussing the first of these findings, though, we want to outline the local context of homelessness in these two rural districts.

The local context of homelessness in Cotswold and Forest of Dean districts

While Cotswold and Forest of Dean districts are situated in the same county, with their borders separated by less than 15 miles, there exist a number of important differences between them. Much of Cotswold district corresponds to dominant ideas of rural idyll (see Cloke and Milbourne, 1992). Its settlement structure is dominated by small 'picture postcard' villages built from distinctive Cotswold stone, and many parts of the district are designated as special landscape or conservation areas within which new dwellings are generally prohibited. The attraction of the Cotswold village environment has led to strong competition for its housing stock, with in-moving affluent groups, particularly from London and the South-east, escalating local property prices. In addition to such housing competition, the tourism sector is particularly strong in the district, with

Figure 5.3: Cotswold and Forest of Dean districts

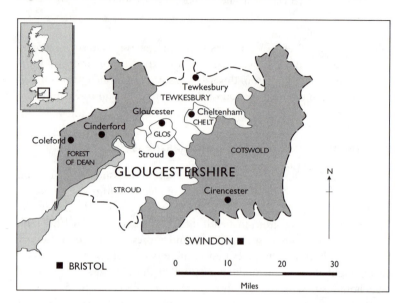

a range of service industries (such as hotels, shops and attractions) geared towards meeting the needs of visitors. Furthermore, the tourism sector impacts directly on local housing markets, with 3% of all housing stock in the district consisting of second/holiday homes. The outcome of such processes has been to transform many villages within Cotswold district into gentrified middle-class spaces, with lower-income groups excluded from village spaces by the high prices of private housing (accounting for 65% of all housing in the district) and low levels of social accommodation[4] in village locations. Furthermore, while Cotswold contains an above-average level of private rental housing – at 17% – a significant proportion of this is tied to particular (agricultural) employment or connected with the local tourism sector, which makes it inaccessible to large numbers of households.

The nature of Forest of Dean district differs somewhat. Bounded by two rivers and containing a high proportion of wooded land, parts of the district are popular with in-moving groups and tourists. In fact, the north-eastern rural areas have been colonised by middle-class commuters working in the major employment centres of Cheltenham and Gloucester. However, other parts of Forest of Dean are characterised by a range of socioeconomic problems, linked mainly to the decline of coal mining in the area. Recognising these problems, much of the south-west of the district has been designated as a 'rural development area' by central government, which makes it eligible for support funds. As such, Forest of Dean has a higher level of households experiencing different forms of economic disadvantage than Cotswold district. There are also strong cultural and political differences between the two districts, with Forest of Dean characterised by working-class cultures and Labour politics, while in Cotswold, middle-class cultures and Conservative/Independent politics dominate. Some of these economic, cultural and political differences are reflected in the structure of local housing markets. For example, in Forest of Dean, average house prices are lower and the proportion of second/holiday homes is one third that in Cotswold. However, the level of owner-occupation in Forest of Dean, at 75%, is much higher than in Cotswold; a reflection of the increased significance of private rental housing in the latter district.

The scale and nature of local homelessness in these two rural districts would also appear to reflect key socioeconomic and housing differences outlined thus far. In relation to the extent of official homelessness, it is a much more significant issue in Forest of Dean. For example, in 1996, the level of homelessness in the district stood at 5.4 per 1,000 households, almost double the rate of 2.9 per 1,000 recorded in Cotswold. Furthermore, over recent years, the level of homelessness in Forest of Dean has increased significantly, rising by 62% during 1992-96, while in Cotswold the homeless total fell by 2%. Similar differences are evident in terms of the causes of local homelessness. While the loss of private rented or tied accommodation represents the main cause of homelessness in each district, this factor accounts for a much higher proportion of homeless cases in Cotswold (58%) than in Forest of Dean (38%), reflecting the increased significance of private rental housing, tied accommodation, and seasonal tourism lettings in the former area. Another important difference exists in relation to levels of mortgage arrears, with Forest of Dean recording a level around four times higher than that of Cotswold (13% compared with 3%). Such a difference connects with the higher level of private ownership and socioeconomic problems in Forest of Dean.

Rural homelessness and local housing structures

It is clear from the analysis of homelessness statistics set out above that key features of rural homelessness are bound up with local structures of housing in rural areas. Here we want to examine these connections in greater detail by considering the characteristics of private and social housing provision in the two study districts. We begin with a consideration of the nature of local private housing provision.

Interviews with local authority homelessness officers and voluntary agencies dealing with homelessness in these rural districts highlight important processes of gentrification of local private housing markets resulting from in-movements of middle-class groups. The scale of this gentrification was viewed as more pronounced in Cotswold district, where many villages are socially constructed in idyllic terms. Interviewees pointed both to retirement in-migration and to an in-movement of groups employed in service-class occupations in the South-East. As one officer commented:

> "The area has become a commuter belt, no doubt about that, for people that ... come here from outside the district but still work outside ... whether it be in London or all up the M4; Reading, Basingstoke, all the way up there, where there is plenty of work going on." (officer, Cotswold)

In Forest of Dean, processes of gentrification are more locally specific. Here, in-movements of higher income service-class groups have largely been confined to those north-eastern parts within easy commuting distance from the employment centres of Gloucester and Cheltenham. As one officer commented, "There's a clear divide within the Forest between north and south ... in the north there are greater links to Gloucester and there is more affluence".

These processes of gentrification clearly impact on the nature and scale of housing problems and homelessness in the two districts. Property prices in many village locations have escalated to such an extent that it is not only residents on low incomes who cannot afford to purchase local houses, but also those on average earnings. For many of these residents excluded from property purchase, then, the only option for remaining within the local property market is renting. However, renting through the private market can be problematic on two main grounds. First, the buoyant tourism sector in these two rural districts increases demand for private rental accommodation. This not only results in higher private rental levels but also allows landlords to be more selective about potential tenants:

> "Because there are people about who will rent at ... market level rents, they [private landlords] don't have trouble renting them. So you know

they're not within easy reach of ... those people who actually require social housing.... The other thing of course is that a lot of private landlords in this area ... will not take people on Income Support.... They want high deposits which can be perhaps two months' rent, and when you're looking at rents of £400 plus [a month] for two bedrooms, then that's a high deposit." (officer, Cotswold)

A second problematic feature of the private rental sector concerns supply-based issues. One issue here relates to the limited stock of private rental accommodation in Forest of Dean, where it comprises only 7% of the local housing stock. However, even though Cotswold has 17% of its housing stock in the private rental sector, two fifths of this stock is 'tied' to particular forms of employment, most notably farming, and so is beyond the reach of most local residents. Another supply-based issue concerns the nature of local private rental housing. There exists relatively little one- and two-bedroom accommodation, such as flats and apartments, in these areas, which is often the type of housing required by young people moving out of the parental home. This pattern of private rental housing has particular implications for young single people whose entitlement to housing-related state benefits is limited to the average rental of single room or bedsitter accommodation (single room rent). As an agency worker in Cotswold commented:

"... bedsits and shared houses ... you can't find any in the north Cotswolds. The estate agents don't do them [and] landlords rarely do them. You know, it's not bedsitter land by any stretch of the imagination. And those bedsitters that are there are like £55 plus [per week] and our single [room] rent is £40." (voluntary agency, Cotswold)

The nature of homelessness in these two districts also connects with the localised provision of social rental housing. At 18%, the level of social housing in each area is below the mean for England as a whole (23%). Furthermore, provision of social accommodation has fallen dramatically over recent years as a consequence of policies introduced by Conservative governments (see Milbourne, 1998), with Cotswold witnessing a decrease of such stock of 27%, and Forest of Dean one of 25% between 1981 and 1991. However, these reductions in social housing stock have been characterised by a great deal of spatial unevenness, with highest levels of loss in the smaller and gentrified villages in each district. As one officer commented in relation to Cotswold district, "In the really 'Cotswoldy'-

type villages we have got very little [social housing] stock left ... we have really suffered through the Right-to-Buy"[5].

Low levels of social housing stock impact on local homelessness in two main ways. First, households experiencing housing need have to wait long periods before being allocated social housing. For groups other than those deemed to be in priority need, social housing now represents an unrealistic option, as this agency worker in Cotswold district illustrates:

> "When I first started in the Cotswolds [2 years prior to the interview] the average time for a single person going on the housing need register and getting accommodation was 15 years." (voluntary agency, Cotswold)

With such long periods on social housing waiting lists, some households may enter into situations of homelessness while on these lists, while others realise the futility of registering for social housing and rarely come to the attention of statutory housing agencies.

A second impact of the limited provision of social housing in these districts relates to local authority responses to homelessness. With relatively few vacancies within the social sector, authorities are forced into rehousing homeless groups in private rental accommodation – the availability of which is limited for homeless people – or moving them into hostels located outside their districts. As the homelessness officer in Cotswold district commented, "If they [homeless people] want hostel-type accommodation, they've got to go to Swindon, Cheltenham and Gloucester". We will return to this issue later.

Rural homelessness and local cultures of rurality

Homelessness in these two districts is strongly connected to what we might call 'cultures of rurality'. It is possible to point to two main types of rural cultures present in our study districts. The first relates to dominant notions of rurality as idyll, bound up with traditional, peaceful, healthy and problem-free life-styles (see Cloke and Milbourne, 1992). With their picturesque land- and village-scapes, and strong tourism sectors, much of Cotswold and the north-eastern areas of Forest of Dean have come to be constructed in idyllic terms. The realisation of such constructed idyllic life-styles often represents a key motivation for in-moving groups (Milbourne et al, 2001) and, consequently, local issues that contradict these images can be denied any form of legitimacy within the social imagination of in-movers. For example, one of the voluntary agency workers in Cotswold described how ex-urban in-movers tend to 'block out' a range of local social problems, including homelessness:

"Well, it's idyllic isn't it when you drive through it. My God, the Cotswold stone and the sheep in the fields and the rolling hills ... I mean, if you are coming in from London, your issue is, well I have been in the big city and I [now] want the nice house and the nice roses; that's what I have paid for. I don't necessarily want to be hearing about homelessness problems." (voluntary agency, Cotswold)

More generally, officers and agency representatives considered that in many parts of Cotswold there exists a dominant construction of rurality which views poverty, housing problems and homelessness as threatening in economic and cultural terms. In economic terms, such issues pose a threat to local tourism and the continued accumulation of domestic property capital. In cultural terms, these issues act to complicate assumed ideas of problem-free rural living.

These types of everyday cultures of rurality also connect with the ways in which agencies dealing with local homelessness are able to operate. In particular, several voluntary agency representatives stated that their projects had been initiated under housing rather than homelessness titles. As one worker in Cotswold commented, "If you start raising the issue of homelessness it's very easy to lose the confidence of people in that area, very easy for them not to provide you with any support". This worker described how, at an early stage in the development of a project to help young homeless people, he was advised that support from local councillors and private landlords would only be secured if homelessness did not feature prominently within the project's public image.

This 'out-of-place' nature of homelessness in much of Cotswold is also reinforced by the actions of key actors within local housing markets. Of particular note here are local estate agents that are engaged in letting properties, who it was claimed by several voluntary agency workers, held negative attitudes towards homelessness. In one case, a voluntary agency was unable to secure any rented accommodation for its office in Cirencester even though local estate agents were advertising suitable properties. In other cases, homelessness workers reported that estate agents were generally reluctant to consider homeless people for vacant rental accommodation.

In addition to the presence of these cultures of idyllised rurality within these districts, our research has also highlighted the importance of more localised constructions of rural identity. Interviews with officers and agency workers in both districts revealed strong attachments to local places and more limited associations with other spaces within these districts. In the case of Cotswold, a clear North–South cultural division was apparent:

> "We tend to have a north–south divide line [in the district], and once you come south of the line, then it's like another country to them [homeless people], whereas in the south the people are probably a bit more willing to live in other adjacent villages. If you go into the north Cotswolds the adjacent village is just like a totally unknown world." (officer, Cotswold)

In Forest of Dean, reported cultural divisions were much more localised and complex:

> "People have strong links with their locality ... [and] people within the Forest [of Dean] are very parochial, very insular. People from Cinderford won't talk to people from Lydney." (officer, Forest of Dean)

These strong feelings of localism have important consequences for agencies responding to homelessness in these rural districts. People made homeless often reject offers of support from homeless agencies if these offers involve relocations to 'other' spaces within these districts. For example, workers in Cotswold reported difficulties in rehousing homeless people from the north of the district, as the only units of temporary accommodation are located in Cirencester, in the south (see Figure 5.3). In the case of Forest of Dean, the situation appears to be more serious for homelessness agencies, with one of the officers reporting that many homeless people "want to live not only in the same village, but in the same street". However, the limited provision of affordable rental accommodation and emergency support services in village spaces mean that local homeless people are faced with two options; they can either remain in their local area and seek out alternative accommodation arrangements, or relocate to urban areas where housing and support options are more numerous. It is to these options that we now turn.

Coping with homelessness in rural areas: 'moving on' or 'staying put'

For most people made homeless in villages within these two districts, the only rehousing option offered by homeless agencies involves relocation to urban places. In most cases this concerns a movement to those towns within the district that offer most of the social and (affordable) private rental housing and all the temporary accommodation provided by agencies. In Cotswold, for example, all units of temporary accommodation are located in Cirencester, while in Forest of Dean such housing is present in Cinderford, Coleford and Lydney. And while for many, these movements involve relatively short distances, homeless people in the northern villages of Cotswold can be faced with relocations of around 30 miles to Cirencester (see Figure 5.3).

In other cases, though, movements of homeless people from rural to urban spaces involve longer distances and different types of urban destinations. These two districts have no emergency support provision for homeless people, such as shelters and hostels, so homeless people requiring such accommodation are forced to travel to other (larger) urban spaces located outside of Cotswold and Forest of Dean. In the former, homeless people have to make use of hostels in Cheltenham and Swindon, while those in the latter have to travel to Gloucester (see Figure 5.3). These types of rural-to-urban movements of homeless people are highlighted in the following commentaries provided by agency workers:

"The particular problem in rural areas is rural drift. There is a lot of evidence of young people having to seek accommodation or help in the towns when they don't want to, because there is so little affordable accommodation in their own area.... People are having to be brought to hostels in the towns by project workers and it's causing real problems.... Many homeless people are having to go to Cheltenham from the Cotswolds." (voluntary agency, Gloucestershire)

"[There is] a lot more choice in an urban area. When it comes to the crunch you are more likely to find a wider range of accommodation options. There are cheap B&Bs, there are grotty, cheap little bedsits which, okay, you wouldn't want to put a hamster in there, but it's an option for a couple of weeks until you can find something else. The private rented sector is bigger [in urban areas], there are more hostels, there are more night shelters." (voluntary agency, Cotswold)

In attempting to deal with the homelessness being experienced by people in rural areas of these two districts, however, agencies are helping to push homeless people and the issue of rural homelessness out of rural spaces. Indeed, several workers were acutely aware that their actions are self-defeating in that the more successful they are at securing rehousing options for homeless people in urban spaces, the more they reinforce cultural and political constructions that homeless people are not a feature of the rural spaces of their districts. However, as one agency worker in Cotswold commented: "You are helping that [homeless] person find accommodation ... you are also helping them move out of the area, but there's no choice in that".

Homeless people in rural areas are not forced to accept the help provided by local agencies and move to emergency accommodation or rented housing in urban places within or beyond these two districts. Instead, many homeless people seek to remain in their rural localities. However, 'staying local' involves the employment of a range of 'coping tactics', some of which place them in precarious housing situations:

> "... I recall one young person who said he was sleeping rough. I said 'OK, I will put you in B&B', but ... he was from the south of the district and I only had something in the north. [He said] 'I am going to sleep in my car or in the woods' ... I have known [other] people sleep in cars but they have been parked outside other people's accommodation and they have used their facilities." (officer, Forest of Dean)

Attempts to remain in the local housing market were also viewed by officers and agency workers as contributing to housing problems and homelessness. As one worker suggested:

> "They don't want to go into the local authority place 30 miles away. They want to stay in the area and will move into either poor quality [or] expensive accommodation; accommodation that is often too small and which Housing Benefit won't cover the full amount [and] so find themselves getting into rent arrears [and] threatened with eviction...." (voluntary agency, Cotswold)

Homeless people are also forced into complex and difficult movements through local spaces in an attempt to cope with their situations. The nature of the local housing market, the local geographies of emergency homelessness support facilities, and the inadequate provision of everyday services mean that homeless people in rural parts of these districts often experience a range of problems in dealing with their homelessness. One voluntary agency worker in Cotswold felt that knowledge of her agency's work with young homeless people was limited in many villages "because there isn't an information point ... if you're living in a tiny village which has probably lost its shop and its pub, it's difficult to find things out". She continued:

"If they [young homeless people in villages] haven't got the money for
the bus fare to come to Cirencester ... they can be quite stuck. We
have had people turn up on our doorstep who have walked from a
village to us. They have found out about us and they have walked five
miles." (voluntary agency, Cotswold)

Evidence from Forest of Dean points to similar types of enforced
movements of homeless people and their attempts to cope with these
situations. In the following example, which is taken from case notes
provided by a voluntary agency, we highlight the experiences of 'David',
a young man who was made homeless in a village in Forest of Dean:

"He slept in a car for two nights in mid-winter before approaching the
project. He went on Nightstop[6] for four nights and then to a hostel 40
miles away [in Gloucester] when Nightstop was not available. During
this time landlords were approached but there was no affordable
accommodation available. David stayed in the hostel for four days but
found it very isolating as it was too far from his friends and family.
David decided to walk the 40 miles back to the Forest of Dean. He
stayed with friends for a few days but had to leave after Christmas. In
order to find shelter David broke into a caravan for the night. The
police were called and David was charged with criminal damage and
placed in a bail hostel in Gloucester." (voluntary agency, Forest of Dean)

Conclusion

A major theme running through this chapter has been the spatial
unevenness of rural homelessness. While it is important to be able to set
out the overall extent and profile of homelessness in rural England, it
should be recognised that rural homelessness is bound up with a great
deal of regional and local diversity. At the regional spatial scale, a North–
South divide is evident, with levels of homelessness much higher in the
three southern regions of England, where pressures from population in-
movement and high property prices are greatest. Homelessness also appears
to be more a feature of accessible rather than remote rural areas, where
processes of gentrification are usually more pronounced.

Cutting across these regional variations are the local geographies of
rural homelessness. Any understanding of rural homelessness needs to
take account of the local contexts within which homelessness occurs and
homeless people find themselves. By focusing on two proximate rural
districts in the same county, we have been able to highlight how the

scale, profile and experiences of rural homelessness differ not only between these two districts but also between different spaces within them. Again, the structure of local housing markets represents an important component of these differences, as particular spaces become gentrified, others are deprived of new housing through planning processes, and affordable housing opportunities are effectively restricted to the larger settlements. However, the case-study material also points to the important role played by localised cultural and political processes in influencing social constructions of homelessness and homeless people in rural spaces. In the next chapter we discuss the ways in which these cultural and political processes connect with agency responses to homelessness at the local level.

Notes

[1] For reasons of consistency, our analysis of official homelessness data uses the spatial categories developed by Lambert et al (1992). This categorisation includes four types of local authority area: London; urban; mixed rural; deep rural. Rural England includes all those 'mixed' and 'deep' rural local authority areas.

[2] Of the 35 rural local authority areas that recorded proportional increases of more than 25% over this period, 32 recorded *absolute* rises of more than 20 homeless households, and 16 witnessed *absolute* increases of more than 50 households.

[3] Losses of private rented accommodation accounts for a higher proportion of homelessness in rural than urban authority areas, even though levels of this type of accommodation are extremely similar (a recent Cabinet Office [1999] report states that private rented housing accounts for the tenure of 11% of all households in rural areas and 10% in urban areas).

[4] While the average for the district is 18%, spatialised historical patterns of provision and more recent Right-to-Buy sales have meant that many villages have much lower levels of social housing.

[5] The Right-to-Buy policy was introduced as part of the 1980 Housing Act and enables social housing tenants to purchase their properties at discounted prices.

[6] A scheme that allows young homeless people in this district to stay for short periods with households who have signed up to this scheme.

SIX

Local welfare governance and rural homelessness

In Chapter Four we provided a detailed discussion of the central policy context of rural homelessness. In particular, we considered the early legislation on homelessness in Britain and traced through some of the key features of restructuring initiated by the 1996 Housing Act. In this chapter we continue with this focus on homelessness policy but examine it from a different perspective. Here we consider the ways in which the implementation of central homelessness policy has become entangled with sets of local rural policy and political structures, and we discuss the important role played by new systems of local welfare governance – based on partnership working – in dealing with homelessness at the local level.

Local welfare governance and the shifting nature of homelessness support

The centralised provision of welfare and homelessness support in Britain is clearly bound up with complex sets of local socioeconomic, political and policy structures. Cochrane (1993), for example, has noted that local variation in welfare provision has long been a feature of the British welfare state reliant as it has been on local government as a key vehicle for its delivery. In a wider discussion of emerging systems of local governance, Stoker and Mossberger (1995) have pointed to two important components of the spatial differentiation of policy implementation – one involving 'vertical' linkages between central and local states; the other consisting of more 'horizontal' interconnections:

> Change and particular models of operation and organisation are imposed
> by central government. Local authorities react in different ways to this
> imposition. Equally there is a horizontal dimension as circumstances
> and actors create the conditions for specific alliances and particular
> ways forward in different localities. (p 220)

In relation to vertical processes of policy imposition, Stoker and Mossberger (1995) have proposed a typology of local authorities based on the ways in which they react to centrally imposed policies, with reactions bound up with complex mixes of localised political and socioeconomic structures. These types of local mediations of central policy are clearly evident in relation to policy dealings with homelessness, with a number of recent studies highlighting widespread variations in the ways in which local authorities interpret central homelessness legislation (see Evans and Duncan, 1988; Audit Commission, 1989; Niner, 1989; Greve, 1991; Butler et al, 1994). Niner's study, based on research with nine English local authorities in the late 1980s, concluded that:

> The sheer visibility of local policies and procedures suggests that there is ample scope within the legislation and guidance for flexibility of interpretation. The case study authorities varied in, for example, the stage at which households were accepted as homeless, working definitions of the ways of assessing vulnerability, the application of intentionality provision, and the nature and duration of investigation undertaken. They also varied in the scale of use of temporary accommodation and in the types used and the levels and methods of charging for temporary accommodation. The authorities differed in the proportion of all council house allocations made to homeless applicants and in the ways in which allocation decisions were made. While such variations undoubtedly reflected differential demands placed on the service and differential resources available to meet these demands, some of the variation was due to policy differences. (Niner, 1989, p 95)

This research also highlights that decisions on homelessness tend to be taken by small groups of homelessness officers operating independently from local elected councillors and without procedure manuals, monitoring or any form of appeals procedures for applicants. Furthermore, local authorities included within these investigations appear to have adopted definitions of homelessness that fit more with local political constructs of homelessness as an issue than any 'objective' assessment of the nature and extent of housing need.

Findings from some of these homelessness studies lend support to Stoker and Mossberger's (1995) idea of a typology of local reactions to centrally imposed policies. For example, Evans and Duncan (1988) and Butler et al (1994) have highlighted the existence of less restrictive practice towards homeless groups in Labour-controlled London and metropolitan authorities than those in non-metropolitan areas. The extent of these types of localised interpretation of centralised homelessness policy has led Mullins and Niner (1998) to suggest that any "totally consistent homelessness service might be a chimera" (pp 183-4). Whether a chimera or not, it is clear that central government has made two attempts – one in 1977, the other in 1996 – to overcome the local specificity of support for homelessness groups. Those studies undertaken in the 1980s and early 1990s have demonstrated that the first attempt was not particularly successful, although very little research has been undertaken to assess local responses to the 1996 Housing Act.

Discussion of the horizontal components of welfare policy delivery has been much more limited. However, an insight of the key processes involved emerges from recent literatures on the shifting nature of local governance. Here attention has been given to the uneven roles played by local government in emerging networks of local governance and the complex nature of power relations that are bound up with these new forms of governance.

Recent conceptualisations of governance (see, for example, Jessop, 1995, 1997a; Judge et al, 1995; Goodwin and Painter, 1996; Rhodes, 1996, 1997; Rose, 1996; Stoker, 1996, 1997a) suggest a new interdependence of governmental and non-governmental agencies, a new collectivity of action, and a move away from assumptions about the primacy of the state as the site of political activity. A governance perspective therefore theorises a 'blurring of boundaries' (Stoker, 1996) between distinct private sector and public sector activities, and poses important questions about the changing nature of power, decision making and agency interaction. It emphasises how a wide range of actors and agencies are now required to contribute resources and skills to a tangled web of policy making, and how in so doing the very meaning of government is being altered. In some cases new forms of governance can be seen as being associated with the New Right ideologies of the 1980s, which promised a rolling back of government but delivered instead a shift in the form of government, characterised by the rise of quangos (Cloke, 1992). To this context should be added the increasing importance of European Union funding which, as Ward and McNicholas (1998) suggest, results in "local, regional and national actors ... being required to work in new ways to plan for and administer rural development programmes" (p 27). Equally important in rural areas, however, is the long-standing ethic and cultural package of self-help, and the rather convenient reliance on voluntary agencies to provide services that previously were either provided by the state, or were never 'state-ised' at all.

What interests us particularly in this book is the way that governance is characterised by the development of new localised policy networks. According to Rhodes (1997) a policy network is "a cluster or complex of organisations connected to one another by resource dependencies"(p 37) and can range from "highly integrated policy communities to loosely integrated issue networks" (p 38). A network is rooted in resource exchange:

> ... the distribution of resources between actors in a specific network remains central to any explanation of the distribution of power in that network. Equally, the different pattern both of resources and their distribution between the several actors in networks explains, in part, the differences between networks. (p 37)

In the post-1979 period in Britain, the nature of policy networks has changed significantly. The previously functional networks based on central or local government departments have been made more complex with the addition of new actors and agencies from the private and voluntary sectors. Government institutions have been differentiated and pluralised, with the result that service delivery systems have become fragmented. Increasingly, the key role of central and local government has been reduced to one of seeking to coordinate or manage policy networks through facilitation and negotiation. As Rhodes (1997) indicates, these changing networks pose new issues for public managers:

> Is their role to regulate networks (in the sense of maintaining relationships)? Do they act as guardians of the public interest? Do they still have the authority and legitimacy to claim a privileged position in the network? Can they be privileged actors in the network without undermining the discourse? (p 58)

This mention of discourse reflects an alternative understanding of policy networks. Thus far they have tended to be viewed in the light of powerful actors or agencies controlling networks through resource or position or both. There is scope, however, for the new fragmented networks to act as arenas of more pluralist participation. Fox and Miller (1995), for example, argue that some contemporary policy networks and inter-agency consortia represent sites where discourses on particular issues can be influenced by a variety of interests, including less powerful ones. Here, they envisage a situation where "think tank experts, legislative staff, policy analysts, public administration, interested citizens, process generalists, even elected officials

[are] participating together to work out possibilities for what to do next" (p 149).

The generation of complex policy networks is also often characterised by the valorisation of 'partnership'. Lurking close to the surface of partnership discourses is the vague promise of citizen self-government – an opportunity to participate in these new forms of governance and an opportunity to raise the profile of issues, interests or client groups by entering into 'partnership' (see, Stoker, 1997b). For some, the new partnerships of governance offer an opportunity for revitalised systems of bargaining, negotiation and collaboration in the 'fragmented post-Fordist context' (Mayer, 1994). As Murdoch and Abram (1998) suggest, however, only those citizens and voluntary groups with the requisite resources and skills are likely to be able to discharge the responsibilities that partnership entails. Moreover, the very proliferation of experimental and often competitive partnership initiatives (see Bassett, 1996) can be seen as further undermining the potential for policy and action from within the state, at the same time achieving precious little in terms of establishing an effective alternative service delivery system.

At the heart of recent discussions of the shifting nature of (local) governance has been the extent to which these systems of governance represent a new form of decision making. For some, new forms of governance are considered as "self-organizing inter-organizational networks" which represent a break from conventional hierarchies of government decision making (Rhodes, 1996, p 659), while others point to the increasing role played by government within these emerging networks of governance, so that decision making "take[s] place in the shadow of hierarchy" (Jessop, 1997b, p 595). In relation to emerging networks of welfare provision, O'Brien and Penna (1998) would appear to support Jessop's perspective on shifting modes of welfare governance:

> The new mode of welfare governance comprises a transfer of responsibility for delivering the services combined with a centralisation of state power over their organisation and distribution. (p 157)

While the nature of power relations embedded within emerging systems of (welfare) governance is subject to debate, there is general agreement that the increased diversity of agencies involved in these new local networks is leading to greater levels of local differentiation associated with the implementation of policy. Several writers have considered the emergence of these new local coalitions of policy agencies in the context of urban regime theory (see Stone, 1989; Thomas and Imrie, 1997; Goodwin, 1998).

Central here is the notion of local regimes which, for Goodwin, consist of:

> ... informal yet relatively stable coalitions (or partnerships), composed of elites drawn from the public and private sectors. A regime is formed when a variety of local interests mesh together to form a relatively stable governing coalition, and involves a number of groups co-operating behind a certain set of policies to achieve their own ends (which may well vary from one group to another). (1998, p 9)

However, given that urban regime theory has been developed in the US by political scientists concerned with new private–public sector coalitions established to steer local economic development, there remains considerable doubt about their suitability in explaining the emergence of new forms of local welfare governance.

Notions of regimes have also emerged within the welfare literature, and have been particularly associated with the work of Esping-Andersen (1990) who has produced a threefold typology of welfare regimes associated with different nation states. Within this typology, the UK is positioned on the boundary between liberal and social-democratic models of welfare, defined as an individualistic semi-welfarist variant. However, discussing the nature of welfare provision in a UK context, Cochrane (1994) has suggested that we need to move beyond a sole focus on notions of national welfare regimes, and instead consider the possibility of "local welfare regimes" that may be able to connect central and local welfare issues, and allow for the existence of localised variations in welfare provision within an "overarching national welfare regime" (p 134). However, little research has been undertaken that has explored in any depth the appropriateness of the notion of local welfare regimes for understanding the nature of welfare provision in the UK.

In the next section of the chapter we want to engage with key issues raised thus far in our review of the local spaces of welfare provision. In particular, we want to examine the vertical and horizontal processes of the implementation of welfare support for homeless groups in our two rural study counties, in an attempt to highlight the local specificities of agency responses to homelessness in these areas. We want to do this in four main ways. First, we consider the ways in which responses to homelessness are bound up with historical local structures of welfare and the distinctive nature of local rural homelessness. Second, we explore how the imposition of central homelessness policy is complicated by local homelessness practice. Third, we move on to examine the formation, composition and actions of new networks of welfare delivery for homeless groups at the local level, before finishing with a detailed discussion of a partnership scheme established in a market town in Somerset.

Homelessness welfare governance in local rural space

The local context of welfare and homelessness provision in Gloucestershire and Somerset

Welfare provision for homeless groups in our two study counties is very much bound up with historical patterns of welfare provision and the distinctive nature of local homelessness. In relation to the first of these issues, local councils within these two counties were controlled by coalitions of Independent and Conservative politicians for most of the 20th century, including the critical immediate post-war period when key aspects of the welfare state were being established. As late as 1979, three of these councils were under Conservative control, three were controlled by Independent councillors, and Independents formed the majority group on two councils that were in situations of no overall control[1]. And as Newby et al (1978) have highlighted, the domination of Conservative politicians, who typically were farmers and landowners, within these types of rural councils has been associated with a restricted provision of welfare services for two important reasons. First, Conservative politicians were reluctant to increase local taxes to provide welfare services, and second, farming and land-owning politicians had a vested interest in controlling their workers through existing paternalistic systems of tied accommodation, estate villages and other forms of informal welfare provision.

The provision of social housing is a good example of the reluctance on the part of these types of rural councils to engage positively with the expanding welfare state. In our case studies, levels of social housebuilding in the post-war period were considerably below the national average. The impacts of these past patterns of social housing provision are very much evident today. With the proportion of social housing in eight of these nine local authorities below the average for England, this limited stock of social housing clearly creates problems for these local authorities in rehousing homeless households within social accommodation.

Specific negative attitudes towards welfare provision for homeless persons were mentioned by some of the local authority homelessness officers interviewed in the course of our research. In the following quotation, a Somerset officer describes the 'old-fashioned' and generally unsympathetic political and policy culture associated with homelessness among both councillors and officers in the 1970s:

"Going back a few years I must admit that the attitude wasn't particularly receptive [to homeless people], it wasn't very encouraging to [homeless] people ... I think it's just a shift in age if that makes sense. When I first came here it was a very old-fashioned housing department. Things were done because they always had been done." (Somerset local authority 5)[2]

Even though the political control of these councils has shifted to the centre-Left in the period since the 1970s, several officers suggested that they were still having to deal with the legacy of conservative attitudes towards homelessness, including a limited recognition of homelessness issues among councillors, under-investments in homelessness support services, and an apprehension on the part of officers about dealing with homeless people. As this officer in Gloucestershire commented, other officers often marginalise homelessness issues:

"People are so scared of homelessness – fellow colleagues, absolutely petrified, don't want to dabble, do not want to know.... So you are left very much isolated, very much left on your own ... [They] are frightened of being sucked into something that's really personal, something that's really technical, that [could result in] judicial review. If you get it wrong, good God, you get penalised for it and they don't want to accept that responsibility. So they are frightened of it." (Gloucestershire local authority 2)

These past and present attitudes towards homelessness are reflected in the nature of welfare provision for homeless people. Unlike most urban and metropolitan local authority areas, our case-study areas contain relatively few advice and support facilities for homeless people, such as hostels, shelters, temporary accommodation and advice centres. Instead, homeless people who need to make use of such emergency facilities are often required to travel out of these local authority areas to other towns and cities. In Cotswold, for example, homeless people have to access hostel and shelter-type accommodation in Gloucester or Swindon. And while we are not suggesting that these authorities are not concerned about homeless people or that they are not involved in local schemes to deal with homelessness, it remains the case that contemporary attempts to respond to local homelessness are bound up with previous political and policy processes that effectively de-prioritised homelessness issues.

A further reason why homelessness has not been prioritised by these case-study authorities relates to the nature of local homelessness. As we have discussed in Chapter Three (see also Cloke et al, 2000a, 2000b), homelessness in these types of rural spaces tends to be much less visible than its urban counterpart. Rural homelessness is dispersed widely across small and scattered rural settlement structures, and there are fewer opportunities for homeless people to become visibly concentrated, for example, through sleeping in shop doorways or residing in shelters and hostels. The hidden nature of homelessness in these case-study areas further acts to marginalise homelessness as a local political and policy issue among local councillors, officers and residents[3].

While homelessness occurs across a wide range of villages and small towns in these counties, the main response by local authorities has been heavily spatialised and involves the main administrative centres, for example Taunton in Taunton Deane and Cirencester in Cotswold (see Figure 2.1, p 37). It is in these places that any advice centres, temporary accommodation and voluntary sector services are situated. It is also in these larger towns that rehousing options in the social sector are more realistic as much of the already limited supply of social housing in village locations has effectively been sold under the Right-to-Buy legislation.

The local implementation of central homelessness policy

Having set out the local context of homelessness welfare provision in the two study counties, we now want turn to consider vertical processes of welfare policy imposition and examine the ways in which the homelessness components of the 1996 Housing Act have impacted on our case-study areas. In doing this, we want to explore the extent to which central welfare policy intermixes with the local policy context in these areas. The analysis that follows is based on in-depth interviews conducted in 1998 with homelessness officers in each of the nine local authorities in the case-study areas.

The 1996 Housing Act had resulted in a dramatic restructuring of homelessness policy and practice among our case-study authorities. Homelessness officers recognised that the Act represented "a significant break from previous homelessness policy" (Gloucestershire local authority 3) and necessitated a great deal of local internal reorganisation and increased administration loads. As another Gloucestershire officer commented, the Housing Act was "a pain in the ass in just implementing it really"

(Gloucestershire local authority 2). For each of these nine officers, this new legislation was viewed initially as a threat to their abilities to meet the needs of homeless people in their local areas. Furthermore, most stated that they had objected to the underlying principles of the 1996 Act; that there were problems with the previous system of allocating social housing.

Having been prevented from treating homelessness as a 'reasonable category' for rehousing and compelled to respond to homeless households through the general social housing allocations route, these nine local authorities set about searching for ways of re-prioritising homeless cases. In the words of one officer, "We tried] to continue to respond positively to all households facing the crisis of homelessness ... to continue housing families as before" (Somerset local authority 5). The main means by which this was achieved was by adjusting the number of points awarded to different categories of housing need on the general housing register. Previously, homeless households had been dealt with outside of the general allocations system and so no points were awarded for situations of homelessness. However, local authorities were prohibited from including homelessness as a category within the social housing allocation pointing system, and so other surrogate categories needed to be brought in. As a homelessness officer in Gloucestershire explained:

> "... we changed our policies, obviously, because previously they [the homeless] haven't had the points and so we had to look at ways that we could give them preference without just giving them preference outright. So we gave them points for insecurity of tenure and for being in temporary accommodation ... we had to have a way of them accruing points so that they were moving on." (Gloucestershire local authority 2)

While each local authority adjusted its pointing system to include surrogate indicators of homelessness, it should not be assumed that homeless applications are treated consistently by each of these authorities. In fact, individual authorities have introduced different surrogate categories of homelessness and awarded these categories different levels of importance relative to general housing needs. However, what is clear is that while key facets of the 1996 Housing Act have been imposed onto local homelessness practice in the case-study areas, these nine local authorities have effectively neutralised its effects, so enabling them to "change as little as possible [and] to ensure that the same people were getting housed at more or less the same point in the process" (Somerset local authority 3). In other words, our case-study research would appear to indicate that this national system of welfare provision has been actively subverted by the actions of the local welfare state.

In addition to these efforts by our case-study local authorities to minimise the effects of the 1996 Housing Act on homeless people in their area, it is possible to point to other situations in which the imposition of new centralised welfare policy has become complicated by different sets of local circumstances. We want to provide three examples of these central–local policy entanglements.

The first relates to a recent voluntary transfer of social housing stock by one of the Gloucestershire local authorities to a local housing association. A condition of this transfer was the merging of the two systems of housing allocation operated by the authority and the association, and the development of a common housing register and points system. Discussions between the authority and association focused on ways of improving the allocation system to take into account a broader range of locally relevant social welfare issues. These discussions also coincided with the introduction of the 1996 Housing Act, which prompted a further phase of adjustments to ensure that cases of homelessness were reflected in the new points system:

"Everything came at once. So we did an interim measure ...by changing a few definitions with a view that we would review it to take on board the requirements of the 1996 Act in more detail. And that's what we did when we reviewed [the local authority's] and our own points.... And we've ... taken on board various issues that the old points system didn't cover ...you know, mainly the social welfare issues.... It [changing the pointing system] had to come, but I think probably the 1996 Act did push it along a little bit." (Gloucestershire local authority 1)

Here, then, restructuring of social housing policy was brought about by an amalgam of local and central welfare circumstances, with the latter accelerating ongoing processes of change. For this homelessness officer at least, the resulting system of social housing allocation not only included homeless people but also a wider range of vulnerable groups and situations of vulnerability which had previously remained locked out of the local welfare state.

A second example of central–local welfare policy entanglements concerns elements of local homelessness practice operated by these rural authorities prior to the 1996 Act. Contrary to claims made by the then Conservative central government, officers in our case-study authorities stated that in allocating social housing, a careful balance had been maintained between the needs of homeless and general housing needs groups. In the view of one officer in Gloucestershire, the 1996 Housing Act was embedded with particular spatio-political assumptions about homelessness practice which corresponded more to pre-1996 allocation procedures of a small number of Labour-controlled metropolitan authorities than with practice in other non-metropolitan and rural local authorities. As such, the impacts of this legislation in relation to social housing allocation would inevitably vary at the local level. For example, in the case of this officer's authority, allocations from the waiting list "had always been prioritised allocations hand in hand with homelessness, so in a way it [the 1996 Act] didn't have that dramatic effect ... on our allocations policy" (Gloucestershire local authority 2).

Local homelessness practice in our case study has acted to complicate the imposition of the 1996 Housing Act in a third way. This relates to the use of private rented accommodation in responding to homelessness. Fitting within the New Right project of welfare privatisation, the 1996 Act sought to make greater use of the private rental sector in rehousing homeless groups. For sets of more pragmatic reasons, most notably a limited supply of local social housing, our case-study authorities have come to place considerable reliance on private sector housing in dealing with local homelessness. In fact, in many villages within the two study areas, the private rental sector represents the only option for rehousing homeless people locally, given that almost all of the social housing stock has been privatised through the Right-to-Buy legislation. Consequently, this aspect of the Housing Act has had less of an impact on local homelessness practice in our study counties than in other areas. As a Gloucestershire officer commented:

> "The Housing Act really hasn't sort of hit our homelessness applications quite as badly as in other areas. Obviously, I can imagine that some authorities, possibly London boroughs ... are just giving out lists of private rented, [saying] that's my discharge, off you go. [But] I never discharge my duties unless I know they are in there and they are settled." (Gloucestershire local authority 2)

New local networks of homelessness welfare support

Welfare support for homeless groups in each case-study area is not only provided by local government, although it does play a significant role in delivering services to statutorily defined groups of homeless people. Over recent years, new coalitions of statutory and voluntary welfare agencies have emerged to meet the needs of homeless groups excluded from state support. In this third case-study section we examine the formation, composition and activities of these alternative local networks of welfare support for homeless people. In particular, we want to consider the power relations bound up with these new networks and the extent to which they can be seen to represent new forms of local welfare. This section is based on in-depth interviews with the nine homelessness officers and a further 19 voluntary agency representatives.

At the time of our research, a total of 15 projects were operating in the case-study areas, with almost all geared towards the needs of young homeless groups and involving partnerships between local authorities, other statutory bodies and voluntary welfare agencies. Typically these projects consisted of homelessness advice and support services, rent deposit and bond schemes, and the small-scale provision of emergency accommodation. The scale of these partnership projects for young homeless people, though, is remarkably different in the two case-study counties, with two thirds based in Gloucestershire.

The main reason for this imbalance in the number of homelessness projects relates to the level of involvement of local government. In Gloucestershire, the county and district councils have played a significant role in establishing these new networks of welfare provision, while in Somerset local authorities have been less prominent. In the former county, a new network of welfare support for young single homeless people was initiated by key officers in the county council (following a review of its responsibilities under the Children Act) and developed in consultation with district council officers and representatives of voluntary agencies. Local government has also provided much of the initial funding for these projects. By contrast, most of the informal projects of support for homeless groups in Somerset appear to have been initiated and developed through smaller-scale networks of concerned individuals and voluntary agencies. This is not to say that key departments in local authorities have not played a part – in fact, they have provided financial support for several projects – but their role has been less pronounced than in Gloucestershire.

The case remains that in both counties local authorities play a pivotal role in funding and coordinating projects, even though most are 'fronted' by voluntary agencies. As such, it would appear that these new networks of welfare provision are closer to Jessop's (1997b) hierarchical model than the 'self-organising, inter-organisational network' of governance proposed by Rhodes (1996). The partnerships of different agencies involved in these projects appear to provide tangible benefits to both local authorities and voluntary agencies. Local authorities are able to extend welfare provision while working within a restrictive financial environment, and voluntary sector agencies require the involvement of local authorities – usually in a funding capacity – to ensure that projects continue. Indeed, partnership working was viewed by almost all officers and agency representatives as the most effective way of responding to different situations of local homelessness. As one of these officers commented:

> "I think it's an understanding from all the agencies that the only way that we can move forward is together. The rules and reg[ulation]s get more restrictive and so if we are all working in partnership, we are better off than being at loggerheads.... I think we would all just ground to a halt if we didn't work together." (Gloucestershire local authority 2)

Furthermore, these new networks of welfare provision were viewed by many of the voluntary agency representatives as capable of wrenching entrenched (conservative) local homelessness agendas and policy initiatives away from the sole control of local authorities, influential officers and councillors. They were also able to highlight and work to rectify important differences in homelessness policy and practice between local authorities on a countywide basis, and also deal flexibly with the different local geographies of housing markets, housing problems and homelessness in these areas.

However, while these new networks of welfare provision provided benefits for both statutory and voluntary sector partners, it is difficult to describe them as in any way stable and consensual on a number of grounds. First, these networks are reliant on complex and often short-term patterns of funding which not only include contributions from local government but a range of other sources, including central and local agencies, and local fundraising. Consequently, many of the individual projects operate on a year-to-year basis under a great deal of uncertainty about their medium-term futures. Second, the instability of these networks is linked to their constantly shifting compositions, patterns of funding, and relationships between partnership agencies.

A third area of instability concerns sets of tensions between different partnership agencies, and particularly between statutory and voluntary agencies. Local authority representatives complained that they were viewed by voluntary agencies as hierarchical and inflexible in dealing with homelessness. In the words of one homelessness officer, "we are seen as the bureaucratic establishment that ... sits on keys, doesn't give out houses, very much the same sort of perspective as their clients" (Gloucestershire local authority 2). By contrast, several voluntary sector representatives considered that their homelessness projects were being funded by local government to patch up ever-growing holes in the formal local welfare net. In some cases, local authorities were accused of discharging their responsibilities to particular homeless groups, and placing additional burdens on the workloads of voluntary agencies. As one of the voluntary sector workers in Gloucestershire commented:

> "Sometimes we get young people who say, 'Oh I went to [housing] but they told me to come here' and sometimes I think they are actually put off from making homelessness applications. We have instances of people being told, 'Oh the waiting list is so many yards long, so there is almost no point in applying', which makes me a bit cross.... My personal view is that they are shifting the responsibility." (Gloucestershire agency 4)

Homelessness and begging in Taunton, Somerset: a partnership approach?

In the final part of this chapter we want to discuss a series of important issues associated with the development of a partnership scheme in Taunton – the main town in Taunton Deane, Somerset (see Figure 2.1, p 37) – which was established to deal with a perceived problem of increased numbers of homeless people and beggars on the town's streets.

In October 1996, concerns that improvements to the town centre could be spoiled by "the influx of beggars and homeless on the streets" led the local authority – Taunton Deane Borough Council (TDBC) – to draw up a 'Six Point Initiative' "to ensure that the enhanced town centre continues to be a safe and pleasant environment for all members of the public" (Taunton Deane District Council, 1996). The initiatives proposed involved: information gathering with two surveys, one of homelessness and begging and the second to establish the attitudes of town centre users towards vagrancy and the consumption of alcohol in public; practical measures with improved street cleaning and plans to introduce a system of diverted giving (in which so-called 'begging boxes' are placed in a number of stores as an encouragement to shoppers to help 'the homeless' in this way rather than giving money directly to people on the street); and moves towards greater official regulation of public space with investigation of the possibility of introducing a local bylaw to restrict the sale and consumption of alcohol and proposals to establish a licensing scheme for street trading.

The proposals were drawn up jointly by leaders of the three main political parties and involved a number of organisations, including: the police; the Town Centre Partnership (set up in response to an identified need for the business sector and TDBC to work more closely together for the benefit of the town, and consisting of representatives from major national retailers within the town, the Chamber of Commerce, TDBC and Somerset County Council) and voluntary organisations such as Shelter, Taunton Association for the Homeless and Open Door. Here is clear evidence of the establishment of 'partnership' within contemporary local governance. However, it is important to recognise that this partnership arose under particular circumstances. Discourses of the 'problem' of homelessness in Taunton had already been formed and negotiated in the local press, and although two 'sides' to the issue had been aired, the loud voices of local business people and some elected representatives had successfully framed the problem in terms of 'unacceptable' street behaviour. Moreover, dominant discourses also pointed to a *regulation* of the problem (that is, by a stricter 'policing' of public space) rather than a response to the needs, which some voices suggest underlies the problem. In particular, the interests of local capital and consumers were set against those agencies who were seeking to enhance the welfare of homeless people. This, then, was a partnership in which, initially at least, there seemed to be little willingness to relinquish control or resources in order to fulfil the aspirations of other partners in the policy network. Partnership in the network was undertaken from a platform of pursuing key sectoral interests.

The role of a key local government officer – TDBC's housing officer – was crucial in the establishment of a wider policy network with which to engage in homelessness partnership in Taunton. Soon after the 'Six Point Initiative', he brokered a 'Town Centre Inter-Agency Meeting' which brought together more than 40 individuals representing 19 or so agencies including the Town Centre Partnership, the police, the Private Landlords Association and local business (those, perhaps, most interested in regulation 'solutions'), but also including local housing associations, Citizens Advice Bureaux, Shelter, the homeless agencies (Taunton Association for the Homeless; Open Door), local churches, *The Big Issue*, detached youth workers and TDBC itself. There was a strong sense that by calling together these potential partner agencies something was being done about the 'problem'. There was also a sufficiently wide constituency to allow participants the prospect of participatory citizenship with partnership. A sense of pluralism within partnership was fostered in this and subsequent meetings by the organisational gambit of going around the room asking each participant for their particular views and reactions.

It would be overly simplistic to define the various interests represented in terms of business interests, housing agency interests and council interests, with the last being a complex amalgam of concerns relating not only to housing and homelessness responsibilities but also to maximising local economic growth and to the need to maintain voter support. However, although such categories are by no means mutually exclusive, they do illustrate the varying motivations for the involvement of individuals and agencies in the partnership approach and the different priorities that are likely to result. What emerged most clearly from the meetings, therefore, was the concern of the business community that homelessness and begging have a detrimental effect on trade. So far as the voluntary agencies are concerned, while it might be considered that the motivation for their involvement in the partnership approach is fairly unequivocal – a desire to help those in need – talking of the voluntary sector as a whole disguises differences between the organisations within the sector. Although there was no evidence of this in the Taunton case, other studies (Hutson and Liddiard, 1994; Oldman, 1997) have pointed to inter-agency rivalry where there is competition for limited funds, and tensions may also arise over differences in approach – for example, the extent an individual is considered responsible for their situation – and in the nature of an organisation's response to homelessness – for example, whether they simply react to the situation in hand, through, for instance, the provision of overnight accommodation, or whether they are more concerned to prevent homelessness occurring in the first place.

Perhaps the most complex motivational influence was that of TDBC, whose officers and members were positioned so as to attempt to balance the needs and demands of a number of different constituencies – including local electorates, businesses and people in need. However, although the council leader stated a belief that the Six Point Initiative "gets the balance between caring and the need to ensure a viable and prosperous town centre just right", it is perhaps not overly cynical to regard the council's pursuit of an inter-agency/partnership approach in tackling the problems of the town centre as being primarily financially driven. Indeed, at the Inter-Agency Meeting, the borough housing officer spoke of "maximising existing resources" and, having highlighted the constraints on public expenditure, stated, "it is therefore imperative that we make the best use of existing provision and services and *hence* the encouragement of this inter-agency network approach".

The council is also under pressure from the public and business community to show that something is being done to address the problems of the town centre and to counter claims in the press that they are taking no action to resolve the situation. There is thus a political dimension to their response, with the failure to achieve a satisfactory solution liable to lead to a loss of public support. As a correspondent to the *Somerset County Gazette* warned, "If Jefferson Horsley [the council leader] really believes bylaws about dogs on leads coupled with sanctimonious platitudes are in any way an adequate response from the Deane Council leader to an extremely serious and growing problem facing Taunton, then the sooner his party makes way for an alternative administration willing and able to take decisive and positive action the better" (6 June 1997).

Missing partners?

It should also be recorded that key individuals and groups were absent from the Inter-Agency Meeting, and hence from the partnership process. In particular, despite being the focus of discussion, homeless people and beggars were not present and it was left to workers from agencies such as Taunton Association for the Homeless and Open Door to represent their interests and speak on their behalf. This emphasises their position as 'other', with the exclusion of homeless and other vulnerable people from mainstream society reflected and indeed reinforced by their exclusion from the political process. Barriers are consequently strengthened when, it could be argued, the opportunity provided by such meetings for "engaging with the other, what bell hooks calls repositioning, might lead to understanding, a rejection of stereotype and a lesser concern with threats to the boundary of community" (Sibley, 1995, p 29). In addition, it could be argued that such exclusion may lead to an incomplete or inadequate understanding of the needs and requirements of homeless people and consequently may result in inappropriate strategies for dealing with the problems.

Having said that, excluding homeless people themselves from the partnership process is not necessarily wholly disadvantageous. As Sibley (1995, p 29) warns, there are drawbacks if contact with 'the other' is only partial or brief and limited engagement, or that superficial encounters "might result in the presumption of knowledge which could be more dangerous than ignorance, if this were in the province of state bureaucracies or academia". In addition, the voluntary agencies lend a degree of respectability to the issue of homelessness which perhaps ensures a greater receptiveness, especially among a Conservative audience, to the views and needs of homeless people than they themselves would be able to achieve.

In terms of other 'groups' who were missing from the Inter-Agency

Meeting, although all the participants there were members of the public, they were representing specific organisations and there was no one who was there simply as a resident of Taunton and/or a town centre user. Yet the 'public' also need to be part of the partnership approach. As the Director of Taunton Association for the Homeless pointed out, in an article in the *Somerset County Gazette*, "continued multi-agency work between voluntary and paid agencies in the Deane will produce results *if* supported by public support and understanding" (9 May 1997) (emphasis added). Of course there is no such thing as the 'general public' in the sense of a homogenous mass of people with shared aims and ideas, but this did not prevent some members of the business community from claiming to speak on their behalf. In particular, the manager of the local Marks & Spencer speaking at the Inter-Agency Meeting stated: "In a sense, Marks & Spencer's can claim to represent a constituency of 25,000 people a week, all of whom have legitimate views about the environs of the town centre". But he gave no indication of what, if any, research had been carried out to establish these views and consequently it is at least questionable how far he can claim to represent public opinion.

Louder views

Partnership will be characterised not only by who is included and excluded, but also by the power of particular voices over others. The management of the Inter-Agency Meeting seemed to reflect a model example of the partnership process at work. Seats were arranged in circular form and, following an introduction from the chairman, contributions were invited on a 'round-the-table' basis. Yet this spatial configuration belied a clear hierarchy of power. While ostensibly about partnership, it very soon became obvious that some interests were more powerful than others. In particular was the dominance of business concerns in the debate – even though, in numerical terms, agency representatives far outweighed these.

The primacy accorded to business interests has been evident from the outset of attempts to tackle the problems in the town centre. Despite requiring the involvement of a whole host of organisations, a meeting of the council's Policy Committee (3/10/96) a few days after the Six Point Initiative was drawn up, recommended that the proposals, "be passed onto the Taunton Town Centre Partnership for comments and endorsement with suitable action and funding being made available through both the council and the Town Centre Partnership itself". Consultation with other bodies and, in particular, voluntary agencies in the town was limited and on a more informal basis. This is not perhaps surprising given the council's dependency on the business community, particularly in the light of constraints on public expenditure. Right from the beginning of discussions, the Town Centre Partnership were accorded with a degree of financial responsibility for the programme to deal with the problems in the town centre, as is apparent from the minutes of the meeting of the Policy Committee (3/10/96) which recorded: "Clearly ownership must be shared with the Town Centre Partnership who if they approve the thrust would be expected to pick up some of the costs".

In addition, local traders constitute a powerful lobby force, with the economic well-being of the town and its citizens resting on the jobs and direct financial support they provide. This is a lever which companies have proved themselves willing to use. For example, speaking at the Inter-Agency Meeting, the manager of Marks & Spencer, referring to pressure to move out of town, seemed to make a veiled threat to withdraw from Taunton and suggested continuing investment was incumbent on action to address the problems, commenting: "Marks & Spencer are investing millions in Taunton but expect a return". Consequently, the council is reliant on the approval of the business community before embarking on a course of action, but has less need to take account of the opinions of the voluntary agencies who have no financial hold over it and little or no power to exercise in order to ensure that their voices are heard.

Discursive incompatibilities

To some extent presenting a division of interest between the business community – who seek to protect trade in the town centre – and the voluntary agencies – whose concerns are more geared towards the needs of the beggars and homeless people identified as the cause of the town's problems – is something of an artificial distinction. These two objectives are not incompatible and both groups seek, albeit for different reasons, to end homelessness and begging on the streets. Nevertheless, the different priorities and motivations of the business community and the voluntary agencies are reflected in the very different discourses of homelessness that they promote. While the business community tend to see the people involved *as* problems, the voluntary agencies are much more likely to see them as people *with* problems. This is not simply a semantic distinction but has an effect on the type of approach and strategies adopted to deal with the situation in the town centre. The presence of incompatible discourses was highlighted most graphically at the Inter-Agency Meeting in discussions of plans to conduct a survey of homelessness and begging.

Both the council and the business community seemed unable to grasp the ethical issues and complexities involved in conducting such a survey and failed to understand the concerns of the agencies, expressed most forcefully by workers from Shelter, Taunton Association for the Homeless and the *Big Issue* with regard to the use to which information might be put once it was in the public domain and its potential as political ammunition. Although a considerable amount of time was spent at the Inter-Agency Meeting discussing the matter, it is salient to note that the minutes prepared by the TDBC do not record, even in passing, the reservations of the agencies with regard to the survey, perhaps reflecting the lack of recognition of the importance of ethical issues and the legitimacy of the concerns expressed. (An alternative reading is that omission of the discussion from the minutes was less an oversight than a conscious attempt to gloss over what were, at the time, quite heated differences of opinion.)

The discursive distance between the commercial and the voluntary sector was also apparent in their different reaction to some of the measures proposed by the council to deal with homelessness and begging in the town centre. In particular, plans to implement the 'diverted giving scheme' referred to earlier (whereby shoppers place donations for 'the homeless' in collection boxes placed in stores rather than giving money directly to people on the street) were strongly supported by representatives from the Town Centre Partnership. In contrast, a number of the voluntary organisations expressed their suspicion and reservations about such a scheme with the most vehement opposition coming from the *Big Issue* who were concerned about homeless people being 'further' stigmatised and alienated. Despite such opposition, a diverted giving scheme in Taunton was launched at the end of June 1997. Although it is too early as yet to assess its effect, the fact that a local dogs' home collected money outside ASDA for a day and raised £700 while Taunton Association for the Homeless did the same and collected only £80 perhaps raises doubts about the fundraising potential of the scheme.

The outcomes of partnership

There were three main outcomes from the Inter-Agency Meeting in 1996. First, there was a commitment from the council to hold a further meeting in a year's time "to review the position at that time and to consider what developments have occurred in the intervening period" (TDBC minutes). Although the council suggested that some of the organisations who attended the meeting would continue to meet in the meantime, "with a view to maximising existing resources and developing new initiatives where this proves possible", the council could be seen, from this statement, as effectively relinquishing any responsibility as coordinator of the inter-agency approach to dealing with the problems in Taunton.

Second, the meeting led to the creation of a directory of agencies, which provided a brief summary of the work of each of the organisations represented. Such information is essential to the success of a partnership approach. An awareness of the existence and remit of other organisations can lead to more effective and efficient provision both by preventing an unnecessary duplication of services and by facilitating the referral of clients to the organisation best able to meet their needs. In addition, such a directory provides the opportunity for contacts to be established and may enable different organisations with similar concerns to come together to lobby for policy changes and financial support.

However, the main outcome ('the substantive commitment') of the Inter-Agency Meeting as the minutes record "was an agreement to prepare a survey of the people who are on the street". As the meeting progressed, it was fairly obvious that the council had a clear idea of what it wanted to achieve from the meeting, namely a survey carried out by the voluntary sector with minimal, if any, local authority funding, to which end a sub-group was established. Subsequent meetings of this group once again highlighted the differences between the different bodies involved and the consequent difficulties encountered in pursuing a partnership approach. Representatives from the voluntary agencies reiterated the reservations they had expressed previously regarding the purpose of the survey and to what use the information would be put, and their concern not to alienate the people they were trying to assist. While the council officers present argued that the survey was not intended to stigmatise homeless people, they were at something of a loss to explain exactly *why* a survey was required. As a result, the idea of conducting a survey of homelessness was eventually (after several meetings) abandoned in favour of carrying out a simple count of the number of people on the streets as the basis for a bid to obtain funds under the government's Rough Sleepers Initiative, with any further information required by TDBC being supplied by the voluntary agencies present, so long as this would not breach their codes of confidentiality or infringe the rights and privacy of their clients.

The restricted nature of these outcomes is perhaps understandable. TDBC seemed very committed to a partnership approach, but resource constraints limited their ability to provide directly for homeless and other vulnerable people. Therefore, at the Inter-Agency Meeting, the borough housing officer noted that expenditure constraints and a shortage of affordable accommodation meant that priority was given to households with children and "concern for the single homeless has to take its place within those priorities". The council acknowledged at an early stage that "development of a multi-agency programme towards reducing homelessness would be extremely resource intensive" and that "extra funding would be required, possibly for additional staff", but this appears not to have been forthcoming. Indeed, the two principal providers of support for homeless people in Taunton – Taunton Association for the Homeless and Open Door – have struggled to maintain their current levels of service, and have both faced financial problems sufficiently severe to have had to contemplate cutbacks or even closure.

The lack of financial support from TDBC and the business sector for voluntary agencies dealing with homelessness provides a significant indicator of the limitations of their commitment to partnership. These 'loudest voices' are clearly pursuing their own goals through the partnership approach. If partnership is a sharing of interests, risks and resources – collaboration of players on the same side of the game – then the Taunton partnership has made relatively few gains. Indeed it could be argued that participation in partnership has allowed the most powerful and loudest voices to continue to (re)construct discourses of homelessness which are principally motivated by self-interest and profit. In other words, partnership has provided a further platform where exclusionary social practices are legitimised discursively while the parties concerned can wear the clothes of reason and collaboration. Within unequal partnerships such as this, it is much more difficult to deconstruct the discursive power of 'loud voice' groups.

A letter to the *Somerset County Gazette* sums up this dilemma:

> If we allow people motivated by profit to sanitise, normalise and regulate our society we will, by our inaction, support their spiteful tricks. After they have handed over the poor and the unlucky, who will be next? Answer: anyone they cannot see commercial value in. (4 October 1996)

This is not as exaggerated or sensationalist a conclusion as it might at first sound. The latest controversy to embroil Taunton's town centre revolves around the objection of a number of traders to a scheme to improve access for people with disabilities by creating a paved strip across an area of cobbled pathway, on the grounds that it will disrupt pedestrian flow and that the £16,000 cost "would be far better spent on ridding the town of the various beggars and vagrants who continue to pollute the streets" (*Somerset County Gazette*, 13 June 1997). Attitudes to homeless people and those with disabilities are linked in this apparent desire to remove anyone from the town centre who does not conform to a particular brand of 'normality'. As the press officer for Somerset Coalition of Disabled People writes in a letter to the newspaper, "we can see that some traders have extended their definition of undesirables (from homeless people) to include disabled people" and echoes the warning issued by the previous correspondent with his concluding question: "Who will these people want to exclude next?" (*Somerset County Gazette*, 20 June 1997).

Conclusion

In this chapter we have explored the local spaces of welfare and homelessness provision. In Gloucestershire and Somerset, local government has played a crucial role in mediating key intended outcomes of the 1996 Housing Act. Whether or not we interpret these localised interventions as 'acts of resistance', the case remains that these politically mixed councils have successfully challenged key elements of centrally imposed homelessness legislation by altering localised social housing allocation systems. By doing this, these rural authorities have been able to continue to rehouse homeless groups and, indirectly, to undermine central government attempts to standardise local dealings with homeless groups. In this sense, then, key findings from these study areas would appear to confirm the spatial unevenness of welfare provision and recent processes of welfare restructuring.

The local research findings have pointed to the local spatialities of welfare policy in other ways. Contemporary local homelessness practice has been shown to be bound up with previous political and policy structures, and restrictive local systems of welfare. Homelessness practice in our case-study areas is also influenced by the nature of local homelessness, and particularly its more dispersed and hidden features provision, which has led to policy responses that have pushed rural homelessness into particular urban spaces within and beyond these counties. Furthermore, we have been able to provide clear evidence of different types of central–local welfare policy entanglements that have complicated the implementation of central homelessness policy at the local level.

If the imposition of centralised homelessness policy has been complicated by the activities of local authorities, then a further level of complication is evident in terms of the new networks of welfare support that have emerged to deal with the needs of particular groups of homeless people. Not only have these emerging networks introduced new ways of responding to homelessness at the local level, the formation, composition and activities of these welfare networks appear remarkably different in our two case-study areas.

Notwithstanding such differences, it is clear that local government has played an important part in steering or governing these informal networks of welfare support. In Gloucestershire, for example, the prominence of local authorities in initiating, funding and coordinating networks of support for young homeless groups has produced a much more extensive range of provision than in Somerset, where local government has been less active. In the former area at least, it would appear that these new arrangements of welfare governance are being established under the 'shadow of hierarchy' (Jessop, 1997b), with local government strategically positioned as the most powerful player. However, this is not to say that these emerging local networks of homelessness support have not been able to challenge traditional local policy constructs of homelessness, and, to some extent, circumvent existing axes of power.

Last, we want to suggest that the activities of these local authorities and new networks of local welfare provision in the case-study counties constitute what Cochrane (1994) has termed local regimes of welfare. Working within an overarching national[4] welfare regime, the operation of these local regimes has resulted in welfare being dealt with in very different ways, reflecting the distinctive nature of local welfare issues and particular localised political and policy structures and processes. These local regimes of welfare also show some similarities to the local regimes of economic development introduced by political scientists in the US; they constitute new informal coalitions which draw on elites from the public and voluntary sectors, in an attempt to work together to achieve particular local policy goals. However, they are clearly different in relation to the types of goals being pursued and the more limited involvement of the private sector. It is also the case that the local regimes of welfare we have described are characterised by a great deal of instability and fragility – in terms of tensions between statutory and voluntary agencies, and the precarious nature of funding arrangements.

Notes

[1] Data were not available for one of these councils.

[2] To protect the anonymity of interviewees, names of these authorities have been replaced by the county name, agency type and number.

[3] Many of whom have relocated to local rural spaces in search of idyllised life-styles which do not include the presence of homeless people in their locality.

[4] By national we mean English, as national regimes of welfare in Wales and Scotland are taking on different forms in the post-devolution era.

SEVEN

Experiencing rural homelessness

Stories

Rick

We interviewed 'Rick' in his house in a west Somerset village quite close to where he had grown up. Back in the 1970s he had spent time in the US ("living in a shack in the mountains") and had participated in a number of squats in London, in one of which he met his partner, 'Daisy'. He did not like London much, so came back to stay at his father's house in Somerset. Subsequently he and Daisy lived in a woodshed in rural Worcestershire, a wooden shelter, a caravan and (briefly) a flat in the Glastonbury area, and a caravan and a remote cottage in rural Devon. He told us:

> "I just like the variety. I like to live quite isolated. I don't like to be overlooked. Like the caravan I lived in, up this track, up this valley, like right out the back of beyond. And it was really wild. It was just magic."

The seeming idealism of his life-style, however, was tempered with other, more difficult, memories:

> "Sometimes I'd spend half the day just getting firewood, like just to keep me warm at night.... Sometimes it was quite desperate as well, you know, sometimes I just wanted company, and some money or something ... the pay-off is that if you are living like kind of, sort of, like 'on-the-edge' sort of way, sometimes the 'on-the-edge' gets back to you."

Rick and Daisy had a daughter, and after they split up they "lived in orbit around each other because of the kid", finally deciding to settle together so that they could co-parent their child through her teenage years. Rick first stayed with friends:

> "So I moved back up (to west Somerset) and lived in [friend's] – a little
> room above [friend's] kitchen, like a store room. It hasn't even got a
> staircase to it, you have to climb up through a ladder into the ceiling."

Then he briefly moved into a house in the village, but he "fell out with
the bloke that was living there" and when Daisy and his daughter returned
from travelling, they once again shared with friends, until they finally
found a house of their own. Their search was a hard one:

> "We saw several places, but we had a lot of difficulty, bizarre little things
> like agents who said they had a nice house, and when you went round
> it was rubbish. Or agents who took us to a house and it was obvious as
> soon as we turned up that the landlord and landlady were completely
> horrified by the way we looked."

Finally they managed to rent a house from the cousin of one of Rick's
best friends. Rick currently works as a carpenter so is able to pay the
necessary bills. However, he fears for the future. He sees himself as 'local
Somerset boy' in danger of being priced out of rented housing markets:

> "What took me by surprise was the price and everything. Because all
> of a sudden I realised I couldn't afford it. I mean at one time, you could
> get places dead easy round here, you know. If you looked in the free
> press, you'd find somewhere. A cottage, you know, or whatever. Nice
> places. You know, the places were wonderful – and you could get them
> easy, but not any more."

Laura

We interviewed 'Laura' in a young people's housing project in
Gloucestershire. She grew up in a north Gloucestershire village, but in
her words she "didn't get on at home":

> "I fell out with my brothers and sisters and I got a bit moody, then I got
> violent towards my brothers and sisters."

Laura shared her house with her mother and her step-father and six
brothers and sisters, including a half-brother and half-sister, whom she
regarded as receiving constant favouritism in the household. In a series
of family rows, she tried to leave home several times, before finally moving
in temporarily with a friend:

"I didn't want to get violent, but I did. My mum used to say 'Oh fuck off somewhere' and I would, and then she'd ring me at my mate's house and tell me to go back. She did that a couple of times, and then I left and I lived at my friend's for a month. But they were finding it hard to pay for stuff for me as well, so I moved in here."

Laura is now 16 and is setting about the task of finding work, and also trying to establish relationships with other tenants.

Sally

'Sally' lives in a Somerset village. She was a medical student in Bristol, but after a serious accident and a series of operations, she decided to move to the village to recuperate. The move was prompted by the fact that her erstwhile boyfriend lived in the area, but on arrival she encountered a shattering change in her circumstances:

"I came here and unfortunately he'd started a relationship with somebody else whilst I was in hospital, and I didn't know about it. We'd been going out together about eight years.... He didn't like it when I was here because it was making life difficult for him."

Sally's plight was exacerbated by her mother being in Australia, and she had no other family to turn to. So she stayed in the village:

"I went into bed and breakfast, and they closed it down four weeks after I got there. So I ended up going into a small hotel that was opposite, which was in receivership, and I stayed there nearly a year. But I was sold with the property and the new landlord didn't want me to stay there, and he made life very difficult ... he decided to put my rent up by £21 per day."

Sally had to move out and in her words "beg and plead" to the people who ran another little hotel in the village, and they gave her a room which was awaiting refurbishment:

"There was a window missing in the bathroom, there was no heating, there were holes all over the carpets, the sheets didn't fit the beds ... I was sick for three weeks out of the six I was there. It was appalling. Then they just said, look sorry, we've got round to your room now and you'll have to go, or pay the going rate."

There being no other options, particularly since Sally's accident left her with considerably reduced mobility, she had to leave and try to find another place. Not only was there nothing available, but she experienced continuous problems in obtaining Housing or Mobility Benefit. So she had to accept the only available option, which by most definitions represented unfit accommodation – a derelict flat above a garage that hadn't been lived in for at least four years:

> "It was falling to pieces – in a terrible state. When I got there, there was nothing. They'd slapped a bit of paint round but it still had no hot water, no heating, no cooking facilities."

A local friend took one look at the accommodation, suggested that "I wouldn't let my dog stay in here overnight", and took Sally into her home for three weeks. But Sally could not get benefit because she had not taken up residence in the flat and was not paying rent. So she had to return to the unfit housing. Finally, she received Housing Benefit and Disability Living Allowance and that enabled her to move out to a better, but by no means salubrious small cottage, in which she has no security of tenure. Her assessment of her chances of local authority housing leads her not to try:

> "I would get some priority, but I wouldn't get as much priority as somebody who was perhaps slightly less disabled but had a child or a husband out of work maybe. So at the moment I mean my best situation is to stay where I am."

With more surgery in prospect, Sally is really worried that she could lose her accommodation at any time, leaving her with nowhere to go. However, given all of her experiences, she resists the idea that she has experienced homelessness:

> "Once you've been classed as homeless, that gets out and people find that out, and then that makes a difference long after your circumstances have changed, because people *perceive* homeless people to be somebody quite different – usually they are the sort of people you see in the streets in Bath – they're not like me."

Peter

We interviewed 'Peter' in a hostel in a small Somerset coastal town. He grew up in south Somerset, but left home at the age of 16 because in his words "me and me step-mum weren't getting on". He has been homeless on eight or nine separate occasions – in London, in Scotland, in the South-West of England. Being homeless seems to have consisted of two spatially diverse sets of practices. First, he has on many occasions slept on the city streets:

> "All I've got is a pair of trainers, a pair of socks, trousers, underpants and a shirt and jacket, and that's it. I've got no money, I've got no fags, I've got nothing, and I've had to turn to crime so I can feed myself. It's been very hard, and then I got among the wrong people and started to take heroin, and I was going out doing crime to feed my habit, and it got to a stage when I was taking £300 per day."

Peter's urban life-style led to several periods of imprisonment. However, his life history is also punctuated with periods of sleeping rough in the countryside:

> "Living off the streets you are just trying to stay alive until the next day, but in the country it's quite easy ... because I went poaching. I didn't have to go out and rob ... I was sleeping in a hay barn, under a hedge or under the stars."

Peter's training during a short sojourn in the Navy taught him basic survival skills, including how to camouflage himself to become 'invisible' in the countryside (see Chapter Three). This enabled him to spend periods of six months or so sleeping rough in rural areas, usually during the spring and summer. However, at the end of the summer he found himself drawn back into city life:

> "Winter was coming, it was raining, and I was walking up this road, and this girl stopped and picked me up ... and she took me back to her place and me and her hit it off. And then I went to jail and came out, and I was homeless again, and then went back into jail again ... just for stupid things like shoplifting, breaking into shops for clothes or breaking into shops for food."

A break to this spiralling pattern of existence came when Peter met someone in prison who around the time of his divorce befriended him. Peter's friend offered to meet him on his release and help him start a fresh life where he lived; he put him up for 13 weeks and then found him a place in the current hostel. Peter is proud to have kicked his drug habit, and is looking forward to 'making the best' of his life.

These four stories, representing a small sample of the 100 or so encounters we had with homeless people during our research, demonstrate the complexity of rural homelessness. Rick, Laura, Sally and Peter have each experienced periods of homelessness in a rural setting, but for a wide variety of reasons and in a wide variety of circumstances. Rick's transient life-style involved a constant shifting from one form of temporary accommodation to another. His travelling instincts make him difficult to pin down in terms of formal homeless identity. Laura's teenage life in a village is disturbed by the aftermath of family break-up. She turns to rural 'sofa-surfing', and then finds help in an urban housing project. Sally has tenuous local connections, but the lack of obvious kith or kin networks mean that she becomes stranded in rural Somerset because of her medical circumstances. Here she encounters common traps in the benefit system and rented housing sector, but in a particular rural setting. Peter spends some summers sleeping rough in the countryside. His capacity to lead a relatively invisible life-style is in stark contrast to his city street experiences, which lead to different crimes and subsequent imprisonment. His 'new life', however, suggests a different form of 'settling' in the countryside.

To the world outside, Rick, Laura, Sally and Peter may not seem like homeless people, as each is discursively scattered into somehow more acceptable, if stereotypical identity categories: the traveller; the young person leaving home; the medical case with a housing need; and the drug abuser. Indeed, the individuals themselves (particularly in this case Sally) may not want to be recognised as homeless, because of the knock-on impacts of how they are viewed thereafter by members of the local community, and by financial managers who can use such status as a reason to blacklist for credit. This process of discursive scattering works to deny the issue which interconnects the complex and shifting circumstances of people like Rick, Laura, Sally and Peter – that of homelessness. We would certainly not argue here for an artificial lumping together of all possible situations so as to inflate the significance of homelessness. Rather, we suggest that it is important not to allow rhetorical discourses of the problematics in rural areas to effect a denial of homelessness as an issue.

Circumstances

In building up a picture of rural homelessness, it is important to recognise at the outset that many of the experiences of homeless people in rural areas occur as a response to what are largely aspatial circumstances. We suggested in Chapter One that homelessness is often associated with crises associated with loss of work and income, with breakdown of relationships, with processes of de-institutionalisation, and with the often disastrous cocktail of benefit traps and shortage of affordable accommodation. Our encounters with homeless people in rural areas reinforce the importance of these issues. Naturally some of our interviewees were unwilling to divulge sensitive and hurtful passages of their life histories even to interviewers who had got to know them over a period of months. Many others, however, were extremely ready to tell their story, a readiness we attribute in part to the fact that homeless people who are 'in the system' are more or less required to 'tell their story' to any number of public and voluntary managers dealing with benefits, housing, health and counselling. Homeless people are therefore familiar with requirements or requests to lay bare the circumstances of their 'problems'. In addition to this potentially mechanical process of storytelling, however, we believe that many homeless people carry with them the everyday emotional or situational scars of these circumstances, regardless of how recently they have occurred. It is little wonder, then, that the hurts of these scars often emerge very readily in the conversations of research encounters. In this context we would highlight four common sets of circumstances which were strongly represented by the homeless people we encountered.

First, there was very significant evidence of family breakdown, which the manager of one youth housing project in our study area regarded as 'the main cause of youth homelessness'. The disintegration of family relationships not only represents an often crucial prompt to 'leave home', but it also renders the home-leaver bereft of crucial support networks. Our research suggests that rural areas are by no means immune from family breakdowns, despite the cultural constructions of rural idyll which present the countryside as an ideal and safe place to bring up children and to enjoy family life. Laura's story already indicates the potential risk to some young people of radical reorganisation of parental relationships, and this is a story which was repeated in the lives of many of the homeless people we spoke to. For example, 'Adam' was 18 when we interviewed him in a Somerset hostel. He left his village home at 16:

"Well it wasn't a choice. It was more of a mutual decision. Mum didn't want me there. I was getting into a lot of trouble ... I just started getting into drugs and stuff and lost it, just went off the rails.... My step-dad was a tosser. He was – the thing that pissed me off more than anything was that he never shouted. He was just quiet. We never had a conversation. We never said anything at all. The only person he would talk to is *his son*...."

For Laura and Adam, relational breakdown led them to stay with friends, and then into more problematic searches for somewhere to live. Such fault-lines of crisis are by no means, however, restricted to young people. 'Charles' is a retired man who until recently lived in rural Somerset and ran a successful business. Then his wife died, and he moved into a flat:

"I stayed there about a year but wasn't happy there. And then my son was talking about moving into another house, and I suggested to him that if he bought a house with a bedroom and a sitting room for me, you know, I would give him my share of the business. So I gave up my flat, to live with them."

Charles' son then suffered a serious stroke, and the business collapsed as a result:

"Because of this ... his income wouldn't pay the mortgage and all the endowment policies he had ... so he had no option but to go for a smaller house with lower costs. So of course, this put me in the position of being homeless ... I couldn't come on to him for any money back or anything back that I'd loaned him, because of the simple fact that he hasn't got it."

Charles sought help from the local authority, but they were unable to give him immediate priority, and so he found himself in emergency halfway house accommodation, living to some extent communally with people with whom he feels he has little in common.

Some of the most serious consequences of relationship breakdown are often hidden from view, especially in rural areas. Domestic violence seems often to be tolerated in order to maintain pretence of normality, but ultimately can lead to tragic circumstances of distress and upheaval for women and children. 'Angela's' experiences, in her village home, represent an extremely serious aspect of causality in rural homelessness:

"To start with he was brilliant. Then he started working and that is when the grief started, he'd go out drinking. If he'd had a really bad day at work that was it, we were in for it when he got home. It got to the stage where I was putting the kids to bed before he got home at eight in the evening. It got to the stage when we just couldn't cope with it. I called the police out...."

Angela found her way to a city-based women's refuge, as very few such facilities exist in rural areas. However, her partner continued to harass her, so she moved again on several occasions, and has ended up in bed and breakfast accommodation in our study area.

A second strand of causal circumstances of rural homelessness relates to de-institutionalisation. It is sometimes assumed that because many of the institutions concerned – prisons, army bases, psychiatric centres and care homes, for example – are usually sited in urban locations, it follows that the issues of homelessness attendant on release from these institutions are contained within urban settings. Such assumptions are simplistic. As 'Peter's' story suggests, life after prison, for example, may well involve periods of homelessness in a rural area. Another of our interviewees, 'Elsa', was about to be released from a psychiatric ward, where she was attempting to overcome problems of alcohol addiction. 'Elsa' had previously slept rough, and stayed in various B&Bs, but she had been frequently robbed, and had considerable fears about where she would end up after leaving hospital. Having left an abusive relationship with her alcoholic, violent ex-husband, she wanted to find a place well away from groups of men, and was worried that if placed in unsuitable accommodation, she would not be able to receive visits from her three children. People in vulnerable circumstances such as Elsa's tend to get trapped into cycles of recovery and relapse, and such cycles extend beyond urban limits into seemingly idyllic rural communities.

Another of our research encounters was with 'Kevin', whose early years were dramatically shaped by being taken into care. Kevin is currently part of a youth housing project in Gloucestershire, but had previously experienced rooflessness in a number of different locations. Throughout our interview he referred back to the fact that he had been in care. This aspect of his past was offered as the reason why he had been homeless, and why he is unsuccessful in finding settled accommodation. His account of his current life was structured around how the past comes flooding back into how he feels and how he is treated, and that this past is clearly characterised by an overwhelming sense of rejection. Emergence from care into an uncertain and unsettled way of life clearly impacts on rural areas as well as larger urban centres.

Kevin's position clearly represents a mix of the impacts of de-institutionalisation, and such personal crises form a third strand of causal circumstances associated with rural homelessness. Depression, and other forms of not being able to cope, are common features in the experience of being homeless in rural areas. So too are addictions to alcohol and other drugs. Again, the stereotype of urban rooflessness often highlights such addictions – on-street encounters with homeless people in the city will often suggest evidence of Special Brew or cider as part of the scene. We met 'Dave' and 'Suzy' in a small Gloucestershire town; both had recently become tenants in a youth housing scheme. Dave had just been placed on probation after a court case, a condition of which was that he attends alcohol counselling. He suggests that he does not have a drinking problem – it is other people who have a problem with his drinking. Suzy who is 16 tells us that he drinks the strongest beer he can find, and has at least four cans a day if he can get the money. Despite the fact that she is in a relationship with Dave, she is willing to share with us that she is scared by the consequences of his drinking. Many of our respondents have talked freely of the role of alcohol and drugs in their life, their attitudes varying according to whether such substances were 'fun', 'necessary for coping' or 'something to be conquered if I am to get out of this mess'. Personal addiction is undoubtedly part of the moral construction placed on homelessness by the discourses of wider society. Our research strongly suggests that addiction is just as much a part of the experience of some rural homeless people, as it is in urban locations.

The final set of circumstances found to shape the experience of homelessness in rural areas can be summarised as life-style circumstances. Here, our interviewees pointed to key mechanisms associated with employment, housing, and life choices that placed them at risk of being homeless in rural settings. For example, our study area in Somerset includes the town of Minehead where a substantial Butlins holiday centre is located. Butlins acts as a magnet for people seeking work and who are at risk of becoming homeless in the locality if they fail to get a job, or if the job does not last. As the manager of the local community information bureau told us:

> "People come to Butlins thinking there is a job ... they hitch-hike down there ... and that's a whole category of homeless people that we get. People will hang around here and find a floor to sleep on and try to get themselves established down here."

The proximity to Glastonbury is equally magnetic, in this case to people in and around the traveller scene. As Garry explains:

> "It's because it's starting the summer, and you've got your summer solstice as well, where everybody meets up around Pilton and Glastonbury. It's like birds really, they all flock towards a certain area and meet up. And it's just like old friends. You meet up and talk about where you've been...."

These local congregations of travellers inevitably lead to localised experiences of homelessness, as some people decide to 'settle' in the area. For example, 'Heather' told us of her experiences as a traveller. She left home at 14 and had been on the road for 28 years, but finally she was forced to seek localised accommodation because of a threat to take her daughter into care:

> "But because I lived on a bus – I put her into school because I thought every kid ought to have every opportunity.... And they found that a little bit difficult to accept. And in the end they brought social services in and they said they didn't think it was right the way _____ [her daughter] was living."

Heather moved into a council flat, and although her daughter was taken into care, the flat ensured that she could visit. Heather divided her time between the flat (which she kept for appearances so that she could still have visits) and her bus. Finally, she joined a squat in a local market town and was sleeping rough when we interviewed her.

The nature of our Somerset area is also characterised by specific forms of housing – a range of holiday caravans and chalets in coastal and moorland areas, and a bottom rung of the rented housing sector which consists of rundown cottages belonging to former regimes of the agricultural economy. In both cases, the experience of homelessness in the area can be characterised by housing vulnerability. People renting holiday accommodation out of season often embark on circuits of short-term and uncertain tenancies. Those forced by lack of income to rent at the cheapest end of the market often encounter unfit housing conditions. We spoke to 'Mrs Clark' who lives in one such place:

> "There's no windows at the back of the house at all ... half the house is under the hill ... the walls are really really damp.... I get mould all over my clothes ... they get ruined ... upstairs the walls are black. There's an

electric heater, but that's too expensive to run…. At this time of year I just can't sleep upstairs – it's too cold and damp."

As with Sally's story, Mrs Clark's experiences of unsatisfactory accommodation, and the problems of ill health and vulnerability that follow, are fundamental aspects of living in, or on the edge of, homelessness. When we interviewed her, Mrs Clark was not being given priority for rehousing from the local authority, and saw no other option but to 'stick it out' in clearly unfit housing conditions.

Single and family homelessness

The causal circumstances discussed above suggest the kinds of crises which people face in rural areas when experiencing homelessness. The complexity of these experiences renders generalisation problematic and sometimes even unhelpful. But it is possible to interpret particular strands of rural homelessness running through these experiences. First, there is clear evidence of single homelessness in rural areas. Managers of hostel and advice projects in our Somerset study area suggested to us:

"… there's single homelessness – nobody provides housing for single people, so a single person wanting a permanent place to live probably won't find one. So you end up with people sharing.…"

"Rural accommodation is very difficult – there just isn't much of anything when you're looking for a house, and you may find none of them at all will take people on Housing Benefit."

"Single people are not often roofless unless they choose to be – it's easier for a single person to 'solve' the problem, ie doss down on a mate's floor."

"We get people who've been staying on friends' floors … either they haven't got a home to go to or they don't get on with their parents; or their parents want to move and they don't want to go and if they're over 16 they stay here."

The impression given here is that single homelessness affects young local people, especially those without benefits, but also those on benefit. This latter aspect was emphasised to us by 'Stu' who showed us the 'Property to let' column in his local newspaper and read out "no DSS, no DSS, no pets, no DSS. Nearly everything you look at is no DSS". However, during the course of our interviews we have found evidence to suggest at least two other broad types of single homelessness in rural areas. First, the single homeless are not all young people. Perhaps because local projects focus on youth unemployment they underemphasise single homelessness experienced by older people. Stu himself is 44 and used to live in a local authority property with his partner and child. He was compelled by court order to vacate the property, and with no employment or savings, he faced the same difficulties as younger people in finding a place to rent. Stu and Charles (see earlier) represent a rather different set of experiences of homelessness later on in life.

Second, there is some evidence of rural rooflessness, although whether this is 'by choice' is a matter for considerable debate. At least 10 of the homeless people we interviewed had slept rough in rural areas at some point. We reviewed Peter's story at the beginning of this chapter, but others too have been forced to/chosen to endure rural rough sleeping, albeit usually during the warmer summer months. Barns, sheds, woods and hedgerows are the most commonly reported sleeping places, although in the particular circumstances of Minehead, it was reported to us that:

> "The cleaner and his colleague goes and cleans the shelters along the sea front, all the shelters early in the morning, and couldn't get in there to clean them because there were people sleeping in them, young people and old people."

These moments of visibility, either in interviews or more anecdotally, serve to provide glimpses of what is often by nature a series of invisible practices of isolated rural rough sleeping.

Non-single homelessness also occurs in rural areas. Here, people tend to be on Housing Benefit, and find that even when they can overcome the barriers of 'no DSS', the rent required is more than the benefit received. Also, the types of properties available are often not suitable; a house with three bedrooms and two downstairs rooms will incur a Housing Benefit penalty (around £15 in 1998) because there are too many rooms. Families will sometimes approach the local authority for housing, but may well be put off by the prospect of living for a year in a bed and breakfast place while waiting for less temporary placements. The options in these circumstances are limited: find the extra money from somewhere; find a way of 'adding points' to your local authority priority; or move either to a cheaper area or to unsatisfactory or vulnerable housing.

It is interesting to question whether there are geographies of gender in these experiences of homelessness. Certainly we have encountered a significant number of women – at least one third of our interviewees – who have experience of homelessness in rural areas. There are a number of clear first-hand examples of under-18 girls leaving difficult domestic relationships and 'sofa-surfing' in their locality. A local advice centre manager told us:

> "I know a girl in _____ (I live in _____) who wouldn't live with her parents, and social services wouldn't help and told her to go home, and she wouldn't, so she ended up just going from one friend to another. She found people to stay with until she became 18, and then moved on. It means a lot of moving around though from room to room within a community."

Equally, as is evident from the foregoing account, there is strong evidence that women are suffering forms of homelessness associated with unfit and vulnerable housing in rural areas, in addition to the incidences of domestic violence which are overwhelmingly inflicted by men on women, and which can lead to homelessness. However, we have found no evidence of women rough sleeping in rural areas, other than participation in town-based squats, and voluntary involvement in travelling, which predominantly would not be regarded by the people concerned as homelessness. Housing-related professionals and volunteers regularly explained these gendered phenomena to us in terms of two sets of processes. First, women with children, and to a lesser extent single women, are afforded higher priority status than men when presenting themselves to a local authority for housing, though this is not universally so. Second, in the experience of these professionals and volunteers, women have a greater propensity than men to deal with their problems. As one Children's Society worker suggested:

> "Women I think tend to spend longer trying to find their own solutions. With traveller women particularly there is a definite sense that this is them sorting out their lives. Generally, women see themselves very much in control, more so than many of the men."

These interesting observations should again not be regarded as all-encompassing, and certainly should not be used to underestimate the problems faced by many rural women, but they do begin to forge some understanding of the gendered differences in the experience of homelessness in rural areas.

Dimensions of experience

Experiences of homelessness should not be interpreted merely in terms of the circumstances discussed in the previous section. Yes, these circumstances reflect a sense of crisis, loss and emotional turmoil. They also convey the embodied experience of, say, living in utterly damp conditions, sleeping rough in the countryside, or surfing from spare room to spare room while waiting for a new home. There are, however, axes of moral coding which overlie these experiences, and which are active in processes of making homeless people *knowable*, both to each other and within wider community discourses. This process of making people known vacillates (as K. Hetherington, 2000, suggests) between under-determining and over-determining within the public imagination. Where the experiences of homeless people are hidden, such people represent a shadowy and uncertain absence in the collective consciousness and cultural politics of rural people. Where homeless people – usually discursively categorised as something other than homeless – become visible to the public view, they represent an over-determined, often caricatured and sometimes vilified presence in both consciousness and politics. This interaction between under- and over-determination does not presuppose a fixed or pre-established moral map of rural order. The out-of-placeness of homeless people and the purification of rural space are both fluid. The endless series of beginnings of representation of social space and social order will be different in different places. However, both the hiddenness of under-determination and the visible presence of over-determination are likely to conspire against any discursive categorisation of 'rural homelessness'.

In this section we discuss briefly three such axes of moral coding which serve as key distinctions in the appreciation of rural homelessness.

Local/in-migrant

Local people in rural areas will, as this chapter has demonstrated, often have experienced a personal, family, financial or medical crisis which means that they are no longer able to, or cannot afford to, stay in their previous home. In some cases, rural people will 'make do' with what may be an unacceptable set of circumstances. A local representative of the Children's Society suggested that "rural young people will actually tolerate more, and put up with more difficulty in (I hesitate to say it because it has other connotations), 'not a good family environment', because of the lack of available options". Other people are forced to stay in unfit housing, even though doing so poses a threat to their safety or health. Where 'sticking it out' is not an option, the first step for some was to go to the local authority for help. For others it was not considered worthwhile doing that because it was perceived that either the authority did not have any stock to offer, or what was on offer would be 'miles away' from home. Such impressions, whether correct or not (and many were generally confirmed to us by local homelessness officers), reproduce local cultural constructions of the futility of applying to the local authority unless conforming to a certain stereotyped pattern of need.

For those who have to move out, housing options are usually few – bed and breakfast, a room somewhere, an unfit flat above a garage, a temporary billet on a friend's floor, a caravan, a tent. People fortunate enough to find accommodation of reasonable quality will often experience a rent trap. Many of our respondents were state beneficiaries for whom single room allowances and rent assessments meant that Housing Benefit did not cover the cost of the accommodation and this rent-benefit trap caused them to leave for more inexpensive and temporary accommodation, often several times within their life histories. Such people will tend to move in and out of homelessness, with the less fortunate trapped into a downward spiral ending in more permanent homelessness. If life crises are seen to be caused by external factors, then such homelessness among local people can be viewed as deserving by a local community that will rally round. Others, however, are regarded as undeserving, and responsible for their own demise.

Homelessness in rural areas also involves non-local people, and homelessness among non-local people was perceived locally as almost entirely undeserving. Some rural areas do attract work-seekers, or people simply attracted to the environment and associated life-style, who subsequently encounter problems of homelessness. These non-locals are often vilified in local representations of homelessness. Our research in and around Taunton (see Cloke et al, 2000a) traced the discourses used by local politicians reported in local newspapers to discern the moral code-lines being surveyed in public debates on homelessness. One dominant theme concerned 'outsiders' coming to Taunton to scrounge from local people. Such in-migration was painted as morally indefensible, as if to suggest that it was out of the question that residents and taxpayers of Taunton should be asked to deal with a problem that was 'not their own'. Such protestations would perhaps have seemed less empty if greater efforts had been apparent to deal with the needs of local homeless people!

Vilification of outsiders was also in evidence in our interviews with local homeless people. Thus Charles complains that:

"Someone can come down here from Birmingham or from Liverpool or Newcastle and get housed almost immediately."

And Mrs Clark suggests that:

"One of the problems about the girls that come down to Butlins, and they have a good time, and they have too much to drink and they get themselves pregnant, and then just dump themselves on the local council. The problem is that they've got more priority than any of us ... the locals are the last priority for the council."

Regardless of the truth or otherwise of these claims, they figure consistently in the perceived experiences of many local homeless people. The moral suspicion of outsiders even extended to those homeless people who were more likely to be rough sleeping periodically. Jim is a long-term rough-sleeper in Taunton, and in our interview he was very concerned to tell us about another rough-sleeper 'Scouse' from Liverpool:

"The general feeling is that Scouse needs sorting. He's been bullying and intimidating. He thought he could get away with it in a country town, coming here to shit on people, but he's just got other people's backs up."

Jim's emphasis on Scouse's status as an *outsider* from Liverpool, operating differently from the perceived codes and norms of homeless people in a *country town* re-emphasises the importance of local/non-local as an axis of moral representation.

Settled/passing through

As we discussed in Chapter One, cultural constructions of idyllic rural life often focus on the importance of the settled home as an axiomatic indicator of rural community and rural living. Any form of homelessness will transgress these cultural assumptions to some extent, although it is possible to regard some homeless people as in the process of becoming settled, while others display stronger markers of restlessness and transience. The distinction between 'settled' and 'passing through' is therefore at one and the same time of great significance in the moral coding of homeless people, and an uneasy differentiation in that many of the homeless people we interviewed lived in such a way as to iterate frequently between settling and moving on.

In our encounters with homeless people, we recognised many different facets of being 'unsettled' that refer both to 'settling' and to 'passing through'. For example, both 'Sonya' and 'Kirsty' were able to convey the unsettling restlessness both within shared accommodation and in the moves between different houses. Kirsty's story is typical:

> "I was living in a one-bedroom flat in _____ [a Somerset village], it was damp and everything. I worked at Butlins, but they shut down for three weeks every year, so I went on the dole for three weeks ... my claim [for Housing Benefit] was then treated as a new claim, and cut to £40 ... so I could no longer afford my rent there ... I stayed until March, but I couldn't afford to live there any more. I moved because it was stressing me out. And all I could do was to move into a bedsit, but from there I got made homeless. The landlady sold the house and they gave us notice to leave [Kirsty goes to stay with a friend in another let, but this property too is sold]. From there on, the council put me in this hostel."

Kirsty's wish to stay 'settled' means that she 'passes through' four different places in a short period of time, ending up in hostel accommodation. Similarly, Sonya talks about how settling down actually means moving around:

> "At the first house I was there from May last year to December, it was a nice house, the landlord was okay ... but it got a bit too untidy in the end and we had someone try to break in once. We had a girl there whose boyfriend was into drugs and things, and he stole our payphone twice. Then we had a lot of trouble, and it got into a mess there, so I decided to leave."

This pattern is then repeated in Sonya's story:

> "So they found me another house in _____, it was in the middle of nowhere ... it all went well for a month or two. The landlord tried to make it a home for us, but things [pictures, vases] went missing and they found [one of the residents] trying to sell them to antiques dealers.... Then the others started having parties like at two in the morning, and trying to break into other people's bedrooms ... I moved out in April."

Sonya was eventually housed by the local authority, and has a job nearby. Her struggle to settle might be seen to conform with the expectations of rural life, but restless shifting from accommodation to accommodation may well be interpreted by people around her as an inability to settle, even though (according to her account) the housing uncertainties were not of her making.

Other people we interviewed suggested that periods of being homeless (including those in rural areas) were much more associated with a deep-seated sense of restlessness. 'Heather's' account illustrates this phenomenon, connecting sojourns and journeys in the countryside into a wider account of an emotional aversion to 'settling':

"I left home when I was 14. And I enjoyed it … I couldn't settle. I can settle for a couple of months and then I've got to go again. Even if it's moving from one bedsit to another, to another. There's nothing like thinking 'I need to change my view'. So you fire up the engine and you drive and you wake up next morning and you've got another view, you know? And in the countryside there's wooding, there's logging. You know, there's always work, farm work. There's always picking of some sort. You know. You don't have to sign on."

Interestingly, Heather's 'needing to change her view' is interconnected with an enjoyment of the countryside, and an ability to cope within it. For 'Dan', the emotional freedom of a life without financial concerns and responsibilities has prompted a 'doing what your heart tells you to do' which has resulted in periods of homelessness in rural Somerset:

"I'm happy without it. If I wake up skint in the morning, as long as I've got … the dogs are fed and that, that's it … I mean, at the end of the day you're all going to die anyway. I mean, why work your bollocks off? I dunno, be happy. Travel. Do what your heart tells you to do."

These aspects of an itinerant life-style are by no means novel, but in the rural context they allow us to begin to develop a picture of the importance of different forms of mobility in a wider understanding of homelessness in rural areas. There are those, such as Kirsty and Sonya, whose wish to be settled is problematised by a shifting series of places to live. And there are others, such as Heather and Dan, who, for periods of their life, will always be 'passing through' a particular rural area. During our interviews, for example, we heard from homeless people for whom rural Somerset was but a stopping-off point on a bigger journey. For 'Garry' and others, it is the place they stay "three or four times a year". Sometimes such stays are a planned *circuit* – a deliberate moving from place to place, mixing rural and urban experiences. Sometimes it is more random – "half the time I just put my thumb out – where are you going?". At other times a short period of homelessness in a particular rural place is a result of 'visits' to friends and family, as with 'Olly', whom we met during a two-night period of rough sleeping and who was "just passing through to check up on a mate who's not well". We discuss the complexities of mobilities underlying rural homelessness in the next section.

Visible/invisible

In Chapter Three we argued that there are morphological and socio-cultural reasons why people experiencing varying forms of homelessness in rural areas will tend to remain 'invisible'. Rural homelessness becomes visible when people decide that they may elicit a positive response from local authorities or advice agencies, or when some external factor can be blamed for their crisis. However, local people who are in crisis may well be regarded by the community around them as undeserving, and will thus attempt to hide the crisis from local gossip, or will move away to another place (often an urban location) to escape the visibility that their crisis would bestow on them. A local advice worker emphasised to us: "I think they're all hidden actually – they're staying with friends or relations or people they've met, or else they're in accommodation they can't afford to live in … or that's unfit to live in". Moreover, those living in mobile or temporary accommodation seem often to locate themselves in lonely sites, out of sight of centres of population (see Chapter Three). These forms of homelessness are therefore also hidden, often invisible both to generalised public and political discourses, and to the imaginings of local rural people about social problems that require action. As Peter's story (quoted at length in Chapter Three) suggests, homeless people who sleep rough in rural areas engage in specific tactics of invisibility. Interviewees provided us with details of how to live and move about in the open country incognito, involving wearing camouflaged clothing, poaching food, careful cleaning away of cooking fires, using isolated paths and buildings and so on.

One further way by which homelessness is rendered invisible is wrapped up in the tendency to deny that any of the cases and situations described in this chapter actually constitute homelessness. Many rural people who would be defined normatively as homeless do not accept that label for themselves. As one local advice worker in rural Somerset discussed:

"The difficulty is identifying people who will define themselves as being homeless. I mean, most people have an image of what it means to be homeless, and that means sleeping in a cardboard box. So you get people saying 'Oh no, I'm not homeless'. So you say 'Where are you living?' And they say, 'Oh, I'm staying with a friend'. They are clearly homeless but don't actually identify themselves.... People living in caravans or tents didn't want to be identified. They wanted to blend in, really, and not be spotted."

Many of our interviewees, especially those contacted outside of formal facilities for homeless people, or who were encountered in advice centre case files, did not want to be identified as homeless. To do so would be to stand out as visibly unable to sort out their own problems, and as having lost control over their life. This elective invisibility through refusing the label of homelessness occurred throughout the spectrum of people interviewed, and adds significantly to the hidden nature of homelessness in rural areas.

Conclusion

Each of the distinctions discussed here – local/in-migrant, settled/passing through and visible/invisible – contributes to the degree to which homelessness is made knowable in rural areas. The question of visibility is crucial. By staying hidden, homeless people become a shadowy absence in the cultural politics of rural people, something to be denied or coped with under different discursive headings. In fact, most of the 'coping with' is thereby thrown back onto the individual(s) concerned. Where homelessness becomes visible, people are again discursively categorised not as homeless, but as 'leaving home' or 'in housing need'. In the market towns, where the first spatial signs of on-street homelessness appear in a rural region, the visibility of homeless people becomes exaggerated in the public consciousness.

In these different situations of visibility, being 'local' or being 'settled' can be regarded as positive moral indicators in rural society, although this is by no means always the case, and as the preceding discussion demonstrates, the ideas of 'local' and 'settled' are complex and constantly in flux. Being local and showing signs of wanting to be settled offers a conformity to cultural doxa which *may* lead to a sympathetic acceptance of a homeless person's 'deserving' nature. Often, however, the crisis leading to homelessness will involve other local people – partners, parents, landlord, employer and so on – who will also be representing themselves in moral terms within the local community, a process which can reinforce the otherness of the homeless person concerned. Being non-local and unsettled predominately equates with 'undeserving'. Local discourse deems to 'know' such people as outsiders, coming into *our* area and scrounging what is not theirs, even to the extent of jumping over *local* people in the benefit and housing queues. This perceived moral contamination prompts the re-purification of rural space and thereby further overshadows the needs of less visible and what might be regarded by local people as more 'deserving' cases.

EIGHT

Tackling rural homelessness: the way ahead

Rural homelessness and policy

We began this book by arguing that the very invisibility of rural homelessness constitutes the principal barrier to effective policy responses. In most public and policy discourses rural homelessness is a mysterious concept – for some unknown, for others unbelievable, for most incompatible with what they know and believe about rural living. Our contention was that without appropriate encounters with the needs of homeless people in rural areas, and indeed with homeless people themselves, the mystery of rural homelessness will continue, to the detriment of the individuals and families who find themselves in circumstances of being homeless. Our survey of local authority homelessness officers in rural areas gave grounds for pessimism in this respect. The story we were repeatedly told was that local authorities in rural areas struggle to present informed discourses of the scale and scope of homelessness within their jurisdiction, let alone generate innovative policy responses. Given that local authorities are given considerable latitude in determining how to prioritise particular individuals and households within statutory definitions of homelessness, such struggles point to very significant policy issues for rural homelessness.

In Chapter Three we developed a series of ideas about why homelessness is so invisible in rural areas, focusing first on socio-cultural constructions of rurality itself. Here we argued that rurality is subject to popular imaginings which are often dominated by notions of idyllised places and life-styles, in which the benefits of close-knit community and environmental quality are intimately bound up with traditional moral values which emphasise the naturalised importance of home and settlement. Against this background, homelessness becomes dysfunctional – a series of out-of-place people and practices which cannot be envisaged as part of the idyll. Inability to envisage can lead to passive invisibility, but it can also lead to a more active purification of rural space through

191

diverse political and cultural means that together deny the coupling together of rurality and homelessness in rural areas. The silence on rural homelessness in rural policy is deafening. As a result, those wishing to see innovative policy responses to rural homelessness recognise the need for a considerable shift in the ways in which these notions of spatiality and social problems are combined in the hearts and minds of rural people, and in the actions of policy makers.

Such a shift seems a long way off. As discussed in Chapter Four, the wider policy context within which homelessness is being tackled is itself urban-centric and thereby represents a contributor to the invisibility of *rural* homelessness. There are, however, a number of broader-scale issues in this policy context which seem to us to have peculiarly 'rural' effects. For example, much of the effectiveness of responses to homelessness depends on the adequacy of accommodation available for the rehousing of homeless households. Adequacy here refers to the quality and type of accommodation and to its location. In rural areas, the shrinkage of affordable housing stocks has been well documented. Equally significant, however, are the localised geographies of housing in rural areas. As we found in Chapter Six with the examples of Cotswold and Forest of Dean districts, a lack of suitable accommodation in rural areas invariably necessitates the shift of homeless individuals and households in these areas to an urban location, sometimes as far as 30 miles away. The impact of such displacements is arguably exaggerated in rural areas where notions of home, belonging, local roots and familiarity of environment can be very localised compared to the city.

Throughout this book, we have sought to recognise the dramatic restructuring of homelessness policy and practice that has been brought about by the 1996 Housing Act and looks set to be augmented through the current (2001) Homelessness Bill. For example, the Bill responds to previous calls for local authorities to take a more progressive approach in tackling youth homelessness. Not only does the Bill offer greater protection for young people from becoming homeless, but for the first time local authorities will be required to adopt a more preventative approach to homelessness. The Bill also encourages housing departments, social services and the voluntary sector to work together. Although there remain limitations in this legislative approach we applaud the progress being made.

However, our experience in researching rural homelessness strongly suggests that tackling homelessness in rural areas cannot be left to these generic legislative measures. It is widely recognised that homelessness is often about much more than the lack of somewhere to live. As a result, tackling homelessness requires not just ensuring an adequate supply of affordable accommodation, but measures that address a panoply of other issues including poverty, unemployment and support needs. Housing initiatives are fundamental to combating homelessness but so too is action to address issues around welfare (social security) benefits, employment, transport, and the provision of treatment services for those with drug or alcohol problems.

As well as requiring a response across a range of policy areas, tackling homelessness involves different *scales* of response. Both local and national action is required. Local initiatives, for example rent deposit schemes, are vital in tackling rural homelessness, but so too are national initiatives – for example, the allocation of resources to provide affordable housing. This is, of course, to create something of a false dichotomy. The local and the national interrelate. As we saw in Chapter Five, local government mediates central government policy – although some policies (such as the allocation of housing) are more amenable to local mediation than others (such as benefit levels and entitlement). In some instances, local responses may be facilitated by national initiatives – for example, central government funding for establishing rent deposit schemes. Central government also has an important role to play in ensuring local authorities take a proactive and progressive approach to tackling homelessness. Here we would cite the duty on local authorities to draw up housing strategies – contained within the 2001 Homelessness Bill (discussed in Chapter Four) – as a particularly good example of central government's ability to determine, or at least strongly influence, what happens at a local level.

The policy response requires both the implementation of policies that *tackle* homelessness and the abolition or reform of policies that are instrumental in *causing* homelessness (for example, the single room rent). As this suggests, action is needed to prevent as well as combat homelessness. Permanent solutions need to address both the structural causes of rural homelessness – in other words those causes which lie in generally experienced social and economic factors (such as poverty, unemployment and lack of affordable housing) – and individual causes (such as drug and/or alcohol misuse, and mental health difficulties). Often these factors overlap and interrelate. Homelessness is seldom rooted exclusively in either structural or personal problems but stems from interactions between the two.

Our argument for tackling rural homelessness, then, is that it requires a mix of national and local responses, which cover an array of policy areas, including but stretching well beyond housing issues, and which take full account of rural factors. In the remainder of this chapter we lay out an agenda for policy intervention. The agenda arises not only from interviews with these specialist agencies, and informative discussions at our inter-agency conference, but also from the interviews with practitioners and service receivers which were undertaken as part of our research project. The chapter looks first at the housing aspect of tackling rural homelessness, moving on to address the rural dimension and concluding by looking at more general welfare issues. The intention here is not to provide detailed examples of specific schemes or projects, but rather to set out some of the building blocks that would go some way towards providing a foundation for both tackling and preventing homelessness. Many of these 'solutions' are generic and pertain to tackling homelessness irrespective of where it occurs; others have a particular relevance to tackling homelessness in rural areas. In the second part of the chapter we look at more general issues surrounding the practicalities and difficulties experienced in responding to homelessness on the ground. Here we examine issues of funding, cooperation and collaboration (joined-up working) and the way in which rurality impacts upon tackling homelessness.

Housing policy solutions

Increase provision of affordable housing

Although we recognise and have highlighted throughout the book that homelessness is often about much more than a lack of housing, housing remains fundamental to its resolution. This is particularly the case in rural areas where there are quite simply not the housing options that exist in urban areas. Indeed, our research suggests that homelessness in rural areas is much more closely related to housing difficulties than it is elsewhere. As one of the key speakers at our national conference on rural homelessness eloquently put it:

> I think the argument that we need 'housing plus' was won a long time ago, but we should not pretend that there is not a huge level of housing need. The options are just not there in rural areas. 'Housing plus'? – Yes, but try doing the 'plus' without the housing, is my response. I have got too many colleagues who are trying to do the 'plus' without the housing; supporting people who are going round that sort of chain and are losing hope. Homeless people cannot establish themselves in education, in training or in employment, because their biggest concern is 'where am I going to be tonight?'. (Macklin, 2000, p 69)

This was a view also encountered at a local level. An agency worker in Gloucestershire for example, told us:

> "Let's hope they knock some bricks and mortar together, it won't be a magic wand and it won't solve the problem because homelessness is more than just needing a home.... But if the homes were to exist then that would be a start." (agency worker, Gloucestershire)

Although we acknowledge and welcome the increased funding for social housing announced in the Rural White Paper (see Chapter Four), we share the concerns of organisations such as the Countryside Agency that this does not go far enough. The increased levels of social housing provision envisaged is likely to still fall short of what is required and will do nothing to address the outstanding backlog of need.

Prevent further diminution of stock

The Right-to-Buy legislation has had a considerable impact on the availability of affordable accommodation in rural areas. Many authorities have lost a considerable proportion of their social housing stock. One of the homelessness officers interviewed for our research, for example, noted:

> "... something like 48% at the moment of all our houses have been sold and I don't include flats and bungalows, just houses, and that's a lot, a heck of a lot to lose, a lot of lettings." (homelessness officer, Somerset)

Given the detrimental impact that Right-to-Buy has had on the ability of low-income households to access property in rural areas we are sympathetic to calls for its abolition. However with the Labour Party having abandoned its opposition to this policy in the mid-1990s, it is unlikely that any current or future government will take such a course of action. Consequently, and in lieu of abolition, we would recommend that the government extends restrictions on the resale of Right-to-Buy properties (outlined in the Rural White Paper – see Chapter Four) to cover *all* properties or at the very minimum properties in rural or urban areas where affordable accommodation is in short supply.

Like Right-to-Buy sales, as we saw in Chapter Four, holiday and second homes can have a detrimental impact on the availability of housing for local people. According to research by housing consultant, Lori Streich, in some areas landlords can get more in a summer season renting to tourists than they can by renting to local people in housing need throughout the year (Streich, 2000). Abolition of the 50% Council Tax discount on second homes is imminent in England. While we support this initiative, there is more that could be done to reduce the number of rural properties being sold off as second homes in areas with high levels of unfulfilled local needs. For example, councillors in the Isles of Scilly – where an estimated one in five residential properties are owned by people not permanently resident – have lobbied the government to agree legislation under which the purchase of a property as a second or holiday home would be regarded as a change of use requiring planning permission (Gibbs, 1999). This measure is also supported by Plaid Cymru who in 1998 (unsuccessfully) introduced an amendment to planning law which would have required buyers to seek planning permission if they were not using a home as their main residence (Leake and Brennan, 1998). However, we would caution against a blanket implementation of restrictions on second home ownership. In some rural areas, holiday and second homes may utilise property which would otherwise be empty and at risk of falling into disrepair. Local communities may also benefit from the money second home owners, and holidaymakers in particular, may bring into an area through their use of local shops, pubs and other facilities.

Facilitate access to accommodation

In some areas, where demand for social housing is high and private rented accommodation is in short supply, tackling rural homelessness requires an absolute increase in the provision of affordable accommodation. Elsewhere, however, considerable progress can be made through measures to facilitate access to the accommodation that is available. As a worker from Shelter commented in relation to one particular group of households:

> "I think that's what this [tackling homelessness] is about, really, is trying to make the existing accommodation work better for young people, try and find ways of getting them into it."

In terms of the public sector, this involves removing the restrictions which currently prevent households from either accessing the housing register (also known as the waiting list) or being considered for housing. There is now a considerable body of research highlighting the way in which certain individuals and groups are excluded from access to the housing register and hence prevented from gaining access to social housing (see, for example, Niner, 1997; Bacon, 1998; Goodwin, 1998). In a recent

Shelter research project examining local lettings policies, just 4 out of 65 organisations surveyed had a totally open housing register. Instead, the study revealed that local authorities and Registered Social Landlords (RSLs – principally housing associations) applied a wide variety of exclusions, most commonly excluding households from the housing register or from consideration for rehousing on the grounds of rent arrears and past anti-social behaviour (Smith et al, 2001). Proposals in the Housing Green Paper to end such blanket exclusions are thus widely welcomed and we would endorse Shelter's recommendation that exclusions and suspensions from both local authority and RSL housing registers should only occur in exceptional circumstances.

Facilitating access to the private rented sector requires measures to overcome both financial and attitudinal barriers. In terms of financial obstacles, although private rental accommodation forms a greater proportion of stock in rural areas than in urban locations, it is often at rents which local people are unable to afford. One of the homelessness officers we interviewed commented:

> "There's not a lot [of private rental properties] available in the villages and particularly in the north side of the district it's very expensive because it's commuter distance to Bath and Bristol, which obviously bumps up the price.... If we have people working in the cities that can afford to pay it, the landlords are going to charge it. People working in the rural economy can't afford it, the majority of them are on fairly low income, farm workers or that type of thing." (homelessness officer, Somerset)

Rents are often particularly high in the more picturesque rural areas, where local people often find themselves having to compete for property against not only wealthier incomers who commute to jobs elsewhere but, especially in the summer months, from the accommodation demands of holidaymakers.

Even where households can afford the rent demanded, access to the private rented sector may be hindered by difficulties in providing the deposit and rent in advance which landlords generally require. In recognition of this problem, local authorities have attempted to facilitate access through some form of rent deposit and/or guarantee scheme. Such schemes can play a vital role in securing accommodation for homeless and other low-income households. However, the viability of these schemes has been severely undermined by the single room rent which restricts the amount of Housing Benefit payable to young people under the age of 25 to the average cost of renting a room in a shared house. A number of the homelessness officers and agency workers we interviewed reported a low take-up of rent bonds/deposits by young people, not because of lack of need or demand but simply because such shared accommodation was not available and access to self-contained (and indeed some shared) accommodation was frustrated by the shortfall between rent levels and benefit payments. Evidence suggests that this is a common experience across the country. A survey for Centrepoint in Devon, for example, found that the average discrepancy between the single room rent level and the average rent level for self-contained accommodation was £27 per week.

The single room rent has also had less tangible effects. In particular, awareness of shortfalls between rent and Housing Benefit levels has further deterred some landlords from letting property to younger tenants. As one interviewee told us:

> "It's hard enough persuading landlords anyway to even think about letting out to young people but then knowing that they are not going to get the full whack of Housing Benefit so 'are they really going to be able to afford it [and] therefore aren't we going to get rent arrears?', it's a real disincentive." (project worker, Gloucestershire).

Although government proposals to extend the forms of accommodation covered by the single room rent (outlined in Chapter Four) may ease some of the difficulties homeless households face in accessing private rental accommodation, we share the view of Shelter and other homelessness charities that it would be much more productive to abolish the restriction altogether.

Facilitating access to private rental accommodation also involves tackling attitudinal barriers. Our research uncovered a particular reluctance to rent property to young people, as highlighted in the quotation above. More generally, advertisements stating 'no DSS' remain commonplace, further limiting the ability of many homeless households to secure accommodation. Some local authorities have attempted to address landlord reservations about letting to benefit-dependent households through establishing a landlords' forum. This provides the opportunity for the housing department to explain some of the difficulties low-income households face – hopefully encouraging landlords to deal with their tenants in a more understanding manner – and for landlords to feed back any problems that they are experiencing, particularly in relation to the receipt of Housing Benefit payments. While such forums are unlikely to solve rural homelessness, if they can reduce discrimination against homeless households and ease access to the private rental sector then they undoubtedly have a role to play in its resolution.

Increase provision of emergency accommodation

While it is clearly important to ensure the availability of long-term, permanent housing for homeless households, there is also a desperate need in many rural areas for emergency accommodation. As one homelessness officer told us:

> "I mean, there just is nowhere to go if all you want is a bed ... a lot of people when they come to us, all they want is for you to tell them somewhere where they can stay the night, have a cup of tea, whatever, and we have to say 'Well I'm sorry but the nearest refuge is in XXX', you know that's the nearest place that somebody can go and XXX from here again is like a world away." (homelessness officer, Somerset)

Even where emergency accommodation is available, the level of provision is often inadequate to meet demand. A project worker we interviewed explained:

> "We are constantly juggling. Earlier this week, for example, I had one lad on an emergency placement and we had to put him back on the street because we then had a 16-year-old girl who was more vulnerable." (project worker, Somerset)

Although by no means a long-term solution, hostels and other forms of temporary accommodation such as bed and breakfast facilities can provide a valuable respite for homeless households with nowhere to go, as well as – in the case of the former – a useful means of gaining access to other services such as benefit advice and drug treatment facilities.

There is a tendency to equate emergency provision with direct access hostels. However, although such accommodation may be appropriate in some areas, there is no necessity for emergency provision to take this form. A number of rural authorities have introduced Nightstop schemes which provide a safe place for young people to stay within a family home for one or two nights, allowing advice workers and the individuals involved time to secure more permanent accommodation.

These schemes are particularly valuable in rural areas lacking more concrete forms of emergency provision, enabling homeless households to remain in the local area (where they are often linked into various informal support networks) rather than having to move away to urban locations, often to the detriment of these networks and the disruption of other local connections such as schools and place of employment. In Stroud district, for example, prior to the establishment of a Nightstop scheme in 1998, homeless households requiring emergency accommodation had little alternative but to go to Gloucester.

The type and amount of emergency accommodation required will obviously vary across the country, but we would strongly encourage an expansion of the Nightstop schemes to other parts of rural Britain and to other groups of homeless households – at present schemes cater only for young people. Local authorities obviously have a key role to play in establishing and managing such schemes but would undoubtedly benefit from central government financial support.

Increase provision of move-on accommodation

In those areas where some form of emergency provision is available, a common complaint – made by a number of our interviewees – is the lack of move-on accommodation. Not only does this prevent currently homeless households from moving on to more settled accommodation and beginning to rebuild their lives but it also leads to a silting up of emergency provision with consequent problems for future homeless households. As one project worker commented:

> "We've got 15 places and if they're not emptying you know, that's it isn't it? Life's not going to stop outside because this place is full, people aren't going to not be homeless." (project worker, Somerset)

In some areas there is a need to increase the provision of various forms of supported accommodation; elsewhere it is more a question of removing the barriers that prevent households from gaining access to local authority housing or property in the private rented sector (such as the eligibility requirements and single room rent discussed above).

Rural policy solutions

Without an adequate supply of accessible, affordable accommodation, rural homelessness can never be solved. However, while housing is a basic requirement, measures to address other (non-housing) issues have an important role to play in both facilitating the resolution of rural homelessness and ensuring that solutions are sustainable.

Better transport provision

Tackling transport difficulties in particular is a key issue. A worker from one of the national homelessness charities for example, reflected:

> "I do think you can't actually address any of this stuff [homelessness] unless you have got some idea about what we are going to do about transport because it doesn't go away." (Centrepoint)

Inadequate transport impinges on the ability to access accommodation and employment. Indeed, difficulties surrounding housing, transport and employment are intimately related. The ability to obtain and retain accommodation is highly dependent on being employed. For some people the loss of a job is a prime factor in their becoming homeless (with inability to make rent or mortgage payments leading, in the extreme, to eviction or repossession) and lack of employment also makes it difficult to find accommodation, limiting the number of properties a household can afford. Yet access to employment in rural areas is invariably restricted by a lack of public transport. As a project worker in Gloucestershire noted:

> "The places that you can apply to for work are severely restricted because you have got to look first of all, can I get there?" (project worker, Gloucestershire)

Measures that facilitate mobility such as 'Jump Start' in Cirencester, which loans out mopeds to allow rural residents to get to their place of employment, and the 'Cars for Work' scheme in Scotland, which provides cars to long-term unemployed people who are offered jobs but who cannot rely on public transport[1], can thus make a valuable indirect contribution to preventing and, in some cases, resolving rural homelessness.

Transport difficulties also hinder access to the kinds of advice and other services (such as family mediation and addiction counselling) that may help to prevent households from becoming homeless. Households may be unaware of the various options available to them or require professional assistance in accessing different forms of support. In addition – as a number of our interviewees pointed out – it is much easier for problems to be resolved (and homelessness prevented) if these problems are dealt with at an early stage prior to a crisis point, such as the receipt of an eviction order, being reached.

While improving public transport will help households in rural areas to gain access to larger settlements where advice and other services are generally located, other initiatives – in particular mobile and outreach services – in which services and workers come to the clients rather than vice versa have a particular role to play in these areas. However, there can be drawbacks to such forms of provision. As a worker from Centrepoint noted in relation to mobile services:

> "The trouble with mobile services is they can only be in one place at a time. I helped with a mobile advice project in Oxfordshire called The Van which is really brilliant when you are there but … it only comes to you about once every 12 weeks and then you might be out that night and you missed it and your problem might have gone away by then or whatever." (Centrepoint)

The provision of outreach services in village halls, doctor's surgeries and so forth by organisations such as Shelter and the Citizens Advice Bureau are similarly limited. In addition, households may be deterred from taking advantage of both mobile and outreach services, which may be highly visible (as in The Van project just mentioned) by the kinds of cultural barriers discussed in Chapter Three.

Local authorities and other agencies are well aware of these limitations and have begun to explore ways of delivering advice and other services which are not so time and place dependent and offer households a greater degree of anonymity. In the late 1990s, the national homelessness charity Shelter launched 'Shelterline', an advice service providing access to housing advice over the telephone free of charge, and an increasing number of authorities and organisations are looking towards using the internet in the delivery of advice and other services. For example, it is now possible in some authorities to apply to join the housing register electronically.

Improved employment and training opportunities

The close links between accommodation and employment are recognised and built on in the establishment of foyers, which seek to meet the related needs of young people for accommodation and opportunities for training and employment. Originating in France, there are currently just over 100 foyers across the UK, providing accommodation, linked with access to education, training and job opportunities for around 5,000 homeless and disadvantaged 16- to 25-year-olds (http://www.foyer.net). While the majority of foyers provide most of their services under one roof, a growing number operate from more than one location in a town or district, or link several smaller projects together to share resources and facilities (The Foyer Federation, 2000, p 4). This so-called 'dispersed model' of provision is particularly suited to rural areas where often it is more appropriate (given the scattered nature of needs) to have a number of smaller developments situated in several different settlements rather than one large development in the main service centre.

A good example of a dispersed foyer development in a rural area is the 'Housing, Employment and Rural Training' – HEART– project, which consists of a network of small linked units in eight Suffolk towns each with between four and eight spaces of accommodation. Services are offered not just to residents but to all young people in the project's catchment area and include life and social skills, access to training and job opportunities, and transport provision to enable local youngsters to get to work and access other services and facilities (The Foyer Federation, 2000, p 4).

Social policy solutions

Address the support needs of vulnerable groups

One of the key issues to emerge both from our study and from the subsequent national conference was the need to provide homeless households with support in their new accommodation. This ties in, once again, with an understanding of homelessness as much more than a housing problem. While support may be provided for people with clearly recognised and recognisable support needs – such as those with mental health difficulties or problems related to drugs and/or alcohol (although such support is often lacking in rural areas) – people with less severe (and therefore less apparent) difficulties may slip through the net. There was a common belief among the homelessness officers and agency workers we interviewed that many young people in particular require some form of low-level support to maintain a tenancy (and that providing accommodation goes only part of the way towards resolving their housing difficulties). In the majority of cases, it is not that young homeless people have support needs which are particularly unusual, rather that the more traditional sources of low-level support provided by family and friends are either not available to them, perhaps because they have moved away from the family home (a particular issue among young people leaving rural areas to move into towns); or family relationships have broken down (one of the principal reasons underlying youth homelessness); or because they have never existed at all (for example, young people leaving institutional care). Without such support – which may be as simple as providing some companionship and training in basic life skills – rehousing can be seen in some respects as setting people up to fail. In general, tenancy breakdown occurs not because of some act of wickedness or wilful negligence on the young persons part but simply because, as one officer pointed out:

> "They just haven't got the skills to keep it going, they can't budget and are not really capable of fending for themselves." (homelessness officer, Somerset).

Agencies emphasised the need for accommodation offering varying levels of support, providing a step-by-step move into independent secure accommodation with speed of progress through the system related to the extent of a person's support needs:

> "There does need to be this flow-through of people coming in and moving from step to step to step and then getting settled accommodation, whether that's in the private sector or whether that's in the social housing sector.... There needs to be a step by step where people actually move through and if their support needs are non-existent then maybe they move through much quicker than somebody that's got high support needs." (project worker, Gloucestershire)

An alternative (and more flexible) mechanism for providing support than these so-called supported housing schemes – and one which garnered particular praise from both interviewees and conference delegates – was the idea of floating support. In this system, rather than attaching support to a particular property, support is tied to the client. This avoids people having to leave accommodation once their support needs are met or change and enables the level of support to be more easily varied over time in accordance with client needs.

Floating support systems allow both an increase in support as well as a reduction, in a way which is not always possible in supported housing schemes where different levels of support are provided in different properties. As well as providing greater stability for the client, floating support systems have a particular value in rural areas. As one interviewee told us:

> "In a way it [floating support] precisely answers the key problem we have got about supported housing in rural areas which is that you don't

want big buildings and you can't, if you put it in one place then you are immediately creating this problem of everyone having to come to you when actually they want to be over there, but if you just get rid of, don't think in terms of buildings at all from the support angle, you just think of getting the support to wherever those people are." (Centrepoint)

Address household poverty

Although support is clearly an important factor in addressing (rural) homelessness, this should not be taken as an indication that homelessness is solely – or even predominantly – a result of individual inadequacies. Structural factors also play a role. In particular, the inability of low-income households to afford to access and maintain good quality secure accommodation continues to be a major cause of homelessness. While we acknowledge and applaud government initiatives to address poverty such as the minimum wage, the Working Families' Tax Credit and the Minimum Income Guarantee (which have undoubtedly improved the finances of many individuals and families), much remains to be done.

The government has placed an emphasis on work rather than welfare as the main route out of poverty. However, in accordance with the mantra 'work for those who can, security for those who cannot', the government should look towards increasing benefit payments to a level high enough to support a reasonable standard of living, including the means to access and maintain decent and secure accommodation. We would also advocate abolition of age differentials in benefit payments that leave many young people unable to secure or retain accommodation especially when combined with the limitations imposed on them by the single room rent (discussed earlier). As one of the project workers we interviewed commented:

"Benefit levels for under-25s are ridiculously low, I don't know why they are so low, the difference between a 24 year old and a 25 year old, I mean they eat the same amount of food, their electricity costs are just the same ... £39.85 a week, that's Income Support or JSA for an under-25 year old. So you could be living in a one-bed flat and having to pay Council Tax, water rates, gas, electric, TV licence, food, clothing, from that, it's almost an impossibility." (project worker, Gloucestershire)

In order to prevent a further widening of inequalities in income and wealth, future increases in benefits (and pensions) should be tied to increases in average earnings. The government also needs to continue its efforts to make work pay by further increasing the minimum wage and raising the earnings disregard (the amount of money an individual can earn before income is 'clawed back' from their benefit payments).

Increase financial support for responding agencies

As well as tackling the poverty of individual households there is also a need to address the 'poverty' of the (voluntary) agencies seeking to tackle homelessness and its related problems. As we noted in Chapter Four, a number of national agencies (such as ACRE, the Countryside Agency and the Local Government Association) have drawn attention to the way in which current indicators of need used to allocate resources to local authorities and housing associations (such as the Index of Local Conditions[2] and Housing Needs Index) are biased towards urban areas and fail to adequately reflect levels of need in rural areas.

There is also a feeling that rural areas lose out in bids for funding which work on 'urban' notions of cost-effectiveness and success and fail to take into account the greater costs entailed in delivering services to a dispersed population across a wide geographical area. According to the Local Government Association, "rural areas often fall foul of the 'numbers game'". So many government targets can most easily be attained by concentrating attention and resources on the areas where most people live, ie urban areas. By contrast the *perceived* return on public investment in rural areas where the populations are smaller and more dispersed is weaker" (Local Government Association Rural Executive, 2000, p 2). For example, one of our case-study authorities – South Somerset – has to deliver services to a population of 142,000 spread over some 370 square miles. As a worker from Shelter commented:

> "I mean, you can't just run projects in a rural area on exactly the same funding as you would run a project in an urban area, it doesn't work. There are issues which make it more costly so it means that you can't just go to the local authority and ask for the normal run of funding as you would do for an urban area, it costs more and there has to be recognition of that." (Shelter)

At a local level, voluntary agencies need not only more funding but for that funding to be placed on a more secure footing. The short-term nature of financial support hinders the development of more strategic long-term services. Voluntary agencies dealing with homelessness in Taunton, for example, face a continual struggle to survive, let alone deal with gaps in existing provision such as the lack of accommodation for homeless people with drug or alcohol addictions.

The impact of rurality

As the issue of funding suggests, tackling rural homelessness may require a different kind of response to tackling homelessness in urban areas. 'Urban' solutions cannot, and should not, be simply transposed onto rural areas. Schemes and initiatives implemented in urban areas are not necessarily appropriate to rural areas and the government needs to take into account the specific needs and difficulties faced by rural communities when developing and implementing policy. For example, it may not be possible to offer the range of options set out in the New Deal – heralded by the government as a key route out of poverty – and take-up may be significantly hindered by transport difficulties.

Several of our interviewees commented on the need to be more creative and flexible when dealing with homelessness in rural areas:

"I think that probably projects within rural areas do need to have, maybe be more innovative in terms of shaping the project to the area instead of taking the model and putting it on top of it." (Crisis)

"I think we were aware of the need to be much more flexible and creative, it [provision of rural advice] does require more resources." (National Homelessness Advisory Service)

Nor is it simply a case of having one set of solutions for tackling homelessness in urban areas and another set of solutions for tackling homelessness in rural areas. Rural areas are not homogenous (any more than urban areas are) and it is important to take into account the *local context*, adapting solutions or adopting different solutions according to local circumstances.

One of the project workers we interviewed suggested that part of the problem in recognising the issues around homelessness in rural areas stemmed from having:

"A bit of a set picture – this is how it is – and not really acknowledging the variety, not acknowledging how quite specific local circumstances can mitigate against the solution working or not working."

She continued:

> "Local context is very important because sometimes it can come down to quite basic things like there might be a perfect solution if there's some accommodation over here and there's some sort of industrial, some sort of work over here, if there's a bus that goes at the right time of day, and if there's no bus and someone's got a job and needs somewhere to live there's nothing you can do about it or if it's the other way round."

Furthermore, taking into account the local context involves paying attention not only to the local (physical) infrastructure but more nebulous factors such as community attitudes. For example – as one of our interviewees commented – in providing services for homeless people:

> "You could get a rural area where it would actually be quite difficult to break into, because they have a very insular attitude, and somewhere else where they might be very welcoming and you really don't know." (national agency)

Such differences in attitudes were highlighted by one project worker we interviewed who noted that, in setting up a network of services for young homeless people in Gloucestershire, local opposition or wariness in parts of the county led projects, elsewhere referred to as homelessness projects, to be established as *housing* projects even though the service provided was the same:

> "I mean, I am not sure how true this story is ... but when they were setting this project up, the local authority, the councillors did not want the word homeless to be in the title so it's interesting that Glofysh are Gloucester Forum for Young Single Homelessness whereas we are XXX Young Single Housing Project, they didn't want it to be young single homeless project, so they wouldn't let it be called that, it had to be called a housing project and the story that's been passed down to me, whether it's true or not I don't know, is that some councillors say, well we don't have a homelessness problem in XXX so you can't call it that." (project worker, Gloucestershire)

Given the specificities of the local situation, it is difficult to proffer any one solution to rural homelessness. As a worker from Shelter commented:

"The housing structure and other factors as well, of employment and location from cities and stuff varies so much that perhaps you can't propose a single solution, you have to look at each area individually really, and there is perhaps different ways you can, different things you can use to help people." (Shelter)

Related to this need to be open to different types of responses, a number of the people we interviewed stressed the need for practical and realistic solutions and emphasised the potential benefit of even very basic measures such as paying for someone to spend a few nights in a bed and breakfast, or giving someone the money to get to a hostel. Although it would perhaps be more accurate to see such measures as palliatives rather than solutions to rural homelessness, their significance and importance for people experiencing difficulties on the ground should not be dismissed out of hand. While such provision should not deflect from attempts to secure better, more permanent solutions, they can provide a necessary stopgap for households with limited options and may – in demonstrating an awareness that difficulties exist – help to obtain future improvements in provision. As one of our interviewees argued:

"I think you have to respond practically to the problem.... If you have got maybe, say, a small voluntary group in the rural area that wants to tackle the problem without a great deal of resources and they are practically not going to get sufficient money to sort of do something to social housing or build a foyer or something, you need to have some kind of practical response. I am not saying it's ideal but at least it's getting something in there where there was nothing and recognising a problem as well, which is a starting point, and perhaps you can build things up from there." (Shelter)

Collaboration and coordination

Homelessness is a multi-dimensional problem that requires a multi-dimensional response. Our interviews with homelessness officers and agency workers and discussions at the national conference on rural homelessness highlighted the need for different sectors (state and voluntary) and different agencies to work together. Indeed, according to one of our interviewees:

"I think that the key to it [tackling rural homelessness] has got to be – it sounds a bit old hat – but it's got to be about strategy, it's got to be about actually having some kind of coordination of thinking and activity and planning between organisations." (Centrepoint)

Our research revealed a considerable degree of joint working between and within the statutory and voluntary sectors in Gloucestershire and Somerset, although links were more developed in some districts than others. Officers were keenly aware of the need for joint working and its potential value. As one officer remarked:

> "If we are all working in partnership we are better off than being at loggerheads ... I think we would all just grind to a halt if we didn't work together."

Another noted:

> "I think ... we realised many years ago it's to our mutual benefit to work together."

This was a view shared by delegates at the national conference. Partnership working was widely regarded as the most effective way of tackling homelessness in rural areas. However, inter-agency working is not unproblematic. Conference delegates stressed the need for partnerships to have clear and identifiable objectives. Aside from the practical problems of coordination, difficulties can arise due to the varying priorities, agendas and responsibilities of the different organisations.

There is often a particular tension between the statutory and voluntary sectors. Several of the homelessness officers we interviewed believed that voluntary organisations viewed the housing department as the enemy. One officer for instance stated that "we are seen as the bureaucratic establishment that sits on keys, doesn't give out houses" and criticised voluntary agencies for 'feeding' this line to their clients. Other officers commented that these agencies tended to be quite 'idealistic' and were often guilty of raising or sustaining unrealistic expectations among their clients.

Yet joint working between the statutory and voluntary sectors was predominantly welcomed and although officers admitted that difficulties did arise from time to time, they stressed that these could usually be resolved:

"I mean, we have our hiccups now and again but I think generally we try and work with them and if it is happening then we get together and try and sort it out."

Often more problematic were links *within* the statutory sector. While most of the homelessness officers we interviewed considered that their relationships with the Housing Benefit Department – a commonly acknowledged source of tension in other studies – as generally adequate or good, links with social services were somewhat more hit or miss. This was attributed in a number of districts to a high turnover of social services staff and different levels of governance with social services operating at county, as opposed to district, level. There was also, however, a sense of competing or conflicting aims. One homelessness officer remarked:

"I hate to sort of continue with this old thing about housing and social services but [again] they have got different agendas and priorities and unfortunately that's how it feels a lot of the time."

Much seemed to rest on the personalities and personnel skills of individuals working within the different agencies. As one homelessness officer commented in respect of her relationship with the Housing Benefit Department:

"There are some fantastic officers over there who ... will provide you with all the assistance you can possibly imagine whereas certain letters of the alphabet come up and you think oh God I am not going to get anywhere here."

Despite such difficulties and tensions, partnerships between different agencies are a fact of life in many authorities. In a number of our case-study authorities, multi-agency forums have been established, bringing together a range of statutory and voluntary groups to address housing-related issues, while one authority in Gloucestershire has appointed an officer purely to promote partnerships and develop relationships between the housing department and other agencies.

The way ahead?

As we reported in Chapter Five, there have emerged over recent years new coalitions of statutory and welfare agencies to meet the needs of homeless people who have been excluded from state support. Typical activities of these coalitions include the small-scale provision of emergency accommodation, development of rent deposit and bond schemes, and more support and general advice services. Local authority involvement varies. In some areas (such as Gloucestershire – see Chapter Five) the local authorities have taken a lead role, both in the provision of initial funding and in the coordination and network development inherent in these emergent conditions. Elsewhere, local authorities seem less willing to bring funding resources to local networks but may well be willing to pivot local interaction around key officers.

The increasing significance of these local partnerships constitutes a crucial adjunct to the statutory policy landscape discussed above. Such cooperation brings tangible benefits. For local authorities, it permits an extension of welfare provision despite a restricted fiscal environment. For voluntary agencies, it brings their distinctive perceptions of need and alternative modus operandi into a more mainstream policy position. We would, however, also point to other, perhaps less tangible benefits of partnership working, which we characterise in terms of the development of new initiatives and mindsets to local responses to homelessness. We believe that changes to local political mindsets are an essential prerequisite for any more progressive response to rural homelessness. So, while we have no doubt that the measures discussed earlier in this chapter are capable of bringing about substantial progress in the tackling of rural (and other) homelessness, we would suggest that local rural political mindsets may act as a significant barrier to these proposals. Local political will is often geared towards a protection of the idyll, by ensuring that rural spaces are purified and that any potentially transgressive policy responses – such as the siting of emergency homelessness accommodation in villages – are effectively rebuffed. We have encountered very little broadscale political will either to develop local responses, or to campaign for national-level changes on behalf of local homeless people.

What we *have* found, however, is that emergent localised networks sometimes appear capable of sponsoring somewhat different sets of local social relations so far as responses to homelessness are concerned. Small groups of dedicated local people who are committed to the task of providing for the needs of local homeless people can (albeit not without considerable struggle) begin to change the local political landscape. Four local agencies are highlighted here as examples of best practice, although there are many others in our study area, and each shines out locally as a beacon of hope that the political and cultural contexts of rural areas *can* accommodate progressive responses to the issue of rural homelessness.

Cirencester Housing for Young People

Cirencester Housing for Young People (CHYP) aims to provide accommodation (and support) for homeless 16- to 25-year-olds. CHYP was started in an attempt to break the problematic cycle of no home – no job, no job – no home. A lot of the young people who approach CHYP have issues other than homelessness that need to be addressed and the project aims to support them in doing that. The project provides a range of accommodation: a core house with seven bed spaces with 24-hour staff cover, a three-bed house, a two-bed bungalow with disability adaptations and a four-bed house about a mile from Cirencester centre. The last three are 'minimum houses', with no on-site support. Depending on the needs of the residents, staff will provide limited short-term support in the form of daily visits although this is unlikely to continue for more than one or two weeks. Part of the Glofysh network (see page 214), CHYP receives referrals from social services, probation and Cotswold Young Single Housing. Housing Benefit is the main source of income, but the project also receives funding from social services, Gloucestershire County Council, as well as the probation service and Cotswold District Council. However, the organisation still has to raise in the order of £20,000 a year simply to keep going.

Tewkesbury Young Single Housing Project

Tewkesbury Young Single Housing Project is part of the Young Homelessness Network which used funding under the Children Act to establish a housing/homelessness project for young people in each of Gloucestershire's six districts. The project aims to offer advice and assistance to young single people aged between 16 and 24 who are homeless but are not in priority need of accommodation (and therefore ineligible for rehousing by the local authority). The project offers advice about housing matters but also about welfare benefits and, because of the lack of other projects in rural areas, about other issues as well.

The project also tries to assist young people to secure accommodation by negotiating with local private sector landlords and housing associations; and it administers the provision of rent in advance or Housing Benefit in advance and runs a deposit bond scheme to assist people into private rented accommodation. This scheme guarantees participating landlords a certain sum in lieu of rent arrears or damage or theft. (However, the scheme has to some extent been rendered redundant by the single room rent, which has prevented young people from being able to access a private sector tenancy at all.) The vast majority of clients are self-referrals, with only around 10% of referrals coming from a range of statutory agencies including social services, Tewkesbury Housing Department, the probation service and the local benefits agency. The project receives funding from social services, Tewkesbury Borough Council and Shelter.

Gloucestershire Forum for Young Single Homelessness (Glofysh)

Glofysh was set up in response to the Children Act to provide housing advice and information for young people aged 16–25. The organisation provides advice services in Dursley, Gloucester, Stroud and Stonehouse and in 1998 appointed a support liaison worker to look at the changing support needs of young people. Glofysh also administers a countywide rent in advance scheme and retains a register of landlords willing to let to young people.

Some clients are referred to the organisation from the council, social services, the probation service, and from other voluntary agencies (such as Cheltenham Housing Aid and Shelter) but Glofysh also receives a large number of self-referrals, reflecting the organisation's good reputation among young people as being approachable and useful. Funding is received from a variety of sources including the district council and social services but is always seeking further resources.

Stonham Housing projects

Stonham Housing Association runs two projects in Minehead providing semi-supported accommodation for 15 people. While mainly aimed at under-25s, the projects will sometimes take older homeless people as well. Residents need varying levels of support – some have very few support needs and are 'just purely homeless'.

Referrals are received from West Somerset District Council, the probation service, social services and the youth service. The tenants have single occupancy (assured) tenancies. However, while they can theoretically stay as long as they want, the organisation likes tenants to move on within a year or two and seeks to enable them to do so (although a shortage of move-on accommodation is a significant barrier to attaining this goal).

The nature of these projects highlights a further potential barrier to the implementation of proposals which tackle issues of rural homelessness.

In Chapters Five and Six, we emphasised the contemporary political context of governance, suggesting that 'action' to address social issues will now inevitably take the form of partnership between different public sector, voluntary or even private sector agencies. Such a partnership has many potential advantages, but as our study of Taunton (Cloke et al, 2000a) shows, partnership also represents a pathway for local authorities to *be seen* to be doing something as opposed to a platform for innovative

Table 8.1: Initiatives/schemes in Gloucestershire and Somerset

1. *Measures to facilitate access to the private rented sector*

All the case-study authorities provide some form of rent deposit or rent guarantee scheme. However, there are differences between authorities in how these schemes are run. For example, some authorities' schemes are open to anyone who is homeless; others are restricted to applicants towards whom they have a statutory duty – in other words homeless households in priority need.

There is also a landlords' forum in a number of the case-study authorities.

2. *Provision of accommodation*

There are a variety of schemes and measures across the districts aimed at providing accommodation for young people including foyers, supported accommodation and the redesignation or conversion of sheltered accommodation into housing for young people. Other groups have yet to receive the specific attention accorded to the young, possibly because their needs are already being met through existing provision. For example, homeless households with children can generally access socially rented accommodation.

3. *Support services*

A number of authorities have in place, or at the time of interview were looking towards, the provision of floating support workers to help (primarily young) people to maintain tenancies – whether in the private or social housing sector. At the time of interview, however, where such support existed it was predominantly provided by non-statutory agencies.

4. *Outreach services (delivery)*

Few authorities operate a formal outreach housing service to smaller locations. However, homelessness officers emphasised that households could gain access to housing advice on the phone and a number of officers stated that they would make home visits to anyone who could not get to the housing office.

5. *Monitoring*

A couple of the case-study authorities actively encourage *all* homeless people to register on the waiting list (even if their chances of rehousing are slim) in order to identify (and demonstrate) the scale and nature of housing need within different parts of the district. Several officers noted that they kept more detailed statistics than those required in the quarterly DETR returns to ensure they retained as accurate a picture as possible of homelessness within their authority.

Two authorities have conducted recent surveys of the needs of young people in the district that included questions relating to their needs for housing.

action. In this era of governance, we believe that local authorities continue to occupy a pivotal position. Table 8.1 outlines the involvement by local authorities in our case-study areas with homelessness issues. It is clear that the delivery of responses to rural homelessness will require new ways of joined-up working to ensure collaboration and coordination of partnership agencies. It is also clear from our research, however, that all of the agencies concerned were struggling to find sufficient sustained finance to continue, let alone expand and innovate their responses.

We return, then, to the barrier of the lack of political will. The current focus on homelessness in the UK appears to be dominated by a desire to reduce the numbers of rough sleepers. What we suggest in this book is that there are other, much more hidden, forms of homelessness which deserve and demand additional public policy focus. Homelessness in rural areas is one such form of hidden homelessness. It exists in the lives and experiences of a significant number of people living in or moving through rural areas. Recognising the problem is a well overdue first step. Further action to respond to the needs of rural homeless people is now an urgent priority.

Endnote

In September 2001, the Critical Geography Forum ran a conference entitled 'Beyond the Academy', at which focus was directed to the ways in which academic researchers could move out of the traditional roles, practices and spaces they inhabit in order to generate a more significant contribution to people, issues and causes. Interestingly, many of the speakers emphasised the importance of applied research in this context. By applying academic research to particular policy areas, or to the task of advocating the needs of particular groups, researchers were seen to be contributing their skills to relevant and important issues. Having carried out this research into rural homelessness, we are only partially convinced by this argument. Undoubtedly we have been motivated to do this research because of deeply held convictions about the people and issues concerned, and it is not inconceivable that our efforts to disseminate the findings of our research may have impacted, however partially, on the invisibility of rural homeless people. But though our encounters with homeless people were ethnographic rather than remote or virtual, they were temporary and difficult to sustain. There must be more that can be done, alongside further programmes of research.

At the 'Beyond the Academy' conference, a number of speakers suggested that the impact of academic researchers on socio-political issues could also be traced through the political and voluntaristic practices of their everyday lives. That is, the wider social practices of individuals – beyond their research – is also a significant measure of the contribution being made 'beyond the academy'. We have considerable sympathy for this view, and indeed are advocates of it (see Chapter Three, also Cloke et al, 2001), for two reasons which are relevant to the conclusion of this book. First, it is our role in voluntary participation with homeless people where we live that has been a key motivational factor in the undertaking of this research. Second, and crucially, it will be the actions of local concerned and participatory volunteers in rural areas that will bring critical impetus to the localised networks of responses to rural homelessness. If we have a final message to bring from this research, then it would be to urge rural people to engage wherever possible in the support of emergent local networks of support for homeless people. Such engagement will bring about genuine encounters with people experiencing varying forms of homelessness, and do more to demystify the issue of rural homelessness than any central legislative dictat. As well as urging government action at central and local levels, we would encourage rural people to recognise that the rural 'idyll' is socially differentiated and that community values also involve responsibilities to others.

Notes

[1] A jobseeker who has been out of work for more than a year chooses a car worth about £1,000, which is taxed and insured for the first year, with the recipient agreeing to pay for the vehicle over the next 12 months (reported in *The Times*, 14 February 2000).

[2] Revision of the Index of Local Conditions in 2000 to better reflect rural circumstances has led to a greater recognition of deprivation in rural areas.

References

Allison, P. (1998) *Whose benefit? The impact of the single room restriction on housing benefit for young people in Devon*, London: Centrepoint.

Anderson, I., Kemp, P. and Quilgars, D. (1993) *Single homeless people*, London: HMSO.

Aron, L. and Fitchen, J. (1996) 'Rural homelessness: a synopsis', in J. Baumohl (ed) *Homelessness in America*, Phoenix, AZ: Oryx Press.

Audit Commission (1989) *Housing the homeless: The local authority role*, London: HMSO.

Bacon, N. (1998) 'Prepared for impact', *Roof*, January/February, pp 34-6.

Barak, G. (1991) *Gimme shelter: A social history of homelessness in contemporary America*, New York, NY: Praeger.

Barnett, A. and Scruton, R. (1998) 'Introduction', in A. Barnett and R. Scruton (eds) *Town and Country*, London: Jonathon Cape.

Bassett, K. (1996) 'Partnerships, business elites in urban politics: new forms of governance in an English city?', *Urban Studies*, vol 33, pp 539-55.

Blake, J. (1993) 'The right to act?', *Roof*, September/October, p 27.

Blasi, G.L. (1990) 'Social-policy and social-science research on homelessness', *Journal of Social Issues*, vol 46, pp 207-19.

Bondi, L. (1999) 'On the journeys of the gentrifiers: exploring gender, gentrification and migration', in P. Boyle and K. Halfacree (eds) *Migration into rural areas: Theories and issues*, Chichester: John Wiley & Sons.

Bourdieu, P. (1979) *Outline of a theory of practice*, Cambridge: Cambridge University Press.

Bourdieu, P. (1989) *Distinction: A social critique of the judgement of taste*, London: Routledge and Kegan Paul.

Bradley, T., Lowe, P. and Wright, S. (1986) 'Rural deprivation and the welfare transition', in P. Lowe, T. Bradley and S. Wright (eds) *Deprivation and welfare in rural areas*, Norwich: Geobooks.

Bramley, G. (1992) 'Explaining the incidence of statutory homelessness in England', *Housing Studies*, vol 8, pp 128-47.

Bramley, G., Doogan, K., Leather, P., Murie, A. and Watson, E. (1988) *Homelessness and the London housing market*, Bristol: SAUS, University of Bristol.

Burrows, R. (1997) 'The social distribution of the experience of homelessness', in R. Burrows, N. Pearce and D. Quilgars (eds) *Homelessness and social policy*, London: Routledge, pp 50-69.

Burrows, R., Pleace, N. and Quilgars, D. (1997) *Homeless and social policy*, London: Routledge, pp 50-69.

Butler, K., Carlisle, B. and Lloyd, R. (1994) *Homelessness in the 1990s: Local authority practice*, London: Shelter.

Butler, S. (1998) *Access denied: The exclusion of people in need from social housing*, London: Shelter.

Button, E. (1992) *Rural housing for youth*, London: Centrepoint.

Cabinet Office (2000) *Sharing the nation's prosperity: Economic, social and environmental conditions in the countryside* (www.cabinet-office.gov.uk/seu/2001/pse/PSE%20HTML/default.htm).

Cabinet Office Performance and Innovation Unit (1999) *Rural economies*, London: The Stationery Office.

Carter, M. (1997) *The last resort: Living in bed & breakfast in the 1990s*, London: Shelter.

Centrepoint (2000) 'Centrepoint responds to the Government's housing green paper', Press release, 4 April.

Chamberlain, C. and Mackenzie, D. (1992) 'Understanding contemporary homelessness – issues of definition and meaning', *Australian Journal of Social Issues*, vol 27, pp 274-97.

Champion, A.G. (1994) 'Population change and migration in Britain since 1981; evidence for continuing deconcentration', *Environment and Planning A*, vol 26, pp 1501-20.

Chapman, P. et al (1998) *Poverty and social exclusion in rural areas*, York: Joseph Rowntree Foundation.

Chartered Institute of Housing (2000) 'Government pledge to protect homeless must be backed with funding', Press release, 6 December.

Clark, D. (1990) *Affordable rural housing*, Cirencester: ACRE.

Cloke, P. (ed) (1992) *Policy and change in Thatcher's Britain*, Oxford: Pergamon.

Cloke, P. (1995) 'Rural poverty and the welfare state: a discursive transformation in Britain and the USA', *Environment and Planning A*, vol 72, pp 433-9.

Cloke, P. (1996) 'Housing in the open countryside: windows on 'irresponsible' planning in rural Wales', *Town Planning Review*, vol 67, pp 291-308.

Cloke, P. and Goodwin, M. (1992) 'Conceptualising countryside change: from post-Fordism to rural structured coherence', *Transactions, IBG*, vol 17, pp 321-36.

Cloke, P. and Goodwin, M. (1993) 'Rural change: structured coherence or unstructured incoherence?', *Terra*, vol 105, pp 166-74.

Cloke, P. and Milbourne, P. (1992) 'Deprivation and lifestyles in rural Wales, II: rurality and the cultural dimension', *Journal of Rural Studies*, vol 8, pp 359-72.

Cloke, P. and Thrift, N. (1990) 'Class and change in rural Britain', in T. Marsden, P. Lowe and S. Whatmore (eds) *Rural restructuring*, London: David Fulton, pp 165-81.

Cloke, P., Goodwin, M. and Milbourne, P. (1997a) *Rural Wales: Community and marginalisation*, Cardiff: University of Wales Press.

Cloke, P., Milbourne, P. and Thomas, C. (1994) *Lifestyles in Rural England*, London: Rural Development Commission.

Cloke, P., Milbourne, P. and Thomas, C. (1997b) 'Living lives in different ways?: deprivation, marginalisation and changing lifestyles in rural England', *Transactions of the Institute of British Geographers*, vol 22, no 3, pp 210-30.

Cloke, P., Milbourne, P. and Widdowfield, R. (2000a) 'Partnership and policy networks in rural local governance: homelessness in Taunton', *Public Administration*, vol 78, pp 111-33.

Cloke, P., Milbourne, P. and Widdowfield, R. (2000b) 'The hidden and emerging spaces of rural homelessness', *Environment and Planning A*, vol 32, pp 77-90.

Cloke, P., Milbourne, P. and Widdowfield, R. (2001) 'Making the homeless count? Enumerating rough sleepers and the distortion of homelessness', *Policy & Politics*, vol 29, no 3, pp 259-80.

Cloke, P., Phillips, M. and Thrift, N. (1998) 'Class, colonisation and lifestyle strategies in Gower', in P. Boyle and K. Halfacree (eds) *Migration into rural areas: Theories and issues*, Chichester: John Wiley & Sons, pp 166-85.

Cloke, P., Goodwin, M., Milbourne, P. and Thomas, C. (1995) 'Deprivation, poverty and marginalisation in rural lifestyles in England and Wales', *Journal of Rural Studies*, vol 11, pp 351-66.

Cloke, P., Cooke, P., Cursons, J., Milbourne, P. and Widdowfield, R. (2000c) 'Ethics, reflexivity and research encounters with homeless people', *Ethics, Place and Environment*, vol 3, no 2, pp 133-54.

Close, J. and Benson, R. (1996) 'Youth homelessness – the rural perspective', in S. Ransley (ed) *Developing effective responses to rural homelessness*, London: Shelter, pp 36-7.

Cochrane, A. (1993) *Whatever happened to local government*, Buckingham: Open University Press.

Cochrane, A. (1994) 'Restructuring the local welfare state', in R. Burrows and B. Loader (eds) *Towards a post-Fordist welfare state?*, London: Routledge, pp 118-34.

Countryside Agency (1999) *The state of the countryside 1999*, Cheltenham: Countryside Agency.

Countryside Agency (2000a) Press release, 28 November, Salisbury: Countryside Agency.

Countryside Agency (2000b) *The state of the countryside 2000*, Cheltenham: Countryside Agency.

Countryside Alliance (2000) 'Response to the Rural White Paper' (http://www.countryside-alliance.org/policy-briefs/ca-response.htm).

Countryside Commission (1997) *Public attitudes to the countryside*, Manchester: Countryside Commission Publications.

Countryside Focus (2000) Issue 11, December 2000/January 2001, London: The Countryside Agency.

Crane, M. with contributions by Warnes, T. (1997) *Homeless truths: Challenging the myths about older homeless people*, London: Help the Aged and Crisis.

Cresswell, T. (1996) *In place, out of place: Geography, ideology and transgression*, Minneapolis, MN: University of Minnesota Press.

Crisis (2000) *Quality and choice: A decent home for all – Crisis' response to the Housing Green Paper*, London: Crisis.

Daly, G. (1996) *Homeless: Policies, strategies, and lives on the street*, London: Routledge.

Dant, T. and Deacon, A. (1989) *Hostels to homes? The rehousing of single homeless people*, Aldershot: Gower.

Davenport, J., Davenport, J.P. and Newett, D. (1990) 'A comparative analysis of the urban and rural homeless', paper presented at the 15th National Institute of Rural Social Work Conference, New York.

Davis, M. (1990) *City of quartz: Excavating the future of Los Angeles*, London: Verso.

De Certeau, M. (1984) *The practice of everyday life*, Los Angeles, CA: University of California Press.

De Certeau, M. (1985) 'Practices of space', in M. Blonsky (ed) *On signs*, Baltimore, NJ: Johns Hopkins University Press, pp 122-45.

Dear, M. and Taylor, S. (1982) *Not on our street*, London: Pion.

Dear, M. and Wolch, J. (1987) *Landscapes of despair: From deinstitutionalisation to homelessness*, Princeton, NJ: Princeton University Press.

Despres, C. (1991) 'The meaning of home – literature review and directions for future research', *Journal of Architectural and Planning Research*, vol 8, pp 96-115.

DETR (Department of the Environment, Transport and the Regions) (1998) 'New strategy will respond to concerns of rural people, says Prescott', Press release 1007, 27 December.

DETR (1999a) *Rural England: A discussion document*, London: The Stationery Office (also at www.defra.org.uk/wildlife-countryside/ consult/ruraleng/index.htm).

DETR (1999b) *Rural England: Summary of responses*, London: The Stationery Office (www.defra.org.uk/wildlife-countryside/consult/ruraleng/ index.htm).

DETR (2000a) *Quality and choice: A decent home for all*, Housing Green Paper (www.housing.detr.gov.uk/information/consult/homes/green).

DETR (2000b) *Quality and choice: A decent home for all: Summary of responses* (http://www.housing.detr.gov.uk/information/consult/responses/).

DETR (2000c) *Housing policy statement: The way forward for housing* (www.housing.detr.gov.uk/information/index18.htm).

DETR (2000d) 'Improving homebuying and helping the unintentionally homeless outlined in Queen's speech', Press release 748, 6 December.

DETR (2000e) *The Homes Bill 2001*, Housing Factsheet No 8, December (www.dtlr.gov.uk/housing/factsheet/bill/index.htm).

DETR (2000f) 'Housing Investment Summary' (www.housing.dtlr.gov.uk/csr2000/summary).

DETR (2000g) *Our countryside: The future – A fair deal for rural England*, London: The Stationery Office.

DETR (2000h) 'Our countryside: the future – summary' (www.defra.gov.uk/erdp/erdpfrm.htm).

DETR (2000i) 'Housing spend to make major impact on town and country living', Press release 492, 24 July.

DETR (2001a) *The Homes Bill 2001* (www.housing.detr.gov.uk/information/homesbill/).

DETR (2001b) 'Statutory homelessness: England Fourth Quarter', News release, SH-Q4, 14 March.

DETR (2002) 'Housing Statistics Postcard', January (www.housing.dtlr.gov.uk/information/keyfigures/index.htm).

DoE (Department of the Environment) (1989) *The government's review of homelessness legislation*, London: HMSO.

DoE (1994a) *Access to local authority and housing association tenancies: A consultation paper*, London: HMSO.

DoE (1994b) Press release 421, 18 July.

DoE (1995) *Rural England: A nation committed to a living countryside*, Cm 3016, London: HMSO.

DoE (1996) *Housing Act 1996: Code of guidance*, London, HMSO.

DoE (1997) '1996 Housing Act Factsheet', April (www.doe.gov.uk).

Donohue, T. (1996) *In the open: Diary of a homeless alcoholic*, Chicago, IL: University of Chicago Press.

Duncan, C. (1999) *Worlds apart: Why poverty persists in rural America*, New Haven, CT: Yale University Press.

Duncan, S. and Evans, A. (1988) *Responding to homelessness: Local authority policy and practice*, London: HMSO.

Dupuis, A. and Thorns, D. (1996) 'Meanings of home for older home owners', *Housing Studies*, vol 11, no 4, pp 485-501.

Esping-Andersen, G. (1990) *The three worlds of welfare capitalism*, Cambridge: Polity Press.

Evans, A. (1999) *They don't think I exist: The hidden nature of rural homelessness*, London: Crisis.

Evans, A. and Duncan, S. (1988) *Responding to homelessness: Local authority policy and practice*, London: HMSO.

Fabes, R., Worsley, L. and Howard, M. (1983) *The myth of the rural idyll*, Leicester: Child Poverty Action Group.

First, R., Rife, J. and Toomey, B. (1990) 'Homelessness in rural areas – causes, patterns and trends', *Social Work*, vol 39, pp 97-108.

Fitchen, J. (1991) 'Homelessness in rural places: perspectives from upstate New York', *Urban Anthropology*, vol 20, pp 177-210.

Fitchen, J. (1992) 'On the edge of homelessness: rural poverty and housing insecurity', *Rural Sociology*, vol 57, pp 173-93.

Fitzpatrick, S. and Stephens, M. (1999) 'Homelessness, need and desert in the allocation of council housing', *Housing Studies*, vol 14, no 4, pp 413-31.

Fox, C. and Miller, H. (1995) *Post-modern public administration: Towards discourse*, London: Sage Publications.

Gans, H. (1994) *The homeless*, Cambridge, MA: Harvard University Press.

Giamo, B. and Grunberg, J. (1992) *Beyond homelessness: Frames of reference*, Iowa City, IA: University of Iowa Press.

Gibbs, G. (1999) 'Scilly house prices alienate islanders', *The Guardian*, 10 September.

Glasser, I. and Bridgman, R. (1999) *Braving the street: The anthropology of homelessness*, New York, NY: Berghahn Books.

Golden, S. (1992) *The women outside: Meanings and myths of homelessness*, Berkeley, CA: University of California Press.

Goodwin, J. (1998) 'Locked out', *Roof*, July/August, pp 25-9.

Goodwin, M. (1998) 'The governance of rural areas: some emerging issues and agendas', *Journal of Rural Studies*, vol 14, no 1, pp 5-12.

Goodwin, M. and Painter, J. (1996) 'Local governance, Fordism and the changing geographies of regulation', *Transactions, IBG*, vol 21, pp 635-49.

Greve, J. (1991) *Homelessness in Britain*, York: Joseph Rowntree Foundation.

Griffiths, S. (1997) *Benefit shortfalls: The impact of Housing Benefit cuts on young single people*, London: Shelter.

Gunner, J. (1999) *Home or away? Tackling youth homelessness in the countryside*, London: Centrepoint/Countryside Agency.

Halfacree. K. (1993) 'Locality and social representation: space, discourse and alternative definitions of the rural', *Journal of Rural Studies*, vol 9, pp 1-15.

Hansard (1996) London, HMSO, 20 March.

Henley, J. (1998) 'Down and out in the cold of Paris', *The Guardian*, 28 November, p 19.

Hetherington, K. (2000) *New age travellers: Vanloads of uproarious humanity*, London: Cassell.

Hetherington, P. (2000) 'Cold comfort for village as housing market woos outsiders', *The Guardian*, 29 November.

Hill, H. (1980) *Freedom to roam: The struggle for access to Britain's moors and mountains*, Ashbourne: Moorland Publishing.

Hoggart, K. (1990) 'Let's do away with rural', *Journal of Rural Studies*, vol 6, pp 245-57.

Hoggart, K. (1995a) 'The changing geography of council house sales in England and Wales, 1978-1990', *Tidjschrift voor Economische en Sociale Geografie*, vol 86, pp 137-49.

Hoggart, K. (1995b) 'Political parties and the implementation of homeless legislation by non-metropolitan districts in England and Wales, 1985-90', *Political Geography*, vol 14, no 1, pp 59-79.

Hoggart, K. (1997) 'Home occupancy and rural housing problems in England', *Town Planning Review*, vol 68, pp 485-515.

Housing (1995) *Analysis: The White Paper*, September, pp 26-31.

Housing Corporation (2000) *Homes in the countryside: A rural position paper*, August, London: Housing Corporation.

Hughes, A. (1997) 'Rurality and cultures of womanhood: domestic identities and moral order in village life', in P. Cloke and J. Little (eds) *Contested countryside cultures*, London: Routledge.

Hutson, S. (1999) 'Introduction', in S. Hutson and D. Clapham (eds) *Homelessness: Public policies and private troubles*, London: Cassell, pp 1-10.

Hutson, S. and Clapham, D. (eds) (1999) *Homelessness: Public policies and private troubles*, London: Cassell.

Hutson, S. and Liddiard, M. (1994) *Youth homelessness: The construction of a social issue*, London: Macmillan.

Jencks, C. (1994) *The homeless*, Cambridge, MA: Harvard University Press.

Jessop, B. (1995) 'The regulation approach, governance and post-Fordism', *Economy and Society*, vol 24, pp 307-34.

Jessop, B. (1997a) 'A neo-Gramscian approach to the regulation of urban regimes: accumulation strategies, hegemonic projects and governance', in M. Lauria (ed) *Reconstructing urban regime theory*, London: Sage Publications.

Jessop, B. (1997b) 'Capitalism and its future: remarks on regulation, government and governance', *Review of International Political Economy*, vol 4, no 3, Autumn, pp 561-81.

Johnson, B., Murie, A., Naumann, L. and Yanetta, A. (1991) *A typology of homelessness*, Edinburgh: Scottish Homes.

Johnson, G. (1997) 'Villagers buy their tramp his own wood', *News of the World*.

Judge, D., Stoker, G. and Wolman, H. (eds) (1995) *Theories of urban politics*, London: Sage Publications.

Katz, C. (1994) 'Playing the field: questions of fieldwork in geography', *Professional Geographer*, no 46, pp 67-72.

Kearns, R. and Smith, C. (1994) 'Homelessness and mental health', *Professional Geographer*, vol 46, pp 418-24.

Kemp, P. (1997) 'The characteristics of single homeless people in England', in R. Burrows, N. Pearce and D. Quilgars (eds) *Homelessness and social policy*, London: Routledge, pp 69-87.

Kennett, P. and Marsh, A. (eds) (1999) *Homelessness: Exploring the new terrain*, Bristol: The Policy Press.

Lambert, C., Jeffers, S., Burton, P. and Bramley, G. (1992) *Homelessness in rural areas*, Salisbury: Rural Development Commission.

Larkin, A. (1978) 'Rural housing – too dear, too few and too far', *Roof*, vol 3, pp 15-17.

Lawrence, M. (1995) Rural homelessness: a geography without a geography', *Journal of Rural Studies*, vol 11, pp 297-308.

Lawrence, M. (1997) 'Heartlands or neglected geographies? Liminality, power and the hyperreal rural', *Journal of Rural Studies*, vol 13, pp 1-18.

Leake, J. and Brennan, Z. (1998) 'Second-home owners face tax penalty', *The Sunday Times*, 31 May.

Lewallen, J. (1998) *The Camp: A story of homelessness – life, death and reunion*, Washington, DC: National Coalition For The Homeless.

Liddiard, M. and Hutson, S. (1990) 'Youth homelessness in Wales', in C. Wallace and M. Cross (eds) *Youth in transition: The sociology of youth and youth policy*, London: Falmer Press.

Lidstone, P. (1994) 'Rationing housing to the homeless applicant', *Housing Studies*, vol 9, pp 459-72.

Little, J. and Austin, P. (1996) 'Women and the rural idyll', *Journal of Rural Studies*, vol 12, pp 101-11.

Local Government Association (1999) 'Memorandum of evidence to Environment, Transport and Regional Affairs Select Committee Inquiry into the Rural White Paper', September.

Local Government Association Rural Executive (2000) 'Social Exclusion Unit's "National strategy for neighbourhood renewal": views from the LGA Rural Executive' (www.lga.org.uk).

Lowe, G. (2001) 'Rural homeless are counted out', *The Big Issue*, 16 July.

Lowe, R. and Shaw, W. (1993) *Travellers: Voices of the new age nomads*, London: Fourth Estate.

McCarthy, P. and Simpson, B. (1991) *Issues in post divorce housing: Family policy or housing policy*, Aldershot: Avebury.

MacGregor, D., Robertson, D. and Shucksmith, M. (eds) (1987) *Rural housing in Scotland: Recent research and policy*, Aberdeen: Aberdeen University Press.

Macklin, J. (2000) 'Rural homelessness: Developments since 1995', in P. Cloke, P. Milbourne and R. Widdowfield (eds) *Tackling homelessness in rural areas*, Cardiff: Cardiff University Press, pp 68-73.

McLaughlin, B. (1986) 'The rhetoric and reality of rural deprivation', *Journal of Rural Studies*, vol 2, pp 291-307.

Malpass, P. and Murie, A. (1990) *Housing policy and practice* (3rd edn), Basingstoke: Macmillan.

Mayer, M. (1994) 'Post-Fordist city politics', in A. Amin (ed) *Post-Fordism: A reader*, Oxford: Blackwell, pp 316-37.

Meikle, J. (1997) 'Deadly serious', *The Guardian*, 10 December, p 9.

Milbourne, P. (1997) 'Housing conflict and domestic property classes in rural Wales', *Environment and Planning A*, vol 29, pp 43-62.

Milbourne, P. (1998) 'Local responses to central state social housing restructuring in rural areas', *Journal of Rural Studies*, vol 14, no 2, pp 167-84.

Milbourne, P. (2000) 'Exporting "other" rurals: new audiences for qualitative research', in A. Hughes, C. Morris and S. Seymour (eds) *Ethnography and rural research*, Cheltenham: Countryside and Community Press, pp 179-97.

Milbourne, P., Mitra, B. and Winter, M. (2001) *Agriculture and rural society*, London: Department for Environment, Food and Rural Affairs.

Mitchell, D. (1997) 'The annihilation of space by law: the roots and implications of anti-homeless laws in the United States', *Antipode*, vol 29, pp 303-35.

Moore, J., Carter, D., Stockley, D. and Drake, M. (1995) *The faces of homelessness in London*, Aldershot: Dartmouth Publishing.

Mullins, D. and Niner, P. (1999) 'A prize of citizenship? Changing access to social housing', in A. Marsh and D. Mullins (eds) *Housing and social policy*, Buckingham: Open University Press.

Murdoch, J. (1995) 'Middle-class territory? Some remarks on the use of class analysis in rural studies', *Environment and Planning A*, vol 27, pp 1213-30.

Murdoch, J. and Abram, S. (1998) 'Defining the limits of community governance, *Journal of Rural Studies*, vol 14, pp 41-50.

Murdoch, J. and Pratt, A. (1993) 'Rural studies: modernism, post-modernism and the post-rural', *Journal of Rural Studies*, vol 9, pp 411-28.

Murdoch, J. and Pratt, A. (1994) 'Rural studies of power and the power of rural studies: a reply to Philo', *Journal of Rural Studies*, vol 10, pp 83-8.

Murdoch, J. and Pratt, A. (1997) 'From the power of topography to the topography of power: a discourse on strange ruralities', in P. Cloke and J. Little (eds) *Contested countryside cultures*, London: Routledge.

Murie, A. and Jeffers, S. (1987) *Living in Bed & Breakfast: The experience of homelessness in London*, Bristol: SAUS Publications.

Neale, J. (1997) 'Homelessness and theory reconsidered', *Housing Studies*, vol 12, pp 47-61.

Newby, H., Bell, C., Rose, D. and Saunders, P. (1978) *Property, paternalism and power: Class and control in rural England*, London: Hutchinson.

Newton, J. (1991) *All in one place: The British housing story 1971-91*, London: CHAS.

Niner, P. (1989) *Homelessness in nine local authorities: Case studies of policy and practice*, London: HMSO.

Niner, P. (1997) *The early impact of the Housing Act 1996 and Housing Benefit changes*, London: Shelter.

Nord, M. and Luloff, A.E. (1995) 'Homeless children and their families in New Hampshire', *Social Service Review*, vol 69, pp 461-78.

O'Brien, M. and Penna, S. (1998) *Theorising welfare: Enlightenment and modern society*, London: Sage Publications.

Oldman, C. (1997) 'Working together to help homeless people: an examination of inter-agency themes', in R. Burrows, N. Pleace and D. Quilgars (eds) *Homelessness and social policy*, London: Routledge.

Patton, L. (1988) 'The rural homeless', in the Committee on Health Care for Homeless People (eds) *Homelessness, health and human needs*, Washington, DC: National Academy Press.

Philo, C. (1986) *'The same and the other': On geographies, madness and outsiders*, Occasional Paper No 11, Loughborough: Department of Geography, Loughborough University.

Philo, C. (1992) 'Neglected rural geographies: a review', *Journal of Rural Studies*, vol 11, pp 351-66.

Philo, C. (1993) 'Post-modern rural geography? A reply to Murdoch and Pratt', *Journal of Rural Studies*, vol 9, pp 427-36.

Philo, C. (1997) 'Of other rurals?', in P. Cloke and J. Little (eds) *Contested countryside cultures*, London: Routledge, pp 19-50.

Piliavin, I., Wright, B.R.E., Mare, R.D. and Westerfelt, A.H. (1996) 'Exits from and returns to homelessness, *Social Service Review*, vol 70, pp 33-57.

Pleace, N., Burrows, R. and Quilgars, D. (1997) 'Homelessness in contemporary Britain: conceptualisation and measurement', in R. Burrows, N. Pleace and D. Quilgars (eds) *Homelessness and social policy*, London: Routledge, pp 1-18.

Pratt, A. (1996) 'Rurality: loose talk or social struggle?', *Journal of Rural Studies*, vol 12, pp 69-78.

PSI (Policy Studies Institute) (1998) *Understanding processes of rural disadvantage*, PSI, Rural Development Commission (now Cheltenham: The Countryside Agency).

Punch, M. (1986) *The politics and ethics of fieldwork*, Beverly Hills, CA: Sage Publications.

Randall, G. and Brown, S. (1996) *From street to home: An evaluation of phase 2 of the Rough Sleepers Initiative*, London: DETR.

Randall, G. and Brown, S. (1999) *Homes for street homeless people: An evaluation of the Rough Sleepers Initiative*, London: DETR.

Raynsford, N. (1986) 'The Housing (Homeless Persons) Act 1977', in N. Deakin (ed) *Policy change in government*, London: Royal Institute of Public Administration, pp 33-62.

RDC (Rural Development Commission) (1996) *Rural needs in local authority housing strategies*, London: RDC.

Redfield, R. (1941) *The folk culture of Yucatan*, Chicago, IL: Chicago University Press.

Rhodes, R. (1996) 'The new governance: governing without government', *Political Studies*, vol 44, pp 652-67.

Rhodes, R. (1997) *Understanding governance: Policy networks, governance, reflexivity and accountability*, Buckingham: Open University Press,

Richards, J. (1992) 'A sense of duty', in C. Grant (ed) *Built to last: Reflections on British housing policy*, London: Shelter, pp 129-38.

Rogers, A. (1976) 'Rural housing', in G. Cherry (ed) *Rural planning problems*, London: Hill.

Rose, N. (1996) 'The death of the social? Re-figuring the territory of government', *Economy and Society*, vol 25, pp 327-56.

Rowe, S. and Wolch, J. (1990) 'Social networks in time and space: homeless women in Skid Row, Los Angeles', *Annals of the Association of American Geographers*, vol 80, no 2, pp 184-204.

RSU (Rough Sleepers Unit) (1999a) *Coming in from the cold: The government's strategy on rough sleeping* (www.dtlr.gov.uk/housing/information/rough/strategy/index.htm).

RSU (1999b) 'Government to help people come in from the cold', press release, 15 December.

RSU (2000) 'Blocking the fast track from prison to rough sleeping' (www.dtlr.gov.uk/housing/rsu/summary/index.htm).

Ruddick, S. (1996) *Young and homeless in Hollywood: Mapping social identities*, New York, NY: Routledge.

Rural Housing Trust (2000a) 'Rural White paper – reaction from the Rural Housing Trust', Press release, 28 November.

Rural Housing Trust (2000b) 'Second home for help for rich outstrips rural housing subsidies', Press release, 5 October.

Scott, D., Shenton, N. and Healey, D. (1991) *Hidden deprivation in the countryside*, Glossop: Peak Park Trust.

Select Committee on Environment, Transport and Regional Affairs Seventh Report (2000) *Rural White Paper*, 3 May (www.parliament.the-stationery-office.co.uk/pa/cm/cmenvtra.htm).

SEU (Social Exclusion Unit) (1998) *Rough sleeping*, Cm 4008, London: The Stationery Office.

SEU (2001) *Preventing social exclusion*, London: The Stationery Office.

Shelter (2000a) 'Homeless people get their Bill: the Homes Bill, second reading briefing', December (www.shelter,org.uk/).

Shelter (2000b) 'Affordable housing key to thriving rural communities: Shelter welcomes Government's White Paper', Press release, 28 November.

Shelter (2000c) 'Summary of Shelter's final response to the Housing Green Paper' (www.epolitix.com/forum/shelter.htm).

Shelter (2001) 'Target needed to get homeless people out of B&Bs', Press release, 14 March.

Shields, R. (1991) *Places on the margin*, London: Routledge.

Shucksmith, M. (1990) *Housebuilding in Britain's countryside*, London: Routledge.

Shucksmith, M., Chapman, P. and Clark, G. (1996) *Rural Scotland today*, Aldershot: Avebury.

Sibley, D. (1995) *Geographies of exclusion: Society and difference in the West*, London: Routledge.

Sibley, D. (1997) 'Endangering the sacred: nomads, youth cultures and the English countryside', in P. Cloke and J. Little (eds) *Contested countryside cultures*, London: Routledge, pp 218-31.

Simmons, M. (1993) 'A house in the country', *The Guardian*, 28 May, p 7.

Smith, N. (1993) 'Homeless/global: scaling places', in J. Bird, B. Curtis, T. Putnam and L. Tickner (eds) *Mapping the futures: Local cultures, global change*, London: Routledge, pp 87-119.

Smith, R., Stirling, T., Papps, P., Evans, A. and Rowlands, R. (2001) *Allocations and exclusions: The impact of new approaches to allocating social housing on those in housing need*, London: Shelter.

Somerville, P. (1992) 'Homelessness and the meaning of home – rooflessness or rootlessness', *International Journal of Urban and Regional Research*, vol 16, pp 529-39.

Somerville, P. (1999) 'The making and unmaking of homelessness legislation', in D. Clapham and S. Hutson (eds) *Homelessness: Public policies and private troubles*, London: Cassell, pp 29-57.

Spackman, A. (1997) 'A window on the countryside is opened', *Financial Times*, 12 April, p xiv.

Spradley, J. (1970) *You owe yourself a drunk: An ethnography of urban nomads*, Boston, MA: Little Brown.

Stoker, G. (1996) *Governance as theory: Five propositions*, mimeo, Strathclyde: Department of Government, University of Strathclyde.

Stoker, G. (1997a) 'Public–private partnerships and urban governance', in G. Stoker (ed) *Partners in urban governance: European and American experience*, London: Macmillan.

Stoker, G. (ed) (1997b) *Partners in urban governance: European and American experience*, London: Macmillan.

Stoker, G. and Mossberger, K. (1995) 'The post-Fordist local state: the dynamics of its development', in J. Stewart and G. Stoker (eds) *Local government in the 1990s*, London: Macmillan, pp 210-27.

Stone, C. (1989) *Regime politics*, Lawrence, KS: Kansas University Press.

Streich, L. (2000) 'Rural homelessness in the South West: recent research findings', in P. Cloke, P. Milbourne and R. Widdowfield (eds) *Tackling homelessness in rural areas*, Cardiff: Cardiff University Press, pp 25-31.

Takahashi, L. (1998a) 'Socio-spatial stigmatization: exploring the local politics of homelessness', Paper presented to the Annual Meeting of the Association of American Geographers, Boston, MA.

Takahashi, L. (1998b) *Homelessness, AIDS and stigmatization: The NIMBY syndrome at the end of the twentieth century*, Oxford: Oxford University Press.

Taunton Deane District Council (1996) unpublished report.

Tewdwr-Jones, M. (1998) 'Rural government and community participation: the planning role of community councils', *Journal of Rural Studies*, vol 14, pp 51-62.

The Foyer Federation (2000) '100 foyers: 25,000 new futures', unpublished document, London.

The Rural Group of Labour MPs (2000) *A Manifesto for rural Britain*, London: The Rural Group of Labour MPs.

Thomas, A. and Niner, P. (1989) *Living in temporary accommodation: A survey of homeless people*, London: HMSO.

Thomas, D. (1989) 'The production of homelessness', *Housing Studies*, vol 4, pp 253-66.

Thomas, H. and Imrie, R. (1997) 'Urban development corporations and local governance in the UK', *Tijdschrift voor Economische en Sociale Geografie*, vol 88, no 1, pp 53-64.

Thompson, L. (1988) *An act of compromise*, London: Routledge.

Thorns, D. (1989) 'The production of homelessness', *Housing Studies*, vol 4, pp 253-66.

Thrift, N. (1989) 'Images of social change', in C. Hamnett, L. McDowell and P. Sarre (eds) *The changing social structure*, London: Sage Publications, pp 12-42.

Thrift, N. (1991) 'Over wordy worlds? Thoughts and worries', in C. Philo (ed) *New words, new worlds: Reconceptualising social and cultural geography*, Lampeter: Social and Cultural Geography Study Group, Institute of British Geographies, pp 144-8.

Tomas, A. and Dittmar, H. (1995) 'The experience of homeless women: an exploration of housing histories and the meaning of home', *Housing Studies*, vol 10, pp 493-515.

Tonnies, F. (1957) *Community and society*, New York, NY: Harper.

Veness, A. (1992) 'Home and homelessness in the US: changing ideals and reality', *Society and Space*, vol 10, pp 445-68.

Veness, A. (1993) 'Neither homed nor homeless: contested definitions and the personal worlds of the poor', *Political Geography*, vol 12, pp 319-40.

Veness, A. (1994) 'Designer shelters as models and makers of home: new responses to homelessness in urban America', *Urban Geography*, vol 15, pp 150-67.

Ward, N. and McNicholas, K. (1998) 'Reconfiguring rural development in the UK: Objective 5B and the new rural governance', *Journal of Rural Studies*, vol 14, pp 27-39.

Wardhaugh, J. (1996) '"Homeless in Chinatown": deviance and social control in cardboard city', *Sociology*, vol 30, no 4, pp 701-16.

Watson, S. (1984) 'Definitions of homelessness: a feminist perspective', *Critical Social Policy*, vol 11, pp 60-73.

Watson, S. and Austerberry, H. (1986) *Housing and homelessness: A feminist perspective*, London: Routledge.

Webb, S. (1994) *My address is not my home: Hidden homelessness and single women in Scotland*, Edinburgh: Scottish Council for Single Homeless.

Welsh Office (1996) *A working countryside for Wales*, Cmnd 3180, London: The Stationery Office.

Whitburn, V. (1996) *The Archers: The changing face of radio's longest running drama*, London: Virgin Books.

Williams, G., Bell, P. and Russell, L. (1991) *Evaluating the Low Cost Rural Housing Initiative*, London: HMSO.

Wilson, A. (1992) *The culture of nature*, Oxford: Blackwell.

Wolch, J. and Dear, M. (1993) *Malign neglect: Homelessness in an American city*, San Francisco, CA: Jossey-Bass.

Wolch, J. and Gabriel, S. (1984) 'Development and decline of the service-dependant ghetto', *Urban Geography*, vol 5, pp 111-29.

Wolch, J. and Rowe, S. (1992) 'On the streets: mobility paths of the urban homeless', *City and Society*, vol 6, no 2, pp 115-40.

Woodward, R. (1996) '"Deprivation" and "the rural": an investigation into contradictory discourses', *Journal of Rural Studies*, vol 12, pp 55-67.

Wright, J. and Everitt, R. (1995) *Homelessness in Boston*, Sleaford: Shelter Lincolnshire.

Wright, T. and Vermond, A. (1990) 'Small dignities: local resistances, dominant strategies of authority and homelessness', Paper presented to the Annual Meeting of the American Sociological Association, Washington DC.

Yanetta, A., Third, H. and Anderson, I. (1999) *National monitoring and interim evaluation of the Rough Sleepers Initiative in Scotland*, Edinburgh: Central Research Unit, Scottish Executive.

Index

Page references for figures and tables are in italics; those for notes are followed by n

237

intentionality 7, 8
Inter-Agency Meeting (Taunton)
 158-66
invisibility *see* hidden homelessness
Isles of Scilly 196

J

Jeffers, S. 96
Jencks, C. 6
Jessop, B. 145, 147, 155, 167
Johnson, B. 5, 6, 8, 70
Johnson, G. 4, 67
Joint Charities Group 87
Judge, D. 145
Jump Start 201

K

Katz, C. 48
Kearns, R. 12, 13
Kemp, P. 18
Kennett, P. 18

L

Lambert, C. 19, 30, 34, 71, 142n
Larkin, A. 69
Lawrence, M. 15, 75, 76, 78-9
Leake, J. 196
Leicester 110
Lewallen, J. 1, 2, *3*, 4, 25
Liddiard, M. 5, 6, 18, 30, 31, 33, 70,
 159
Lidstone, P. 69
life-style circumstances 178-9
Little, J. 80
local authorities 191, 193
 affordable housing 103, 105
 homelessness welfare support
  networks 155-7, 212
 Homes Bill 93-6, 192
 Housing Act 1996 90-1
 interpretation of legislation 7-8,
  144-5
 legal obligations 30
 officers 35, 36
 recording procedures and decisions
  127-8, *128*, *129*

Local Authority Social Housing
 Grant 103
local context 141-2, 149-51, 208
Local Government Association 90,
 206
local people 183-4, 189
local welfare governance 143-9, 166-7
 rural homelessness 149-66
London 18, 58-9
 accepted homelessness 83n, *124*,
  125, *126*
 rough sleepers 29, 109, 110-11
 scale of homelessness *19*, 117, *118*,
  119, 120, *120*
Luloff, A.E. 6

M

McCarthy, P. 88
MacGregor, D. 17
Mackenzie, D. 12, 13
Macklin, J. 194
McLaughlin, B. 17
McNicholas, K. 145
Malpass, P. 87
Manchester 110, 111
Manifesto for rural Britain (Rural
 Group of Labour MPs) 103
market towns 103-4
Marsh, A. 18
Mayer, M. 147
mental illness 72
middle class 56, 132, 134
Milbourne, Paul 17, 34, 39, 135
 ethical issues 44, 47-8
 rurality 55, 75, 131, 136
Miller, H. 146-7
Minehead 178, 181, 214
Ministry of Defence 112
Mitchell, D. 33, 57, 84n
Monmouth 35
Moore, J. 10, 79
Mormont, M. 75
mortgage arrears 20, *126*, 127
Mossberger, K. 143-4
move-on accommodation 200
Mullins, D. 145
Murdoch, A. 61
Murdoch, J. 56, 75, 76, 147